Assessing Autoethnogr

Assessing Autoethnography provides readers with multiple ways to analyze autoethnographies and other forms of personal narrative writing. Given the proliferation of such forms across academic contexts, this book offers a guide of what autoethnography is, why it matters, and how to do it.

Taking each of the three parts of auto-, ethno-, and -graphy in detail, Herrmann and Adams provide criteria and points of discussion to ensure robust assessment of an autoethnographic work as a whole. Every chapter is accompanied with exemplars and considers issues such as ethics, storytelling, and good writing. This book discerns the kinds of personal experiences that often work best for autoethnographic projects and provides ways to evaluate fieldwork, interviews, and representations.

Written by two experts in the field, *Assessing Autoethnography* offers guidance to scholars and dissertation advisors, across diverse disciplines, in producing autoethnographic work and utilizing autoethnographic methods. This book will be of interest to researchers in the fields of Communication Studies, Education, Sociology, Women's and Gender Studies, Critical Race Studies, Mass Communication, English, and other related disciplines.

Andrew F. Herrmann (Ph.D., University of South Florida) is Assistant Professor of Communication at East Tennessee State University. He is the founding co-editor (with Tony Adams) of the *Journal of Autoethnography.* He edited the award-winning *Routledge International Handbook of Organizational Autoethnography* (2020). He is the co-editor (with Art Herbig) of the *Communication Perspectives on Popular Culture* book series.

Tony E. Adams (Ph.D., University of South Florida) is Caterpillar Professor and Chair of the Department of Communication at Bradley University. He has published ten books, including *Narrating the Closet: An Autoethnography of Same-Sex Attraction, Autoethnography* (co-authored with Stacy Holman Jones and Carolyn Ellis), and both editions of the *Handbook of Autoethnography* (co-edited with Stacy Holman Jones and Carolyn Ellis).

Assessing Autoethnography

Notes on Analysis, Evaluation, and Craft

Andrew F. Herrmann
and Tony E. Adams

Routledge
Taylor & Francis Group
LONDON AND NEW YORK

Designed cover image: GettyImages via Carmen Martínez Torrón

First published 2025
by Routledge
4 Park Square, Milton Park, Abingdon, Oxon OX14 4RN

and by Routledge
605 Third Avenue, New York, NY 10158

Routledge is an imprint of the Taylor & Francis Group, an informa business

British Library Cataloguing-in-Publication Data
A catalogue record for this book is available from the British Library

Library of Congress Cataloging-in-Publication Data
Names: Herrmann, Andrew F., 1966– author. | Adams, Tony E., author.
Title: Assessing autoethnography: notes on analysis, evaluation, and craft / Andrew F. Herrmann and Tony E. Adams.
Description: Abingdon, Oxon; New York, NY: Routledge, 2024. | Includes bibliographical references and index.
Identifiers: LCCN 2024007001 (print) | LCCN 2024007002 (ebook) | ISBN 9781032251387 (hardback) | ISBN 9781032251431 (paperback) | ISBN 9781003281771 (ebook)
Subjects: LCSH: Ethnology—Biographical methods.
Classification: LCC GN346.6 .H47 2024 (print) | LCC GN346.6 (ebook) | DDC 305.8—dc23/eng/20240326
LC record available at https://lccn.loc.gov/2024007001
LC ebook record available at https://lccn.loc.gov/2024007002

ISBN: 978-1-032-25138-7 (hbk)
ISBN: 978-1-032-25143-1 (pbk)
ISBN: 978-1-003-28177-1 (ebk)

DOI: 10.4324/9781003281771

Typeset in Galliard
by codeMantra

Dedicated to
Art and Carolyn
and
Bob, Eric, Ron, Laurel, Paaige, Mitch, and Norman

Contents

Acknowledgments

We are grateful to Hannah Shakespeare for conceiving this book and giving us the right amount of push to get rolling. We thank Eleanor Taylor, Adam Woods, and Matt Bickerton for the opportunity to publish with Routledge—without them, this book would not exist. We also thank David Famiano, Cheryl Swope, John Wentworth, and the staff at the University of California Press; without them, the *Journal of Autoethnography* would not exist.

Andrew: Tony Adams! Thank you for your friendship over the last 20 years. I could never have made this academic journey without your support and love. What can I say? You're the best! I'll see you Wednesday for the *Journal of Autoethnography* meeting. Let's keep on keeping on. I want to thank the *JoAE* advisors and reviewers for teaching me so much about assessing autoethnography. To me, you are the unsung heroes of this text. I am grateful for those who have been walking alongside of me on this academic journey, especially Ahmet Atay, Mitch Allen, Abby Arnold-Patti, Keith Berry, Robin Boylorn, Michelle Calka, Sarah Dykins Callahan, Katherine Denker, Jennifer Dunn, Eric Eisenberg, Alec Grant, Stacy Holman Jones, Jeni Hunniecutt, Chris Patti, Chris Poulos, Jimmie Manning, Danielle Stern, Lisa Tillmann, Sarah Tracy, Jillian Tullis, Alix Watson, and Stephanie Young. Special shout out to my good friends and sounding boards: Art Herbig, Adam Tyma, Brian Johnston, and Andrew Dunn. I am forever in your debt. Thank you to my colleagues in Communication Studies and Storytelling at East Tennessee State University. My love to Rob Anderson, Bob Krizek, Paaige Turner, Art Bochner, and Carolyn Ellis: your gifts of knowledge and empathy and ethics are ingrained into the very fiber of my being. You made all this possible. Goodall and Trujillo—I still miss you. Lastly, to the three Herrmann men: Frederick, James, and Garrett; to Mark and Laura; and to the one and only Marianne America Cromeans.

Tony: I am grateful for my dear friend and co-author, Andrew Herrmann—it has been a pleasure living the autoethnographic life alongside you. Our weekly meetings are always a treat—I hope we continue collaborating for many more years. I am also grateful for the many others who have made my autoethnographic life possible, especially Mitch Allen, Abby Arnold-Patti, Michelle Calka, Silvia Bénard Calva, Kakali Bhattacharya, Bernard Brommel, Derek Bolen, Robin Boylorn, David Carless, Devika Chawla, Marcy Chvasta, Cody Clemens, Kathy Denker, Norman Denzin, Kitrina Douglas, Jen Dunn, Tasha Dunn, Sandra Faulkner, Mark Freeman, Craig Gingrich-Philbrook, Alec Grant,

Stacy Holman Jones, Marcin Kafar, Lenore Langsdorf, Patricia Leavy, Jimmie Manning, Ben Myers, Nikki Neuman, Chris Patti, Ron Pelias, Sandy Pensoneau-Conway, Chris Poulos, Carol Rambo, Lisa Spinazola, Danielle Stern, Lisa Tillmann, Jillian Tullis, Jonathan Wyatt, and Stephanie Young; my former colleagues at Northeastern Illinois University and current colleagues at Bradley University; my mother, Sharon Rome; my bestest best friend, Keith Berry; my beloved friends/mentors/collaborators/parents, Art Bochner and Carolyn Ellis, whose care, spirit, and wisdom infuse every page of this text; and my patient and loving partner, Gerardo Moreno, who gifts me time and space to live a writing life.

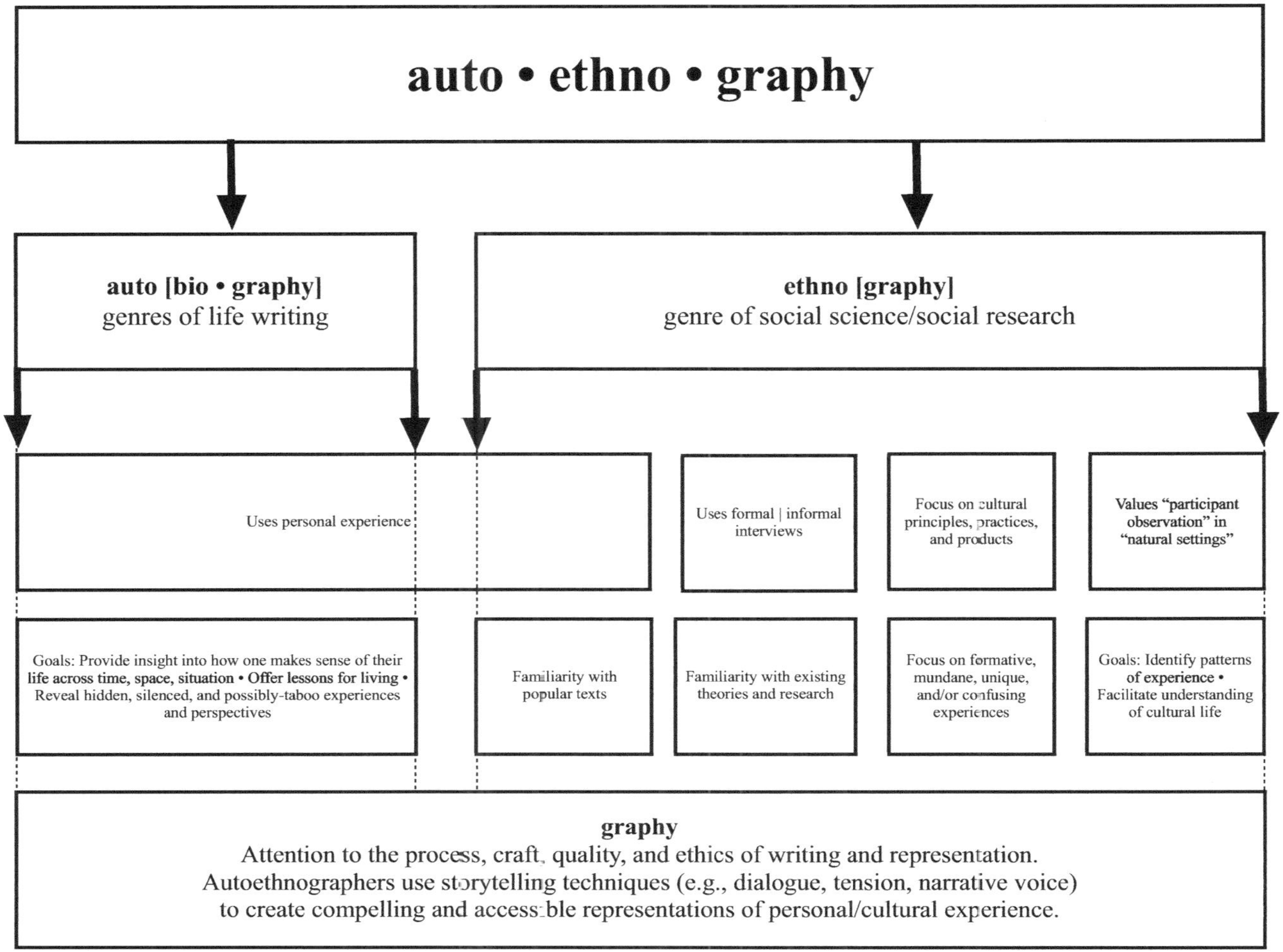

Components of Autoethnography

Introduction

Coming to Autoethnography[1]

SCENES FROM THE EDITORS

ANDREW: This author offers a vivid and vulnerable account of living through an unexpected crisis. They beautifully and brilliantly demonstrate Bochner's "tale of two selves," a criterion for good autoethnography, by offering a "a believable journey" from who they felt they were before the crisis to who they feel they are now, after the crisis.[2]

TONY: Accept.

TONY: This author offers another "life chronology." They share disparate, random moments from their life, a this-happened and this-happened and this-happened reporting style without any focus, organization, or purpose. Also, three reviewers recommend rejecting the manuscript.

ANDREW: Reject.

ANDREW: This author tells an important and compelling story of their experiences with "minor bodily stigma," yet they do not explain or engage Carolyn Ellis' conceptualization of this concept; the manuscript reads as if the author developed it. The manuscript would be acceptable if they explained the concept and cited Ellis' work.[3]

TONY: Revise and resubmit.

TONY: This author uses NVivo to code their personal experiences. They want to remove bias from the manuscript and demonstrate the reliability, validity, and generalizability of their experiences. The authors don't seem to know what autoethnography is or how to do it.

ANDREW: Desk reject.

*

We began this book out of excitement—excitement because, as a method, orientation to research, or, as Art Bochner says, "way of life,"[4] autoethnography has flourished across

DOI: 10.4324/9781003281771-1

disciplines, genres, and regions.[5] Early (1990–2000s) critiques of autoethnography—references to it as narcissistic, self-indulgent, biased, navel gazing, overly emotional "me-search," easy, self-exploitative, and inherently unethical—have since been recognized, at least by serious qualitative researchers, as silly and ignorant.

Autoethnography is now better understood and appreciated. Scholars across numerous disciplines—including, but not limited to, nursing, music, criminology, education, information sciences, sociology, anthropology, psychology, political science, theater, engineering, social work, accounting, communication, and business—have used autoethnography in their research. There are thousands of articles, book chapters, books, and handbooks about autoethnography; a simple Google Scholar search for "autoethnography" yields more than 90,000 results. Courses about autoethnography are taught at several universities, and multiple annual/biennial conferences foreground autoethnographic work.[6] In 2011, Pat Sikes released a four-volume collection of essential readings in autoethnography,[7] and the *Handbook of Autoethnography*—the first comprehensive reference volume on autoethnographic research and practice—is now in its second edition.[8] Andrew completed the *Routledge International Handbook of Organizational Autoethnography* in 2020; *The AutoEthnographer* literary and arts magazine began in 2021, the same year Chris Poulos published *Essentials of Autoethnography* with the American Psychological Association; and in 2019,[9] we started the *Journal of Autoethnography* with the University of California Press, the first journal solely devoted to autoethnographic research.

*

Yet, we also began this book out of frustration.

We are frustrated with the misappropriation of the term "autoethnography" by authors who claim to do autoethnography but disregard the core components of the method—the "auto," the "ethno," and the "graphy"—components that comprise the very term.

We are frustrated by "autoethnographies" that claim to be "indecipherable," and proudly proclaim they don't make sense, and by manuscripts that are poorly written and utterly boring. These manuscripts demonstrate little care for the graphy.

We are frustrated by "autoethnographies" that include a lot of theory and no personal experience. None. These manuscripts disregard the auto.

We are frustrated by "autoethnographies" where the author comes across as wholly narcissistic and unreflexive, as though they were the first and only person to experience [insert topic here]. These manuscripts focus solely on oneself, not one's self in relational and cultural contexts. These manuscripts disregard the ethno.

We are frustrated by "autoethnographies" that claim the use of *others'* personal experiences, such as those gathered in interviews, are autoethnographic. Following this premise, any project using others' experiences as data—e.g., oral histories, surveys, and experiments—could be considered "autoethnographic." These autoethnographies indicate a severe misunderstanding of the auto.

We are frustrated by "autoethnographies" that claim to use "minor bodily stigma," or "sociological introspection," or "relational ethics" yet never cite Carolyn Ellis's vast writing about these concepts[10]; manuscripts that claim to be "layered accounts" but do not engage or follow Carol Rambo's use and description of this form[11]; and manuscripts that use "analytic autoethnography" without engaging Leon Anderson's *multiple* works about this concept, including how the term has been misused.[12] To use these concepts without proper citation or knowledge of their origin and development indicates the little effort one puts in their work. Using these concepts without proper citation also encroaches on intellectual theft and plagiarism.

We are frustrated by authors who suggest we cannot and should not ever assess autoethnography[13] and who, after receiving a rejection for a submitted manuscript, have told us that we shouldn't be able to critique their personal experience. We find this suggestion to be terribly erroneous. People who write memoirs and autobiographies do not write whatever they want without critique. Life writers receive feedback all the time, from neophytes like Britney Spears to experienced writers like Stephen King.[14]

And we are frustrated by so-called "autoethnographies" that include extensive discussions of instrument validation and reliability, statistical significance, sterile coding processes and software, and mitigating bias. Few ethnographers and fewer (if any) autobiographers care about these concepts.

For us, authors who advocate these ideas or engage in these practices and who try to classify their work as "autoethnographic" indicate they haven't read much *about* autoethnography, haven't read many *good* autoethnographies, and do not care much about the quality of their work.

*

Let's begin with the three components of autoethnography, components that comprise the very term: the "auto," the "ethno," and the "graphy." The "auto" of autoethnography relates to an author's lived experience, self, subjectivity, and identity. The auto taps into practices and genres of life writing, particularly what people do when they write autobiographies, memoirs, and personal narratives.[15] From the perspective of research and research methodology, autoethnographers demonstrate and celebrate the epistemic potential of personal experience—they show how personal experience can be used to study specific issues and topics differently, and often more effectively, than other research methods. In an autoethnographic text, the author is present at least some of the time, via their reflections on, and sharing of, formative and meaningful experiences. A text that doesn't engage an author's experience doesn't satisfy the auto requirement for autoethnography. (We will share more about the auto in Chapter 3.)

Yet the mere sharing of personal experience does not make a project autoethnographic. Autoethnography is more than telling a personal story. The "ethno" is also a core component of autoethnography. The ethno pushes us outside of and beyond ourselves; it connects the personal and the political, portrays the self in/as culture, and interrogates intersections of subjectivity and social life. For us, the ethno requires a demonstrated familiarity with the practices of ethnography: conducting fieldwork, interviewing others, engaging existing research, finding and analyzing key artifacts and texts related to a topic or experience, identifying cultural norms and patterns of behavior, and valuing "thick description."[16] A manuscript that does not engage any of these ethnographic practices doesn't satisfy the ethno requirement for autoethnography. (We will discuss the ethno in Chapter 4.)

And then there's the "graphy" of autoethnography. When used as a suffix, graphy indicates the art and practice of writing and representation. We understand autoethnography as comprised of two kinds of graphy: the graphy associated with autobio-graphy, the art of writing and representing one's life; and the graphy of ethno-graphy, the art and science of writing and representing cultural principles, practices, and products. If we consider writing our typical medium of representation, good ethnography requires good writing. Good autobiography requires good writing too. Comprised of both, autoethnography thus requires really good writing.[17] (We'll discuss graphy in Chapter 2.)

Assembled, we have auto-ethno-graphy, the art and science of writing one's life and/or research practices in relation to cultural principles, practices, and products. These components are the first and primary criteria we use to assess autoethnography. If a manuscript claims to do/be/use autoethnography yet disregards any of these components, then we often assess the manuscript as bad autoethnography or not autoethnography at all.

But before we dive into actual assessment, we want to share some formative experiences regarding learning, writing, and autoethnography—experiences that inform how we conceived this project. As we demonstrate here and throughout this book, we cannot avoid assessment—it is a core feature of living and relating.

WRITING OUR WAY IN/TO ASSESSMENT

Andrew

As a kid, I was a solid student. In eighth grade I won a mathematics award and a science award. (I know, right?) I was good at both. And I liked to read a lot. After eighth grade though, I stopped paying much attention. My family started attending a conservative evangelical church that believed the end times were upon us and the apocalypse was moments away. What the hell was the point of learning anything if Armageddon would soon occur and we would die in World War III?

In high school, I passed my classes, but I stopped being interested in teachers' assessments of me. I wasn't that concerned about my grades, as long as I passed. I worried more about the church elders, my parents' friends, and my church friends. And most of all the impending assessment by that church's version of God, the ultimate assessor, who held my final destination in *His* hands. I believed the four horsemen of the apocalypse would come for a visit and judgment would follow.

I wasn't lazy—I just had different interests. Recognizing I would face a final assessment affected everything I did. I became infatuated with biblical prophecies about the end times. I read every book I possibly could, including *The Late Great Planet Earth*, *How to Recognize the AntiChrist*, *There's a New World Coming*, *Armageddon: Oil & the Middle East Crisis*, *The Footsteps of The Messiah: A Study of the Sequence of Prophetic Events*, and *The Revelation of Saint John*.[18] I read books describing the war between heaven and hell and the eventual destruction of everyone but the faithful. I was fully committed. I wanted to be judged righteous and true. I didn't want to be Left Behind.[19]

But I did want to leave behind the stress and chaos of my parents' struggling restaurant and the attendant long hours of work.[20] Since I thought humanity would self-destruct, I didn't put much planning into choosing a college. I started to rebel, listen to a lot of punk music, and develop an attitude.

> I walk into Mr. Argento's office. Mr. Argento is the guidance counselor. I sit in the wooden chair across from his desk.
> "I want to go to college."
> He laughed.
> Loud.
> To my face.
> "You're an asshole," I said.
> He assessed me, and I assessed him.
> I was suspended for a week.

Given my fundamentalist background, I picked a nondenominational Christian college, The King's College, in Briarcliff Manor, New York.[21] I decided to major in chemistry. However, by this time, my math talent had dwindled, and this affected how well I did with science. I failed my first two chemistry exams, and my final exam grade was the worst grade I had ever received.

> My advisor called me into his office. "You need to change your major," he said.
> I slumped in the chair, staring at my purple Converse sneakers.
> "You're never going to make it as a chemistry major. You cannot do math and you can't do chemistry." His assessment wasn't necessarily wrong.
> He pushed a piece of paper across the desk toward me.
> "Here's a change of major form. Bring it to the Registrar's office when you've decided what major you want."
> Was I in a recurring play?

Likely influenced by the nerve-wracking apocalyptic literature I drenched myself in, I had developed a love for horror and existentialism by "The Two SKs": Stephen King and Søren Kierkegaard, respectively. I tried to change my major to philosophy, but I wasn't ready for the repercussions of studying philosophy at a Christian college. "Once you start studying philosophy you've already lost your faith," one friend said. "You can't be a Christian and a philosopher," said another. "What does Athens have to do with Jerusalem?" another asked. "There's no future for anyone with that major," remarked another.

Yet, I loved the philosophy courses and my two professors, Mr. Brönnimann and Dr. Wacome. I loved thinking about the unanswerable. I excelled in my philosophy classes: all As. I realized I might have some acumen for reading hard texts and analyzing philosophical arguments. Mr. Bronnimann and Dr. Wacome pushed me to think deeply and write critically. I wrote a paper arguing that the existential dictum "existence precedes essence" cannot hold for God since, as an everlasting being, existence is *their* essence. I wrote another paper that flipped Descartes' *cogito ergo sum* ("I think, therefore I am") on its head ("I am, therefore I think"). And I wrote a paper about the biblical Book of *Job* from an existentialist perspective.

Despite making the Dean's list, things didn't go well my final two semesters at The King's College. As I've written elsewhere, life got difficult.[22] The College stopped offering the Philosophy major. I acted out, and they threw me out. I lost that fundamentalist version of my faith. (Maybe my peers were right about that happening.) I took a semester off. My parents' family business failed, and I had to make money to transfer to a state school—Ramapo College of New Jersey. On one of my days off from working at a gas station, I returned to my high school. A former teacher yelled "Andy Herrmann? You're still alive?!" The comment offers a sense of how several others assessed my chances.

In 1991, I finished my undergraduate degrees in Philosophy and Literature. That year, the bank foreclosed on our home. I spent the next ten years working in publishing, retail, graphic design, advertising, and information technology. In each position and profession, I felt bored, unchallenged. I read a lot about theoretical physics, including quantum mechanics, Schrodinger's theorems, chaos theory, and astrophysics. I also read more of The Two SKs.

In 1999, I started my information technology job at Saint Louis University (SLU). My office was on the third floor of Xavier Hall, the same floor as the Department of Communication. Between installing faculty computers, ghosting images on lab PCs, and fixing a variety of computer glitches, I was having intellectual hallway conversations with faculty and graduate students. Conversations about interpersonal relationships. Conversations about organizational power. Conversations about work-life balance. About theory. At one point, I had so many "drop-by" conversations with Dr. Paaige Turner that she printed out a placard with "Reserved for Andrew's Elbow" and put it on the bookshelf I used to lean on.

In Fall 2001, I decided to take undergraduate communication classes as a non-matriculated student. As I told Dr. Bob Krizek, "I want to see if I can be the kind of student I could have been as an undergrad." During my lunch hour, I took Communication Theory with Paaige and Interpersonal Communication with Dr. Rob Anderson. In Spring 2002, I spent my lunch hour taking Paaige's Communication Research Methods course and Bob's Organizational Communication course. Under their tutelage, I excelled. Verbally, I was still rough, a combination of punk attitude and New Jersey-aggressive. However, these professors frequently praised my writing.

> I'm walking down the bland hallway on the third floor of Xavier Hall, floppy disk in hand, headed to reinstall printers for Terry, the executive assistant for American Studies. Bob walks towards me.
>
> "Hey Andrew. Come to my office for a second," he says.
>
> "Something wrong with your computer?" I ask.
>
> "It's fine. I want to talk to you about something else."
>
> I need to get to American Studies, I think. Terry hasn't been able to print all morning. Instead, I sit in the dentist's chair Bob has in his office. Good for grilling and drilling, I laugh to myself.

"You should apply to the graduate program."

"What?"

"You should apply to the graduate program. You write well. You read more than we ask you to for classes. You're inquisitive. We think you'd do well."

"Really?" I feel stumped. "Ok, I'll do it. But don't be discouraged by my undergrad transcripts."

Five weeks later I encounter Bob leaving the main communication office.

"Andrew, I just received your transcripts." He chuckles and walks away.

"I warned you," I said.

"Yeah, you did," he replied.

I couldn't help but laugh.

In Fall 2002, I attended my first graduate class with people I had never met before, but who would become a big part of my life for many years, especially Art Herbig. I learned to write in the typical and sterile introduction-literature review-methods-findings-discussion-conclusion formula. I was interested in organizational communication. I wasn't an ethnographer—yet.

In Summer 2003, I took Bob's Ethnography course. This course was life-changing. We read John Van Maanen, Nick Trujillo, Bill Rawlins, and Clifford Geertz. Bob introduced me to key ethnographic practices: picking a site to research and do fieldwork; using, appreciating, and observing with all available senses in the field; writing field notes; going home and writing extended notes, the necessity of thick description; reviewing our notes to discern themes and patterns; making self-reflective notes in the margins of these notes; and writing it all up. Bud Goodall, who was doing research on his father's past work with the U.S. Central Intelligence Agency, gave a talk about narrative ethnography.[23] We did read some autoethnography, but I laughed at it; it just didn't seem like research.

For our final project, we had to do ethnography (process) and create an ethnography (product). I chose to do fieldwork in a local nonprofit organization that put on four punk music shows per week. The fieldwork was exhausting. I worked 40 to 50 hours per week in information technology and would then go home, grab a snack, and head to the field, where I would participate and observe for hours, experiencing everything I could, pulling my little notepad from my back pocket, and scribbling field notes. I would return home and expand on those notes for hours. I'd sleep and then wake to do the same tasks again. My schedule was brutal, but I found ethnography exhilarating.[24]

Originally, I started the master's program at SLU so that I could get promoted at my job. A career move. Yet, I was also becoming an academic. In 2003, Art Herbig said, "You need to get a PhD. You have important ideas to share." I vacillated for months and finally decided to apply to doctoral programs with an emphasis in organizational communication. I had met Eric Eisenberg at an Organizational Communication conference. I'd read a lot of his work, and his research flowed between post-positivistic and interpretive paradigms. Eric was a professor at the University of South Florida (USF), and that program became my top school.

In November 2003, I attended the National Communication Association convention. I met several USF faculty including Carolyn Ellis, Art Bochner, and Ken Cissna, a friend and writing partner of Rob Anderson, my interpersonal communication professor at SLU. I also reconnected with Eric Eisenberg.

> One morning at the convention, as I sip coffee in the hotel lounge, I notice Art and Carolyn sitting comfortably on a nearby couch. Carolyn nods at me and invites me over.
>
> We talk about my thesis research on stockholders. She then asks, "Why do you want to come to USF?"
>
> "I want to come to USF to prove that autoethnography is not a viable method of research," I say.
>
> Art and Carolyn look at each other and laugh.
>
> Besides feeling embarrassed, I remember nothing after this moment. I thought, *Herrmann, for once, could you just stay quiet? You're never going to get into USF now!*

And yet, I was accepted. I never asked USF faculty why they accepted me. Maybe one day I will. Obviously, they had a favorable assessment of me.

In May 2004, I graduated from SLU. My thesis received the "with distinction" moniker and was recognized as outstanding graduate research.[25] Three months later, on a sweltering August day in Tampa, I met Tony.

Tony

I was an average student in high school. I didn't study much; the classes felt silly; and although I didn't care much about learning, my teachers didn't seem to care either. I received mostly As and Bs, took a lot of tests, and can't recall any reading or writing assignments. There weren't many penalties for not doing work, and by merely showing up, I would have likely passed every course. I wasn't lazy—I spent my teens working multiple jobs—but high school just didn't feel serious. Having played the piano and trumpet for several years, the only subject I enjoyed was music.

With music, tests, grades, and written texts didn't seem to matter; discipline, practice, and the ability to read and understand musical texts did, as did realizing how sound could infect and affect audiences. I could practice alone and play music I liked and how I liked to do so, but if I wanted to share music with others—an audience—I had to consider how my sounds might affect listeners. I realized if I decided to share one of my musical creations, and if audiences deemed the creation pleasant, I could generate joy and euphoria. Possibly, subsequently, I might even receive a "standing ovation." I might be asked to perform again, and others might tell others about my talent. But if I decided to share one of my creations too hastily and audiences deemed it unpleasant, I might cultivate discomfort or even hostility.[26] Audience members might leave or fall asleep during the middle of a performance, and possibly, subsequently, laugh, boo, and hiss. I may have fewer opportunities to share my future creations, and my performances might attract dwindling crowds.

During my final year of high school, I told my music instructor I wanted to play trumpet in the University of Illinois at Urbana Champaign marching band. "You are not good enough for the band," she said, laughing. Deflated, I stared at her and agreed, sheepishly. "Okay," I said. "You know best." Having worked with the instructor for nearly a decade, I trusted her; she was an esteemed mentor. And so, at the end of that year, I stopped making music.[27]

After high school, I enrolled at the local community college. Although I cannot remember the actual assignment, I recall the immense fear I had toward writing a two-page paper for Rhetoric and Composition I, one of my first courses. I did not have any formal training in writing, so I sought help from Nicole Neuman, a high school history teacher and one of my best friends. One evening we met for nearly four hours at a diner to work on the assignment. Nicole helped me develop and structure ideas and arguments and taught me about the care required to assemble each word and every line. Nicole's guidance gave me some confidence with writing, and I earned an "A" for the course. However, my limited training in writing would still haunt me.

In August 1999, I transferred to Southern Illinois University Carbondale (SIUC) to major in Radio-Television News. I took courses in news reporting and media writing and production. I wrote stories and scripts, and I learned about message design, delivery, and adapting messages to audiences. If I wanted a story to be printed in the newspaper or shared via radio or television, I had to write at a "fifth-grade reading level" to accommodate and appeal to large audiences. I followed the inverted pyramid format[28] and aphorisms such as "if it bleeds, it leads." I also learned I could attract, or repel, viewers and readers with how I reported a topic. Just as I could have made music by myself, I could have written news reports for myself, but doing so would not have fulfilled the requirements for the public-facing major—the very premise of Radio-Television News was to use media platforms to inform others about social issues and situations. If I wanted others to use, hear, and share my words and if I wanted my ideas to be printed or aired, then I had to care about craft and assessment, as well as accurate and ethical representation. Although I enjoyed studying media processes and products, I found writing news stories, especially about difficult issues and situations, exhausting and often invasive.

In Fall 2001, I started the master's program in Speech Communication at SIUC. I took classes in autoethnography, phenomenology, and performance, and I learned more about telling compelling stories and the aesthetics of representation. I worked alongside contemporary autoethnographers including Keith Berry, Sandra Pensoneau-Conway, Ahmet Atay, Ben Myers, Nicole Defenbaugh, and Adrienne Viramontes, and among a legacy of esteemed autoethnographers such as John Warren, Tami Spry, Lesa Lockford, and Bryant Keith Alexander. I took courses with Ron Pelias, and Craig Gingrich-Philbrook was doing brilliant work with autoperformance. I also taught multiple sections of Public Speaking, a course that prioritized message design and delivery, the importance of logic, emotion, character, and credibility, finding and using extant research, interviewing others, and adapting and presenting information to live audiences.

I quickly realized that writing at a fifth grade reading level wouldn't work in the master's program and my writing and reading abilities were terribly weak. In my first semester, I took Communication Theory with Lenore Langsdorf. Lenore assigned weekly writings—one-page, single-spaced responses to each week's readings. Lenore gave extensive feedback on these writings, and to receive a grade, one had to revise-and-resubmit each writing until she felt the writing was adequate. Once, when I submitted a revision, I disregarded Lenore's prior feedback. She returned the revision and chastised me for disregarding her edits; she said I was wasting my time and her time, and she wasn't sure why I was in the program. Lenore was right—if I wanted to continue, I needed to try harder and do better. I soon asked Lenore if she would be my advisor and help me improve my work. She agreed. I took more classes with Lenore, and out of 40+ weekly writings, I only submitted an adequate first draft a few times. My writing wasn't great, but I was improving.

Near the end of my master's program, I wanted to continue to teach, read, and write, and I applied to four doctoral programs. Three programs rejected my application and the fourth, USF, the program I really wanted, accepted me without graduate funding. I could not have moved without the funding, and I had to decline the acceptance.

Lenore wrote one of my recommendation letters for the doctoral programs. In the letter, she described how I developed as a writer since I started working with her. I later learned that a member of the admissions committee at USF interpreted Lenore's comment negatively—they felt I didn't know how to write and, as such, shouldn't be admitted.

Although the other programs also denied my applications, several folks at SIUC recognized my growth and dedication to learning. Ron Pelias, the graduate director, offered me an additional year of funding so that I could survive; stay affiliated with a university; continue to work on my teaching, reading, and writing; and reapply to doctoral programs the following year.

And that's what I did. I worked more and more closely with Lenore and Ron. I read books about writing, and I began to pursue publication for my work. The next year, I applied to four doctoral programs, including USF. This time, I was admitted to all of them and with full funding. USF was still my first choice so that's where I went. And that's where I met Andrew.

Together

In August 2004, we started the doctoral program in Communication at USF. Art Bochner directed our dissertations, and we worked closely with Carolyn Ellis, who also served on our dissertation committees. Philosopher Charles Guignon, with his courses in phenomenology, existentialism, and identity, was also highly influential.[29] We defended our dissertations in June 2008, within four days of each other. Our graduate cohort consisted of several contemporary autoethnographers including Robin Boylorn, Rachel Silverman, Jeanine Mingé, and Jillian Tullis, and we followed a legacy of autoethnographers including Lisa Tillmann, Christine Kiesinger, Barbara Jago, Jay Baglia, Christine Davis, Elissa Foster, and Michael Arrington. Tony began collaborating with Stacy Holman Jones, a professor in the program, and Andrew continued to have long conversations about organizational ethnography with Eric Eisenberg. As we demonstrate throughout this book, our coursework and close training with Art, Carolyn, Stacy, Eric, and several of these others taught us much about autoethnography, and why we should care about our craft as writers and researchers.

Since USF, we have continued to do a lot of autoethnography, and we continue to work closely with Art, Carolyn, Stacy, and many of our graduate school peers. Together, we have written and/or edited 11 books about autoethnography, published more than 100 articles about, or using, autoethnography, and edited six special journal issues about autoethnography.[30] With Art Herbig, Andrew co-edits the *Communication Perspectives in Popular Culture* book series (Lexington) and with Art and Carolyn, Tony co-edits the *Writing Lives: Ethnographic and Autoethnographic Narratives* book series (Routledge). Both series frequently include autoethnographic manuscripts. We have reviewed hundreds of autoethnographic manuscripts for journals and have served as reviewers of more than 30 autoethnographic theses and dissertations. In 2019, after several conversations with visionary publisher and editor Mitch Allen, we launched the *Journal of Autoethnography* (University of California Press). Nearly every Wednesday for the past five years, we have met to assess manuscripts submitted to the journal. Accept? Reject? Revise and resubmit? We would make these decisions based on our assessment criteria and reviewer feedback. We have had hundreds of in-depth discussions about how to best assess autoethnographic manuscripts, and we have worked with thousands of reviews and hundreds of reviewers. (As of this writing [May 2024], we have reviewed 700+ manuscripts submitted to the journal, many of which were sent to two to three reviewers. As such, we have reviewed 700+ autoethnographic manuscripts and 1,400+ reviews of these manuscripts.) To embrace Art Bochner's framing of autoethnography as a "way of life," autoethnography has been, quite literally, our way of life for more than 20 years.

Since USF, we have also continued our work in communication. Andrew is a professor in the Department of Communication Studies and Storytelling at East Tennessee State University. Tony has been a professor and chair of two departments—the Department of Communication, Media and Theatre at Northeastern Illinois University and the Department of Communication at Bradley University. In our departments, we offer courses on relationships, rhetoric, persuasion, public advocacy, journalism, storytelling, scriptwriting, media production, public relations, organizational consulting, advertising, and social media. Our departments and courses prioritize message design, distribution, and assessment—that's what we do.

Given our disciplinary training and decades of work with autoethnography, Hannah Shakespeare, our esteemed (former) editor at Routledge, asked us to write a book about assessing autoethnography. We initially balked at the idea. It wasn't a bad idea—we were just both finishing big handbook projects and had recently launched the *Journal of Autoethnography*. We weren't sure we had the time to commit to the book. Yet after a few years of editing the journal, we realized that this book needed to be written, and we were well-equipped to write it.

*

You may wonder why we shared these experiences and how these experiences relate to assessment and autoethnography. Here, we offer an explanation, an answer to the necessary "So what?" question we should ask of all autoethnographies (see Chapter 1): How and why do one's experiences matter? Why do we want to share them with others? What insights and lessons should readers learn? Three responses.

First, we wanted to demonstrate various forms assessment might take, the prevalence of assessment in everyday life, and the lessons we can learn from assessment. I (Andrew) learned that I wasn't analytical enough to make a good chemist—an honest assessment of my ability. However, I am an analytical reader who can engage with difficult philosophical and religious tomes. This ability informs most of my writings where I intermingle the ideas of Bakhtin, Buber, Heidegger, Sartre, Weick, and Kierkegaard.[31] I learned the evangelical religious discourses under which I was raised and subjugated are not the only religious discourses under which one can live. There's a freedom to learning that too, including the freedom to interrogate religious cult/ures from an insider's perspective and, if desired, how to challenge or escape these cult/ures.[32] Given my experiences with past instructors, I also learned who I wanted to (not) be as an instructor. I try to be a good assessor for students, especially those who want to write and publish autoethnography.[33]

My (Tony) early training in music taught me about the importance of practice, rhythm, cadence, style, audiences, and feedback/assessment. I observed how I could infect and affect listeners with my music and how others' assessment of my musical ability motivated me to abandon a career in music. However, I soon found writing. Although a different medium, writing is still a craft, and like music, it requires practice, rhythm, cadence, style, audiences, and feedback/assessment. Like music, I could use writing to create feelings, possibilities, and worlds, and I could infect and affect readers with my ideas. I also learned that assessment matters primarily, if not only, if we want to share our work.

Second, we often receive manuscripts that, although claiming to be autoethnographic, merely use first-person voice or describe the author's positionality in relation to a project. Yet such acts do not make an autoethnography. Thus far, we have shared some biographical information about how we conceived of this book and our experiences with autoethnography. Yet sharing this information isn't autoethnography. The experiences we shared are autobiographical "life chronologies" that merely describe our positionalities in relation to this book. To make them more autoethnographic, we would need to connect the topics and experiences to others, extant work, and broader cultural issues, e.g., the significance of religion, being submissive to or challenging canonical educational practices, the importance of practicing one's craft, (in)effective teachers/pedagogy. We receive a lot of autobiographical life chronologies for the journal, but they are often rejected. (We will discuss life chronologies in Chapter 3.) It is important for an author to explain their positionality in relation to a project, but the inclusion of a mere positionality doesn't make a project autoethnographic.

Finally, we share these experiences to establish our credibility as autoethnographers. We care about autoethnography and have devoted our careers to supporting and promoting good autoethnography. We also offer ideas for assessing autoethnographies from the perspective of folks who actually do autoethnography. Early critiques of autoethnography were written by people who had never written autoethnography, and there are many books *about* autoethnography by authors who have never *done* autoethnography. (We do not cite these authors because we refuse to direct attention to their work.) Just as we would question a scholar who wrote about assessing interview research but who had never done an interview, or who wrote about how to play the flute without having ever played the flute, or who wrote about acting but who never acted, we do not trust authors who write *about* autoethnography but who rarely, if ever, have done it. If we want to learn how to play guitar, we are going to consult *actual guitarists* rather than a guitar theorist who cannot play the instrument. We are going to trust Stephen King's advice about how to write fiction much more than someone who writes *about* how to write fiction but who has never written fiction themselves. When we read an article or book about doing autoethnography, we research whether the author has ever done autoethnography. If they haven't, we wonder why they feel credible and entitled to write about it. Worse, these authors often miss the point, misrepresent the method, and mislead readers. So, dear reader, when you read texts about autoethnography, please make sure the author has at least published autoethnography and then whether they did autoethnography well.

ASSEMBLING THIS BOOK

The very notion of assessment suggests judgment and criticism, and writing about how to judge and criticize can feel weird, elitist, and condescending. Being assessed can feel like being attacked; as Bloom notes, "All writing is personal, whether it sounds that way or not, if the writer has a stake in the work."[34] Yet, assessment doesn't have to feel this way. With this book, we have tried to craft a conversational and constructive text about assessing autoethnography, a text rooted in the multiple lessons we have learned across our vast autoethnographic writing, reading, and reviewing experiences. Given the deliberate use and interrogation of our assessment experiences, you could even consider this book an autoethnography of assessing autoethnography.[35] Inversely, this book is also a how-to book about doing and representing autoethnography, a reverse-engineering of sorts. By identifying criteria for assessing autoethnography, we identify techniques a writer should consider when doing autoethnography and crafting autoethnographic texts.

To keep the scope of this book manageable, we prioritize the assessment of *writing* and *written* autoethnographies. There may be different criteria for assessing autoethnographies using other representational media. For instance, what makes a good autoethnographic song, performance, or drawing? We encourage readers who engage these media to consult with resources about how to assess music, performance, and/or visual art. One might make music, performance, and art by oneself, but if they make this work public, share it with others, they should take assessment seriously; they should consider standards for good music, good performance, and good drawing. Assessment matters if one wants others to care about their work.

In Chapter 1, "On Being *Homo Assessors*," we discuss the purpose of assessment and demonstrate why assessing one's work is important and necessary. Although some authors suggest autoethnography should be free from evaluative criteria and criteria can create barriers to entry, we disagree—assessment is a part of nearly every facet of our lives. (Again, we refuse to cite these authors; we do not want to direct attention to their work.) We assess to live better, safely, and comfortably. We assess to create work that will be understood, appreciated, used and engaged, taught, purchased, nominated for awards, cited, and shared. We don't believe authors should ever send out a "shitty first draft" or generally sloppy work.[36] Or rather, authors can do what they want with their work—it is their work, not ours—but they shouldn't be surprised if others do not support sloppy drafts; it's difficult to care about a work an author doesn't seem to care about themselves.

We often understand and explain autoethnography through its three components—the auto, ethno, and graphy—and in that order. Yet here, we will begin with the graphy—one of the most important and challenging facets of doing and assessing autoethnography. Graphy underscores all autoethno*graphy*, which merges the personal writing of autobio*graphy* (and affiliated genres of life writing) with the research goals and techniques of ethno*graphy*. As such, in Chapter 2, "The 'Graphy' of Autoethnography: The Craft of Writing (about Oneself)," we argue good ethnography requires good writing. Good autobiography requires good writing too. Comprised of both, autoethnography thus requires really good writing. Yet, few researchers take formal courses in writing or take writing seriously; instead, they treat writing as a technical, secondary act rather than an epistemic, generative process.

As mentioned, just because a manuscript is written in first-person voice or offers, the author's positionality in relation to a topic does not make it autoethnographic. In Chapter 3, "The 'Auto' of Autoethnography: Narrating the Self and Assessing the I," we identify criteria for assessing the use and representation of personal experience. We explore the kinds of personal experiences that work best for autoethnography, as well as how to assess the use of personal experience without necessarily assessing the person's character—though assessing one's character can and does occur.

In Chapter 4, "The 'Ethno' of Autoethnography: Assessing Culture and (Mis)uses of Others," we discern ways personal experience intersects with others' experiences and, more broadly, with cultural principles, practices, and products. We assess the ethno components of autoethnography including fieldwork, interviewing and including others in our work, and analyzing existing research and representations of an experience, topic, or identity.

In the Conclusion, "Practical Advice and a Few Warnings," we synthesize the various criteria we use throughout the book. We offer some final guidance about doing good autoethnographic work, including developing your authorial voice, and identify several issues to consider before deciding to publish your work.

Although we separate the auto, ethno, and graphy to narrow our focus, these terms are unequivocally connected, mutually reinforcing, intersecting, symbiotic. We isolate them in this book, but, in practice, one cannot do good autoethnography without attending to all three. A work classified as "autoethnography" must demonstrate a care for, and commitment to, the auto, the ethno, and the graphy—for us, this is a rigid, prescriptive, and non-negotiable expectation. We don't intend our other criteria to be as rigid or prescriptive, but rather reflections and ruminations on the kinds of autoethnographic work we prefer to do and read. Yet the autoethnography that we like to do and read may not be the kind of autoethnography that you like to do and read; we have our preferred styles of reading and writing. You likely do too. We are also not the only autoethnographers—there are thousands of us—and our criteria may not be shared criteria.

Further, for decades, scholars have had to defend autoethnography.[37] In the 1990s and 2000s, many autoethnographers cared about legitimizing autoethnography. There were many haters; here is a good summation of their early critiques

> Critics complain that autoethnography is not rigorous, because it is not based on experimental design. *Correct.* Some researchers say autoethnography cannot be research because N=1. *Correct.* Other critics say the findings of autoethnography cannot be statistically valid or generalizable. *Correct.* Concurring with these assessments makes sense, because those are the wrong standards and measures by which to determine the quality of autoethnographic and narrative research. [...] Autoethnography is a narrative approach to research, and therefore to continue to attempt to judge it by the standards of an experimental approach is simply willful ignorance at this point.[38]

In this book, we do not engage in these dated critiques or assess autoethnography from positivist or quantitative perspectives. We don't need to be so defensive anymore. Many of the haters seem to have disappeared. We no longer see the common names of writers who spent so much time bashing autoethnography yet who never did it. Autoethnography has since flourished in many contexts and continues to do so. (Occasionally, we still encounter the errant person who says, "I don't believe in autoethnography," to which we reply, sarcastically, "That's fine. We don't believe in statistics, experiments, survey or interview research.") We don't write in response to past critics; instead, we write for present and future scholars interested in, and excited about, pursuing autoethnographic projects.

We hope this book will serve as a good guide for authors and instructors, students and supervisors, reviewers and researchers who care about doing, creating, and promoting good autoethnography. We want advisors and committee members unfamiliar with autoethnography to be able to support students interested in doing autoethnography. We want instructors and supervisors of autoethnographic projects to have a better sense of the key components of autoethnography, what questions to (not) ask and what criteria to (not) use, and how to assess autoethnographies fairly and constructively.

But first, let's consider when and how and why assessment matters.

NOTES

1 We use this title to pay homage to our beloved advisor/friend/father's book, Arthur P. Bochner, *Coming to Narrative: A Personal History of Paradigm Change in the Human Sciences* (Walnut Creek, CA: Left Coast Press, 2014).

2 Arthur P. Bochner, "Criteria against Ourselves," *Qualitative Inquiry* 6, no. 2 (2000), 270–271, https://doi.org/10.1177/107780040000600209.

3 Carolyn Ellis, "'I Hate My Voice': Coming to Terms with Minor Bodily Stigmas," *The Sociological Quarterly* 39, no. 4 (1998), 517–537, https://doi.org/10.1111/j.1533-8525.1998.tb00516.x.

4 Craig Gingrich-Philbrook writes, "Though sometimes thought of as a 'method,' autoethnography strikes me more as a broad orientation toward scholarship than a specific procedure." Craig Gingrich-Philbrook, "Autoethnography's Family Values: Easy Access to Compulsory Experiences," *Text and Performance Quarterly* 25, no. 4 (2005), 297–314, https://doi.org/10.1080/10462930500362445; Arthur P. Bochner, "Autoethnography as a Way of Life: Listening to Tinnitus Teach," *Journal of Autoethnography* 1, no. 1 (2020), 81–92, https://doi.org/10.1525/joae.2020.1.1.81.

5 Tony E. Adams and Andrew F. Herrmann, "Expanding our Autoethnographic Future," *Journal of Autoethnography* 1, no. 1 (2020), 1–8, https//doi.org/10.1525/joae.2020.1.1.1. Arthur P. Bochner and Carolyn Ellis, eds., *Ethnographically Speaking: Autoethnography, Literature, and Aesthetics* (Lanham, MD: Altamira Press, 2002); Lisa M. Tillmann, "Speaking into Silences: Autoethnography, Communication, and Applied Research," *Journal of Applied Communication Research* 37, no. 1 (2009), 94–97, https://doi.org/10.1080/00909880802592649.

6 Conferences that foreground autoethnographic work include the International Congress of Qualitative Inquiry, the International Symposium on Autoethnography and Narrative, the International Conference of Autoethnography, Critical Autoethnography, the European Congress of Qualitative Inquiry, the Central States Communication Association, the American Educational Research Association, and Contemporary Ethnography across the Disciplines.

7 Pat Sikes, *Autoethnography* (Thousand Oaks, CA: Sage, 2011).

8 Stacy Holman Jones, Tony E. Adams, and Carolyn Ellis, eds., *Handbook of Autoethnography* (Walnut Creek, CA: Left Coast Press, 2013); Tony E. Adams, Stacy Holman Jones, and Carolyn Ellis, eds., *Handbook of Autoethnography*, 2nd ed. (New York: Routledge, 2022).

9 Christopher N. Poulos, *Essentials of Autoethnography* (Washington, DC: American Psychological Association, 2021).

10 Ellis, "I Hate My Voice"; Carolyn Ellis, "Sociological Introspection and Emotional Experience," *Symbolic Interaction* 14, no. 1, 23–50, https://doi.org/10.1525/si.1991.14.1.23; Carolyn Ellis, "Telling Secrets, Revealing Lives: Relational Ethics in Research with Intimate Others," *Qualitative Inquiry* 13, no. 1 (2007), 3–29, https://doi.org/10.1177/1077800406294947.

11 Carol Rambo Ronai, "The Reflexive Self through Narrative," in *Investigating Subjectivity: Research on Lived Experience*, eds., Carolyn Ellis and Michael G. Flaherty (Thousand Oaks, CA: Sage, 1992), 102–124; Carol Rambo Ronai, "Multiple Reflections of Child Sex Abuse: An Argument for a Layered Account," *Journal of Contemporary Ethnography* 23, no. 4 (1995), 395–426, https://doi.org/10.1177/089124195023004001.

12 Many folks who cite Anderson's work on "analytic autoethnography" often only engage Anderson's first (2006) article about the concept. Anderson has further clarified his use of analytic autoethnography; see his opening chapter in the first edition (2013) of the *Handbook of Autoethnography.* We also encourage manuscripts that claim to do/use analytic autoethnography to resemble Anderson's analytic autoethnographies, yet few do; they claim to follow Anderson's arguments and advice but fail to follow the form of Anderson's actual analytic autoethnographic work. We will discuss Anderson again in Chapter 4. See Leon Anderson, "Analytic Autoethnography," *Journal of Contemporary Ethnography* 35, no. 4 (2006),

373–395, https://doi.org/10.1177/0891241605280449; Leon Anderson, "On Apples, Oranges, and Autopsies: A Response to Commentators," *Journal of Contemporary Ethnography* 35, no. 4 (2006), 450–465, https://doi.org/10.1177/0891241606287395; Leon Anderson and Bonnie Glass-Coffin, "I Learn by Going: Autoethnographic Modes of Inquiry," in *Handbook of Autoethnography*, eds., Stacy Holman Jones, Tony E. Adams, and Carolyn Ellis (Walnut Creek, CA: Left Coast Press, 2013), 57–83; Leon Anderson, "Time Is of the Essence: An Analytic Autoethnography of Family, Work, and Serious Leisure," *Symbolic Interaction* 34, no. 2 (2011), 133–157, https://doi.org/10.1525/si.2011.34.2.133; Leon Anderson, "Garfinkeling in Real Life: The Candid Sociology of 'Neon Leon,'" *Journal of Autoethnography* 2, no. 4 (2021), 369–379, https://doi.org/10.1525/joae.2021.2.4.369.

13 Oskar Szwabowski, "Forget All Criteria," *International Review of Qualitative Research* 12, no. 4 (2019), 476–481, https://doi.org/10.1177/19408447211002780; and Andrew F. Herrmann, "The Future of Autoethnographic Criteria," *International Review of Qualitative Research* 15, no. 1 (2022), 125–135, https://doi.org/10.1177/19408447211049513.

14 Jacob Bernstein, "The Many People Behind 'The Woman in Me,'" *New York Times*, October 31, 2023, https://www.nytimes.com/2023/10/31/style/britney-spears-ghostwriters.html; Stephen King, *Danse Macabre* (New York: Gallery Books), 2010.

15 Early works about autoethnography merged the purposes and practices of autobiography and the purposes and practices of ethnography. For example, in their classic chapter about autoethnography, Ellis and Bochner refer to autoethnography as an "autobiographical genre of writing and research." Carolyn Ellis and Arthur P. Bochner, "Autoethnography, Personal Narrative, Reflexivity: Researcher as Subject," in *Handbook of Qualitative Research*, 2nd ed., eds., Norman K. Denzin and Yvonna S. Lincoln (Thousand Oaks, CA: Sage, 2000), 739. See also Lyall Crawford, "Personal Ethnography," *Communication Monographs* 63, no. 2, 158–170, https://doi.org/10.1080/03637759609376384; Norman K. Denzin, *Interpretive Biography* (Newbury Park, CA: Sage, 1989); and Ronald J. Pelias, "An Autobiographic Ethnography of Performance in Everyday Discourse," *Journal of Dramatic Theory and Criticism* 8, no. 2 (1994), 163–172.

16 Clifford Geertz, *The Interpretation of Cultures* (New York: Basic Books, 1973), 10.

17 We revised these paragraphs about the auto, ethno, and graphy from Tony E. Adams and Andrew F. Herrmann, "Good Autoethnography," *Journal of Autoethnography* 4, no. 1 (2023), 1–9, https://doi.org/10.1525/joae.2023.4.1.1.

18 Hal Lindsey and Carole C. Carlson, *The Late Great Planet Earth* (Grand Rapids, MI: Zondervan, 1970); Arthur Edward Bloomfield, *How to Recognize the Antichrist* (Bloomington, MN: Bethany House Publishers, 1975); Hal Lindsey, *There's a New World Coming* (Santa Ana, CA: Vision House, 1973); John Walvoord, *Armageddon: Oil & the Middle East Crisis* (Grand Rapids, MI: Zondervan, 1991); Arnold G. Fruchtenbaum, *The Footsteps of the Messiah: A Study of the Sequence of Prophetic Events* (San Antonio, TX: Ariel Press, 1982).

19 This was long before The Left Behind series, which consists of 16 books, popularized this form of end-times eschatology. See Michael Standaert, *Skipping towards Armageddon: The Politics and Propaganda of the Left Behind Novels and the LaHaye Empire* (New York: Soft Skull Press, 2006); and Barbara R. Rossing, *The Rapture Exposed: The Message of Hope in the Book of Revelation* (New York: Basic Books, 2004).

20 Andrew has written extensively about these parts of his life. See Andrew F. Herrmann, "'Losing Things Was Nothing New': A Family's Story of Foreclosure," *Journal of Loss & Trauma* 16, no. 6 (2011), 497–510, https://doi.org/10.1080/15325024.2011.576982; Andrew F. Herrmann, "The Ghostwriter: Living a Father's Unfinished Narrative," in *On (Writing)*

Families: Autoethnographies of Presence and Absence, Love and Loss, eds., Jonathan Wyatt and Tony E. Adams (Rotterdam: Brill, 2014), 95–101.

21 Andrew is still deconstructing his Chrstian belief system. See Andrew F. Herrmann, "Walking in Kierkegaard's Instant and Walking Out of American Christendom," *Departures in Critical Qualitative Research* 4, no. 2 (2015), 91–119; Andrew F. Herrmann, "Purity, Nationalism, and Whiteness: The Fracturing of Fundamentalist Evangelicalism," *International Review of Qualitative Research* 13, no. 4 (2020), 414–432, https://doi.org/10.1177/1940844720937813.

22 Herrmann, "'Losing Things Was Nothing New'"; Herrmann, "Walking in Kierkegaard's Instant"; Andrew F. Herrmann, "Daniel Amos and Me: The Power of Pop Culture and Autoethnography," *The Popular Culture Studies Journal* 1, no. 2 (2013), 6–17.

23 Goodall was doing research at the National Archives' National Personnel Records Center in Spanish Hill, Missouri. Eventually his research would result in the book, Harold Lloyd Goodall, Jr., *A Need to Know: The Clandestine History of a CIA Family* (Walnut Creek, CA: Left Coast Press, 2006).

24 I published two journal articles from this ethnographic project. Andrew F. Herrmann, "Narrative as an Organizing Process: Identity and Story in a New Nonprofit," *Qualitative Research in Organizations and Management: An International Journal* 6, no. 33 (2012), 246–264, https://doi.org/10.1108/17465641111188411; Andrew F. Herrmann, "Never Mind the Scholar, Here's the Old Punk: Identity, Community, and the Aging Music Fan," *Studies in Symbolic Interaction* 39 (2012), 153–170.

25 Originally, for my thesis, *Sensemaking in Cyberspace: An Analysis of a Financial Discussion Board Online*, I planned to showcase the application of Karl Weick's process of sensemaking in a financial discussion. Halfway through coding, thanks to what Paaige Turner taught me in the graduate organizational communication class, I realized the communicative activity was also gendered. The results of this thesis were published as three journal articles: Andrew F. Herrmann, "Stockholders and Mediated Intertextuality," *Florida Communication Journal* 34, no. 2 (2006), 105–114; Andrew F. Herrmann, "'People Get Emotional about Their Money': Performing Masculinity in a Financial Discussion Board," *Journal of Computer-Mediated Communication* 12, no. 2 (2007), 499–522, https://doi.org/10.1111/j.1083-6101.2007.00335.x; and Andrew F. Herrmann, "Stockholders in Cyberspace: Weick's Sensemaking Online," *Journal of Business Communication* 44, no. 1 (2007), 13–35, https://doi.org/10.1177/0021943606295778.

26 I used to play trumpet for Catholic masses and events. If I played trumpet poorly at a funeral, the grieving family would have been angry with me and/or the church. For another example, see the "Musical Language" episode of the Radiolab podcast. The episode describes how listeners perceive and react to sound and how Igor Stravinsky's "The Rite of Spring" incited a riot among audience members. See WYNC Studios, "Musical Language," *Radiolab* September 24, 2007, https://radiolab.org/podcast/91512-musical-language.

27 I tell a slightly longer version of this story in Tony E. Adams, "Foreword," in *Critical Autoethnography and Spiritual Discovery*, ed., Gresilda A. Tilley-Lubbs (Oxford: Peter Lang, 2017), xv–xvii.

28 The inverted pyramid structure for news reports features the most important information in the opening paragraphs—the who, what, where, when, why, and how. The remaining paragraphs include less important information.

29 For an excellent and accessible introduction to his work, see Charles B. Guignon, *On Being Authentic* (London: Routledge, 2004). Also see Charles Guignon, ed., *The Cambridge*

Companion to Heidegger (Cambridge: Cambridge University Press, 1993); Charles Guignon, ed., *The Existentialists: Critical Essays on Kierkegaard, Nietzsche, Heidegger, and Sartre* (Lanham, MD: Rowman & Littlefield, 2004); Charles Guignon and Kevin Aho, "Authenticity and Social Critique," in *The Cambridge History of Philosophy, 1945–2015*, eds., Kelly Becker and Iain D. Thomas (Cambridge: Cambridge University Press, 2019), 389–398.

30 Andrew has edited two books about autoethnography: Andrew F. Herrmann, *Organizational Autoethnographies: Power and Identity in Our Working Lives* (New York: Routledge, 2017); and Andrew F. Herrmann, ed., *The Routledge International Handbook of Organizational Autoethnography* (New York: Routledge, 2020). He has also co-edited two special journal issues about autoethnography: Sally Sambrook and Andrew F. Herrmann, "Organizational Autoethnography," *Journal of Organizational Ethnography* 7, no. 3 (2012), 222–387; and Andrew F. Herrmann and Kristen DiFate, "The New Ethnography," *Storytelling, Self, Society* 10, no. 1 (2014), 3–118.

Tony has published nine books about autoethnography: Tony E. Adams, *Narrating the Closet: An Autoethnography of Same-Sex Attraction* (Walnut Creek, CA: Left Coast Press, 2011); Jonathan Wyatt and Tony E. Adams, eds., *On (Writing) Families: Autoethnographies of Presence and Absence, Love and Loss* (Rotterdam: Brill, 2014); Holman Jones et al., *Handbook of Autoethnography*; Tony E. Adams, Stacy Holman Jones, and Carolyn Ellis, *Autoethnography* (New York: Oxford University Press, 2015); Sandra L. Pensoneau-Conway, Tony E. Adams, and Derek M. Bolen, eds., *Doing Autoethnography* (Rotterdam: Brill, 2017); Lydia Turner, Nigel P. Short, Alec Grant, and Tony E. Adams, eds., *International Perspectives on Autoethnographic Research and Practice* (New York: Routledge, 2018); Keith Berry, Catherine M. Gillotti, and Tony E. Adams, *Living Sexuality: Stories of LGBTQ Relationships, Identities, and Desires* (Leiden: Brill | Sense, 2020); Tony E. Adams, Robin M. Boylorn, and Lisa M. Tillmann, eds., *Advances in Autoethnography and Narrative Inquiry: Reflections on the Legacy of Carolyn Ellis and Arthur Bochner* (New York: Routledge, 2021); Adams, Holman Jones, and Ellis, *Handbook of Autoethnography*, 2nd ed. He has also edited four special journal issues/sections about autoethnography: Tony E. Adams and Jonathan Wyatt, eds., "On (Writing) Fathers," *Qualitative Inquiry* 18 (2012), 119–209; Tony E. Adams and Stacy Holman Jones, eds., "On Studying Ourselves and Others," *Liminalities: A Journal of Performance Studies* 9 (2013), http://liminalities.net/9-2/; Jimmie Manning and Tony E. Adams, eds., "Connecting the Personal and the Popular: Autoethnography and Popular Culture," *The Popular Culture Studies Journal* 3 (2015), 187–519; and Tony E. Adams and Derek M. Bolen, eds., "Queer Autoethnography" [Forum], *QED: Journal in GLBTQ Worldmaking* 4 (2017), 110–197.

We have also written several articles and chapters about assessing autoethnography: Adams and Herrmann, "Expanding our Autoethnographic Future"; Andrew F. Herrmann and Tony E. Adams, "Learning to be Editors," *Journal of Autoethnography* 2, no. 1 (2021), 1–4, https://doi.org/10.1525/joae.2021.2.1.1; Andrew F. Herrmann and Tony E. Adams, "Autoethnography and the 'So What?' Question," *Journal of Autoethnography* 3, no. 1 (2022), 1–3, https://doi.org/10.1525/joae.2022.3.1.1; Adams and Herrmann, "Good Autoethnography"; Herrmann, "The Future of Autoethnographic Criteria"; Andrew F. Herrmann, "Criteria against Ourselves? Embracing the Opportunities of Qualitative Inquiry," *International Review of Qualitative Research* 5, no. 2 (2012), 135–152, https://doi.org/10.1525/irqr.2012.5.2.135; Arthur P. Bochner and Andrew F. Herrmann, "Practicing Narrative Inquiry II: Making Meanings Move," in *The Oxford Handbook of Qualitative Inquiry*, 2nd ed., ed., Patricia Leavy (Oxford: Oxford University Press, 2020), 285–328.; Tony E. Adams, "Autoethnographic Responsibilities," *International Review of Qualitative Research* 10, no. 1

(2017), 62–66, https://doi.org/10.1525/irqr.2017.10.1.62; and Tony E. Adams, "Supervising, Sharing, and Evaluating Autoethnography," in *International Perspectives on Autoethnographic Research and Practice*, eds., Lydia Turner, Nigel P. Short, Alec Grant, and Tony E. Adams (New York, Routledge, 2018), 201–210.

31 Andrew F. Herrmann, "Kierkegaard and Dialogue: The Communication of Capability," *Communication Theory* 18, no. 1 (2008), 71–92, https://doi.org/10.1111/j.1468-2885.2007.00314.x; Andrew F. Herrmann, "Communicating, Sensemaking, and (Dis)Organizing: Theorizing the Complexity of Polymediation," in *Beyond New Media: Discourse and Critique in a Polymediated Age*, eds., Art Herbig, Andrew F. Herrmann, and Adam Tyma (Lanham, MD: Lexington, 2016), 61–82; Andrew F. Herrmann, "Ghosts, Vampires, Zombies, and Us: The Undead as Autoethnographic Bridges," *International Review of Qualitative Research* 7, no. 3 (2014), 327–341, https://doi.org/10.1525/irqr.2014.7.3.327; and Andrew F. Herrmann, "On Being a Homeless Work of Fiction: Narrative Quests and Questions," *International Review of Qualitative Research* 9, no. 1 (2016), 29–43, https://doi.org/10.1525/irqr.2016.9.1.29.

32 Herrmann, "Walking in Kierkegaard's Instant."

33 Jeni R. Hunniecutt, *Rethinking Reintegration and Veteran Identity: A New Consciousness* (London: Palgrave Macmillan, 2022); Jeni R. Hunniecutt, "Veteran Identity (Perceptions) in Higher Education: A Veteran/Scholar/Advocate's Story," *Journal of Veterans Studies* 8, no. 2 (2022), 36–50; Thomas W. Townsend, "A Groundhog Moment: Examination of a Pivotal Emotional Singularity," *Qualitative Inquiry* 25, no. 2 (2019), 100–110; Thomas W. Townsend, Angela Duggins, Brandon Bragg, Tessa McCoy, Juliette Guerrault, Jessica Newell, and Hannah Tiberi, "The IRB's Stone Wall: Rollercoaster of Doom," in *The Routledge International Handbook of Organizational Autoethnography*, ed., Andrew F. Herrmann (London: Routledge, 2020), 366–382. Thomas W. Townsend and Kallie Gay, "Expendable and Indispensable: Thoughts on Being Non-Tenurable Faculty in These Uncertain Times," *Journal of Autoethnography* 2, no. 2 (2021), 248–255, https://doi.org/10.1525/joae.2021.2.2.248.

34 Lynn Z. Bloom, "That Way Be Monsters: Myths and Bugaboos about Teaching Personal Writing" (paper presented at the Conference on College Composition and Communication, Minneapolis, MN, April 2000).

35 In tone, we approach this book similar to other autoethnographic books about coming to autoethnography: Bochner, *Coming to Narrative*; Trude Klevan and Alec Grant, *An Autoethnography of Becoming a Qualitative Researcher* (New York: Routledge, 2022); and James M. Salvo, *Reading Autoethnography: Reflections on Justice and Love* (New York: Routledge, 2020).

36 Anne Lamott, *Bird by Bird: Some Instructions on Writing and Life* (New York: Anchor Books, 1994), 20.

37 See Arthur P. Bochner, "It's About Time: Narrative and the Divided Self," *Qualitative Inquiry* 3, no. 4 (1997), 418–438; Arthur P. Bochner, "Narrative's Virtues," *Qualitative Inquiry* 7, no. 2 (2001), 131–157, https://doi.org/10.1177/107780040100700201; Norman K. Denzin, *Interpretive Ethnography: Ethnographic Practices for the 21st Century* (Thousand Oaks, CA: Sage Publications, 1997); Carolyn Ellis, "Creating Criteria"; Carolyn Ellis, "Evocative Autoethnography: Writing Emotionally about Our Lives," in *Representation and the Text: Re-framing the Narrative Voice*, eds., William G. Tierney and Yvonna S. Lincoln (Albany: SUNY Press, 1997), 115–139. Carolyn Ellis, "Fighting Back or Moving On: An Autoethnographic Response to Critics," *International Review of Qualitative Research* 2, no. 3 (2009), 371–378, https://doi.org/10.1525/irqr.2009.2.3.371; Carolyn Ellis and Arthur

P. Bochner, *Composing Ethnography: Alternative Forms of Qualitative Writing* (Walnut Creek, CA: AltaMira Press, 1996); H. Lloyd Goodall, Jr., *Divine Signs: Connecting Spirit to Community* (Carbondale: Southern Illinois University Press, 1996); H. Lloyd Goodall, Jr., *Writing the New Ethnography* (Thousand Oaks, CA: AltaMira Press, 2000); H. Lloyd Goodall, Jr., "Commentary: Narrative Ethnography as Applied Communication Research," *Journal of Applied Communication Research* 32, no. 3 (2004), 185–194, https://doi.org/10.1080/0090988042000240130; Pelias, "An Autobiographic Ethnography of Performance in Everyday Discourse"; William G. Tierney, "Life History's History: Subjects Foretold," *Qualitative Inquiry* 4, no. 1 (1998), 49–70, https://doi.org/10.1177/107780049800400104; Tillmann, "Speaking into Silences"; John Van Maanen, "The Fact of Fiction in Organizational Ethnography," *Administrative Science Quarterly* 24, no. 4 (1979), 539–550, https://doi.org/10.2307/2392360.

38 Herrmann, *The Routledge International Handbook of Organizational Autoethnography*, 26–27, emphasis in original.

CHAPTER 1

On Being *Homo Assessors*

Now the wait. I (Andrew) have uploaded my documents into a new evaluation system called Watermark. I must account for the last five years of my academic life. I have included student evaluations of my teaching. I have entered the teaching reviews from other professors who have observed my instruction. I uploaded a "Faculty Activities Report" for each of the last five years, which include assessments by my Chair and my Dean. I have included PDFs of, or provided links to, my publications. I listed every single class I taught, every presentation I gave, every committee I was on, and every award I won.

I am going to be assessed by my departmental colleagues, my chair, my college peers, my dean, my university peers, my provost, my president, and my university's board of trustees. My dossier must pass every level. If it does, I will be Professor Herrmann. If it doesn't, I will remain Associate Professor Herrmann.

Did I forget something? Did I accidentally leave something out? Did I do enough service? Are my teaching evaluations good enough? Some of them aren't great. Are my journal publications of high enough quality? Some of my publications aren't in the highest-ranked journals. This assessment makes me paranoid. I'm not alone feeling this way.[1]

*

As Ron Pelias astutely demonstrated more than two decades ago, we devote much of our waking life to assessment. "What does it mean to live with a critical eye," he asks,

> an eye that's always assessing, always deciding questions of worth, always saying what's good or bad? What does it mean to judge others? What does it mean to say someone else does not measure up? By what right do you set certain standards? How can you not? What does it mean to judge yourself?[2]

Pelias then describes the various assessments he makes in a single day: the quality of a night's sleep, how one views their bodies in the bathroom mirror, what music and sounds one enjoys, grading student work, having one's scholarship reviewed and rejected, evaluating applicants for graduate programs and faculty positions, and choosing not to read boring scholarship.[3]

DOI: 10.4324/9781003281771-2

We can expand Pelias's observations about assessment to other contexts. We determine which foods, drinks, and flavors will quench us, give us energy, make us sick. Many of us appreciate caring and supportive friends, family, strangers, and students, and we try to avoid those who harm us with their words and deeds. We make choices about the places we (won't) visit and the clothing we (won't) wear. We monitor our health and well-being—or are at least encouraged to do so by others. We review employees and restaurants, products and services, books and movies. Some workers are fired because of poor performance; some workers quit because of bad management. We critique politicians and celebrities for (not) espousing certain values or for sending the wrong message. We try to be mindful of the terminology we use to describe persons, populations, and predicaments, and we try to guess how others will evaluate what we (don't) say and do. We may favor exciting and enthralling stories over boring and unrealistic ones, comedies more than scary movies. And, as academics, we often make decisions about good and not-so-good research, journals, publishers. Indeed, across a multitude of contexts, we assess the quality and desirability of choices, objects, and entities, and we make decisions about what and who is (not) worthy of our time, energy, and attention.[4]

If you're reading this book, we assume you have taken a high school or college course—or have at least experienced an educational setting. We assume "reading" and "writing" have been valued practices in these settings and students who can't read and write may not do well. Within the context of graduate programs, those who can't read and write won't be able to complete comprehensive exams, theses, and dissertations.[5] The reading-and-writing bias also assumes linguistic proficiency—we read, write, and teach in a particular language. For example, in the United States, unless one pursues courses in a non-English language, many educational institutions require instruction in English. If someone isn't proficient in English, they may be assessed poorly and have a difficult time excelling with formal education.[6]

The life of/as a student is a life of assessment. Children who haven't mastered a grade level are either left behind or must attend summer school to catch up. Andrew knows someone who didn't graduate from kindergarten and needed to go back for a second year. "I failed playing with blocks," his friend jokes. Were you assessed and able to take advanced placement courses? Or, like Andrew, were you assessed and put in a special class? ("They didn't have diagnoses like they do now," Andrew says. "We were put in a class with other hyper kids who were always bouncing off the walls. We called it the Rubber Room.") We are assessed in our physical education classes. Are you fast enough to be on the track and field team? Tall enough to play basketball? Agile enough to be a wrestler? We take exams (assessments), write papers (assessments), and give presentations (assessments). For each, we might be given a rubric with evaluative criteria. For presentations, a speaker who speaks without enough volume, or who doesn't make enough eye contact, or who takes up too much time—three criteria on many public speaking rubrics—will be assessed negatively and receive a lower grade. Excelling at the same criteria will help one attain a better grade.

If you have ever taught a class, we ask: What criteria do you use to assess student learning? Must students follow certain instructions to complete an assignment? In a specified language? Do you expect students to attend class? What if a student won't attend class—are they assessed the same as those who do? Although many of us try to accommodate variations of student learning, which accommodations are "reasonable," and which are not?

We can consider other kinds of assessment. What do you (not) like to read? What genres and topics captivate you and which ones don't you care much about? Andrew loves to read horror novels. He likes reading stories that wind him up tight, push him to look under the bed for monsters before he tucks himself in, and make him lie awake staring at the ceiling wondering what *that* sound was. He also loves mystery novels with their taught plots, deceptive characters, and surprising twists. (Bud Goodall likened being an ethnographer to being a detective.[7]) Andrew likes to discover new things about the world, about others, and about himself.

How should we approach assessing manuscripts for publication? Is any attempt at writing in a particular language acceptable and praiseworthy? What stories shouldn't be told, shared, and published? How do you feel about stories that dehumanize others, or don't align with your ideas of hope and transformation or promote repressive values and practices? What if you encountered an autoethnography written by a Christian nationalist who spews hatred against Jewish and Palestinian people? Could you ever consider that "good" autoethnography? Conversely, what happens when a civility-bias infuses much of our research, where anger and pain—and maybe even harm and hate—are assumed to have no place in our work?[8] How do we assess good and evil, quality and crap, hasty generalization and practical action?

Every year for nearly 20 years, Tony has taught a course on Persuasion. "Impression management" is a key concept of the course, a concept that, at its core, takes assessment seriously. We do impression management when we consider how others might assess us based on our appearance, words, and deeds. As Erving Goffman demonstrated decades ago, knowing we may be assessed and considering how we might be assessed can allow us to strategically adjust our verbal and nonverbal cues according to audience.[9]

We do impression management when we think about the clothes and scents we (won't) wear, the company we (refuse to) keep, where to (not) publish, topics to (not) write about, and when to (not) stay silent or omit information. We do impression management when we (don't) share political and religious affiliations, past conflicts and crimes, or our love of drugs on resumes and in job interviews. We do impression management when we try to appear friendly and relaxed, not grumpy or nervous, on a first date. We do impression management when we decide to (not) laugh at tragedy or (not) discuss our finances with strangers, students, and supervisors. We do impression management when we desire privacy.

We make choices about what to share and not share with certain audiences, and we make these choices to avoid judgment and risk. If we share everything we think and feel indiscriminately, there would be consequences; as Leary writes, the "tactless person who never impression-managed would have trouble keeping jobs, friends, and lovers."[10] Some people enjoy sharing a lot of personal information on social media, and we can identify dozens of examples of how someone's use of social media has resulted in severe consequences, from being unfriended and cancelled—acts that contribute to social isolation—to being assessed as unfit for a job, and even terminated from a current position. Familiarity can breed contempt, ignorance can be bliss, and disclosure can be a trap.[11]

We begin with these examples to introduce the topic and practice of assessment and to demonstrate how much assessing we do. We don't merely assess when we have big decisions to make. Assessment infuses our mundane lives and happens across myriad contexts. And with assessment comes criteria—criteria for what counts as good and not-so-good stories, food, films, arguments, policies, practices, impressions, etc. We may also have justifications for these criteria: maybe we're vegan out of concern for animal welfare and climate change; maybe we're required to report student attendance to meet institutional and federal standards for learning; maybe we challenge harmful laws to better lives; and maybe we avoid reading, watching, or listening to scary tales because we don't like to feel scared. Although being mindful of impression management isn't a guarantee that others will assess us favorably, caring about it means monitoring our words and deeds and imagining how others might react to them. Assessment is essential to, and required for, satisfaction and survival; just as Walter Fisher called us *homo narrans*, storytelling beings,[12] we call us *homo assessors*, beings who evaluate.[13]

ASSESSMENT MATTERS

We have spent decades doing and assessing autoethnography. We have also spent decades learning and teaching about communication. This disciplinary training informs our approach to assessment. As a discipline, communication foregrounds message design, distribution, interpretation, and assessment; which, how, and why stories matter; the use of various media to convey information; and researching and understanding relationships and audiences. These components comprise the essence of what we teach and study.

We understand that words and deeds create realities, inspire possibilities, and do things. We create texts—advertisements, press releases, speeches, social media posts, news reports, podcasts, and films—to connect with others, generate reactions. We teach about attracting attention and adapting messages to audiences, lessons which, at their core, imply that we care about audiences, especially their reactions to the messages we create and share. Is that a good speech or advertisement? What about that social media post—an arrogant humblebrag or empathetic expression? Why did the author use an insensitive word instead of a more inclusive term? What do we do with the manuscript that denies the Holocaust, praises animal cruelty, or refers to the earth as flat?

We help students and colleagues find and use evidence, as well as create and deliver presentations. We care about authorial intent and credibility, and we discern how texts can generate certain meanings. We assess how our actions and reactions can affect others—just as we are *homo assessors*, we are also *homo socius*, social beings—and we study how and why people (don't) pursue relationships. We learn how to gather and portray information and how to use this information to create stories and construct arguments. We understand the importance of language and how we, as authors, choose terms to describe experiences—terms that "frame" how we understand these experiences.[14]

Although plenty of folks claim to know about "communication" and "writing" because they do it, few have pursued formal training in these areas. (For us, claiming to know about communication merely because one does it is like claiming to know about veterinarian science because one has a pet. Having pets is not equivalent to having formal training in animal behavior or medicine. Yes, we're assessing one's credentials.) Even though many of us produce written texts, many disciplines do not prioritize the creation of these texts; craft is treated as secondary to content, hence the title of Michael Billig's book, *Learn to Write Badly: How to Succeed in the Social Sciences.*[15] Disregarding the craft of message design, distribution, interpretation, and assessment can be careless and consequential. Well-crafted texts have a better chance of being read, understood, used, cited, purchased, and shared; poorly crafted texts might never be found or, if they are, are ridiculed and dismissed—the author's message may not be well-received, if received at all. A poorly crafted text might even be removed from a journal,[16] and an author may encounter personal, professional, and legal consequences for publishing their work.

And regarding publishing: We assume that if someone wants to share their work, they want others to read it; the very concept of "sharing" implies sharing-with-someone. The desire to share is when assessment matters most. Sharing our work means imagining audiences, receiving feedback, and considering ways to adapt our messages for certain readers. Wanting to share our work requires caring about what others might think about or do with it, as well as how they may understand and respond to the ideas and arguments we espouse.

For example, when we write a thesis or dissertation, our advisor(s), review committee, and/or examiners comprise our primary audiences—we write for them, and they assess whether our document is sufficient and if we should pass. If we try to publish an article in an academic journal, our advisors and examiners are no longer our primary audience; instead, the journal editor(s), editorial board, and academics doing similar work become our primary audiences—and we may need to adapt our writing and arguments accordingly. If we write a book manuscript for a particular press, the editor/publisher, external reviewers, and possible readers (customers) become our primary audiences. With each of our book series, some folks try to submit autoethnographic dissertations as books—and yet, these typically fail, not because of quality per se, but because the form and audience of these texts are different; a thesis or dissertation is not an article or a book—each form has different goals and audiences, and different audiences should result in different texts. We often tell these authors to locate and analyze the form and content of a few of their favorite autoethnographic books and then reformat their dissertation like those books, e.g., unlike many dissertations, few good autoethnographic books follow the introduction-literature review-method-findings-discussion-conclusion format.

We assume that when someone writes a manuscript and pursues publication, they care about the messages they convey, and they want to convey these messages to others. We assume authors want readers and authors want readers to understand, engage, and possibly even cite their ideas; use their work in classes; and/or share their arguments on social media. We assume authors value their work—a work that, with their name, represents them. We assume authors understand that publishing a bad manuscript can harm them (and sometimes others), whereas publishing a good manuscript can generate praise and additional opportunities for sharing their work. If an author doesn't care about readers understanding, engaging, and sharing their work, then publishing is a silly endeavor. One might need to publish as a requirement for employment, but if there isn't a need to publish and if there isn't a willingness to be assessed, then why pursue the process and its affiliated stress? Keep the work private. An author may have good ideas and arguments about certain topics, yet these ideas and arguments will only matter if others can access, understand, and respect the work—and the author.

Finally, we want to acknowledge the social justice aspect of assessment. Many autoethnographers, especially critical autoethnographers, share their experiences to call attention to harmful cultural values and practices and to promote social change. If their messages cannot be understood and if they're sloppy and indecipherable, then these messages—and the affiliated calls for change—may be misunderstood and disregarded. If our messages don't make sense, then how can we expect others to use these messages to advocate progressive transformation?

MARKET FORCES

Capitalistic forces also affect our doing and assessing of autoethnography. These forces aren't easily captured by criteria but directly contribute to the infrastructure for assessing autoethnographic projects.

In our book series, there are a few genres of writing we can't publish—not because we don't want to but because books in those genres tend not to sell, and our publisher does not want to devote their resources to support those projects. The publisher knows how many people (audience) purchased books in those genres. (We do not want to mention those genres—we worry that doing so could discourage authors working in those genres. We also know there are publishers for those genres, and we just haven't worked with those publishers.) If a book in a certain genre doesn't sell well, that can affect the ability for others to publish their work in that genre. Further, if a manuscript is too boring or difficult to understand or too complicated to use in classes (e.g., the perceived "course adoption" for books, another assessment of audience and a key criterion for some publishers), then the author may not get their work published; the manuscript has been assessed as unmarketable and thus unpublishable.

Let me (Andrew) offer an example. Art Herbig and I are the founding co-editors of the *Communication Perspectives in Popular Culture* book series. We received a manuscript for an edited collection wherein the introductory chapter ended in the middle of a sentence. It stopped. Abruptly. When we queried the author, they couldn't explain why it ended that way. They didn't care either. The author also wasn't interested in our other feedback. The manuscript wasn't Lamott's "shitty first draft"[17]—it was an incomplete draft. Art and I value the integrity of the research ***and*** the integrity of the series. Our names—and thus our character and reputation—are also tied to every book in the series. We rejected the manuscript.

A similar assessment happens with journals. One way our publisher assesses our ability as editors and the quality, importance, and reach of the work we publish in the

Journal of Autoethnography is by assessing the number of subscriptions to the journal. Subscriptions can indicate who cares about the publication (audience). The journal is also assessed based on citation. Citation affects the journal's visibility and "impact factor," which can influence an author's decision to submit to the journal, as well as affect subscriptions. And if we need an organization like Scopus to bless our work, we must develop and adhere to specific criteria for assessing manuscripts. As such, when we publish an article, we try to cultivate articles of good quality that others (audiences) will access, download, read, use, share, and cite.

We want to accommodate multiple languages in the journal, but doing so is complicated. First, as editors, we must be able to understand a manuscript. Yet we are mostly monolingual. (We can read slowly in Spanish but not with sufficient proficiency, and translation applications, while helpful, cannot capture the nuances of a work.) We must also find reviewers fluent in a particular language and who understand and appreciate autoethnography. As editors, we then must be able to read the reviews. At this stage, translation applications may be sufficient but still cannot give us a full grasp of the manuscript.

The University of California Press (the publisher) pays copy editors to enhance the quality of manuscript—that is the one of the primary purposes of copy editors, to make a manuscript as good as possible. By publishing in more than one language, the journal would have to find editors, reviewers, and copy editors fluent in the other language(s). This is possible, but what if a journal that publishes four issues a year publishes one issue in English, one issue in Spanish, one issue in Portuguese, and one issue in Chinese? By being inclusive, the journal now risks losing subscriptions: the only individuals who would benefit from access to the journal would be those fluent in these four languages. Purchasing a subscription may be less enticing for an individual and institution, yet subscriptions make the very existence of the journal possible.

When we first started the journal, we were limited to publishing 548 .pdf pages every year—with four issues, that's 137 .pdf pages every issue. Even though we only publish the journal online and are not limited by physical space, the press must still hire copy editors who charge by the page and/or their time; pages are therefore limited because of production costs. We received so many submissions the first year, and we requested an increase to our page allocation. Our primary editor, along with the governing board of the press, increased our allotment to 596 pages every year—149 pages per issue. Unlike an online open-access journal, our page limit further affects our approach to assessment. If we are short on submissions and need to fill 596 pages of content, we will assess manuscripts differently than if we had an abundance of manuscripts. For example, if we have a lot of submissions, we will desk reject manuscripts more and more easily; with fewer submissions, we will work with manuscripts that may have previously received a desk reject. Quality may be slightly compromised—we have a page obligation for the journal.

Open-access can be a great option for scholars—we have published several open-access articles—but some publishers now charge excessive "article processing fees." Several of our colleagues have developed and edited open-access journals. These journals require a lot of unpaid labor—not only in everyday management of the journal but also in finding reviewers, creating and maintaining a website, and formatting accepted manuscripts. A modest (under $50 USD) fee may be acceptable, but an author who pays much more than this to publish an article may be viewed as suspect.

Moreover, there are predatory journals and organizations that want to profit off of vulnerable authors. Although traditional academic publishers may function similarly, they also do not charge for publication. Predatory journals and organizations not only charge for publication, but authors may still not benefit from the publication. The folks who run these publishing outlets will accept most anything if an author can pay the article processing fee. Often these outlets do not offer much editorial support either—they may send a manuscript out for review and solicit feedback from reviewers, but this process is more about appearance rather than making the article good. These outlets do not use editors to improve the work, and the author not only has to pay to publish but may publish an article riddled with errors and faulty arguments. And at our universities, an author who paid to publish an article would be assessed as suspect, especially since there isn't much quality control.

Self-publishing may be a good way to distribute our work, but that approach has limitations too. At our institutions, self-published work does not count toward tenure and promotion, and the credibility of the researcher who self-publishes may still be viewed as suspect.[18] Again, these are assessments of a work's—and a scholar's—quality and ability. If an author doesn't care about how a work will be received and merely wants to share their ideas, then steep, article processing fees and self-publishing may be viable options. We would encourage these authors to work with trusted peers or hire a copy editor to make sure their manuscript is of good quality. One could save a lot of money and share their ideas by writing a blog, but blogs introduce concerns about credibility too.

We might not like some of these market forces, and we can challenge them, but we also want to stress the importance of quality. If we don't buy books, then publishers aren't going to exist. Maybe you do not care, and maybe article processing fees will be more common. But again, if an author doesn't care about audiences, readership, and being read, then there isn't a need to publish their manuscript.[19] Unless you contribute something that the system deems worthy, exciting, and of good quality, capitalism may not care about you or your work.

*

Thus far, we have identified facets of assessment—the extent and reason we do it, factors that shape the process, and how and why it matters most when hoping to make our work public. Next, we describe the importance of quality for autoethnography and begin to discern general characteristics of what we consider "good autoethnography."

QUALITY AUTOETHNOGRAPHY

Michael Patton writes, "judging quality requires criteria."[20]

In "Pursuing Excellence in Qualitative Inquiry," Ken Gergen asks, "How can newcomers to [qualitative] inquiry proceed if they cannot ascertain what counts as 'good work?' And how can journal editors and reviewers conduct responsible evaluations if the criteria for excellence are obscure?"[21]

Chris Poulos notes, "Knowing what a reviewer might look for can help a writer construct a text that 'works.'"[22]

And Bob Krizek told Bud Goodall,

> As more and more narrative work hits the pages of our journals we should be able to articulate our reasons why this story worked and this story didn't because in many instances that will be the difference between what gets published and what inhabits the bottom of our file cabinets.[23]

*

We read a lot of bad autoethnographies, ones that have wasted our voluntary time as reviewers and should have stayed in the bottom of a drawer or tucked away in a folder in the cloud. (Andrew has a folder on his computer called "Sh*t." It contains manuscripts he wrote that were rejected from journals.) Yet we need to consider what attributes make an autoethnography bad and the attributes that make one good. Assessment is thus tied to quality, and we need criteria to assess. Once we have these criteria, others—authors, reviewers, editors, and publishers—can better promote and support quality autoethnographic work.

Many others have offered criteria for assessing the quality of autoethnography.[24] We engage several of these others and their criteria throughout this book. The sources we cite are some of our favorite sources, those we find to be the most credible and written by folks who have actually done autoethnography. We encourage you to read the sources we cite.

Quality also matters if we understand autoethnography as "research." In the introduction to the second edition of the *Handbook of Autoethnography*, Stacy Holman Jones writes:

> having our work designated as research not only enables us to meet key performance indicators for tenure and promotion but also shows our colleagues (and critics) that our work contributes to existing knowledge. In addition to a "research" designation, work must also be deemed "quality" to be considered as part of a researcher's body of work. Quality is established by the outlet of the publication (based on the rankings/peer assessment of a journal or a publisher) or by the quality of the work (based on the critical reception of the work, measured by number of citations, reprints, and the like). Again, why is this important? Because having our work deemed to be not only research but also quality research further establishes autoethnography as both an important and rigorous method as judged by a community of academic peers. Paying attention to these elements not only advances the work (and careers!) of autoethnographers who choose to work in the academy but also relies on our community of autoethnographers to do the "heavy lifting" of legitimizing that work.[25]

Note here the various facets of, and criteria for, assessment—e.g., key performance indicators, contribution to existing knowledge, and quality of the publication outlet and the work—and what favorable assessment can do: further establish autoethnography as a viable and familiar research method and allow more folks to do and understand it.

*

As mentioned in the introduction, the three components that comprise the very term—the auto, the ethno, and the graphy—are the primary criteria we use to assess the quality of an autoethnography. (We expand on each component in the next three chapters.) For an autoethnography, we expect to read about an author's meaningful and insightful personal experiences. We expect an author to get outside of themselves, interact with others, connect their personal experiences to cultural discourse, do fieldwork, and/or engage existing research and key artifacts. We expect an author to know how to write and how to write well, use thick description to craft compelling stories, and be a good life writer ***and*** social researcher. In general, if these expectations are met, then a quality autoethnography begins to form; if these expectations are not met, then the so-called autoethnography will be of poor quality.

Once we use these criteria to broadly assess an autoethnographic text, we then apply the "So what?" question.

AUTOETHNOGRAPHY AND THE "SO WHAT?" QUESTION

In January 2020, we launched the *Journal of Autoethnography*. In March 2020, COVID-19 inundated the world. A few months into the pandemic, we began to receive many manuscripts about living through/with COVID-19. Yet many of these manuscripts described the same mundane tasks and didn't offer many new insights about social life. Authors shared their experiences with

(not) wearing masks;
fears of catching the virus;
benefits and consequences of vaccines;
(in)adequate food and healthcare;
joys and struggles with teaching and technology;
frustrations about the inability to travel;
sadness about physical isolation.

Although these topics were (are) important, there were already so many stories about them, and many authors tried to argue that their experiences finding toilet paper, or having to teach online, or being separated from others, were unique to them. They didn't offer new or novel perspectives about the topics and their stories resembled mainstream news reports and editorials. Why should we care about these experiences? That question is the essence of the "So what?" question we must ask of autoethnographies.

We sent a few of the early COVID manuscripts to reviewers, and many reviewers wanted more from the accounts—the mere frustration of wearing masks, or debating vaccines and vaccine access, or the joys and heartaches of Zoom—were insufficient angles for a project. The manuscripts weren't necessarily of poor quality, at least in terms of writing, but they were of poor quality given that they did not contribute to our understanding of COVID—they included common experiences and didn't demonstrate an awareness of other COVID stories. Then (and still now) many reviewers were tired of reading about COVID. When we received a COVID-manuscript, we would often desk reject it unless it offered new and novel insights.

*

Every November and December, Hallmark, a U.S. television channel, features an assortment of holiday movies. In form and content, the stories are similar:

> Successful career ciswoman leaves the city and goes home for the holiday, meets nice-looking down-to-earth cisman, and they show an interest in each other, when there's some mix-up which gets rectified, and they fall in love and she quits her job, and he asks her to marry him, just as the snow begins to fall on Christmas eve.

Change the town, change the characters, change the tension, and change the actors: it doesn't matter—the premise and the plot are the same.[26] If your autoethnography is interchangeable with others, if others have told similar tales, then you're not doing good autoethnography.

In a 2006 interview, Mitch Allen, a visionary editor and publisher of autoethnography, made a similar observation

> [With autoethnography] you have to look at experience analytically. Otherwise I'm telling my story—and that's nice—but people do that on *Oprah* [a U.S. television program] every day. Why is your story more valid than anyone else's? What makes your story more valid is that you are a researcher. You have a set of theoretical and methodological tools and a research literature to use. That's your advantage. If you can't frame it around these tools and literature and just frame it as "my story," then why or how should I privilege your story over anyone else's I see 25 times a day on TV?[27]

For good autoethnography, we must do something more with personal experience. We cannot just share our experiences; we must interrogate the meaning of these experiences and then convey this meaning for others.

*

In the COVID manuscripts submitted to the journal, authors told similar and familiar stories about facets of social life many of us knew and lived. In *Recovering Bodies: Illness,*

Disability and Life Writing, Thomas Couser argues that good life writing portrays stories that haven't been told before. Using autobiographical breast cancer narratives as an example, he notes, "it is symptomatic of the maturing of the breast cancer narrative that new ones evince the need for a new angle; once the genre has been established, the experience of cancer is not necessarily sufficient to justify a narrative."[28]

Be cautious of telling similar and familiar stories. Although no one will tell the exact same story or have the same experience, there might be a story about a theme that is overdone or boring. If you tell a story like others' stories, you also risk being accused of intellectual theft and plagiarism. Offer new and novel insights. And to do so, you must know existing narratives. This is why literature reviews are important. Assess what have others written, and haven't written, about a topic. Doing so will help to establish a market for your work. You're offering audiences something new, and by knowing what others have written about a topic, you can make novel arguments. Engaging others' work will also demonstrate your knowledge of the topic and enhance your credibility—you offer readers a sense that you seem to know what you're writing about. Remember, you can write whatever you'd like by yourself, but if you want to make your work public, offer a new angle. Here, the auto, one's experience, becomes tangled with the ethno and the graphy, the need to know what and how others have written about a topic.

*

While seemingly honest and vulnerable, the COVID manuscripts didn't offer many unique insights. We, and many of our reviewers, found ourselves asking: Who cares? What makes the author's experience unique? We had limited journal page space—why would we waste space on similar and familiar stories? We all had to figure out masks, employment, technology, and isolation; we didn't need multiple manuscripts to tell us that we had to do so.

These manuscripts pushed us to consider the so-what question regarding the sharing of personal experience: Why should readers care about your experiences? How might, and why should, your experiences matter for them? To better address the so-what question, we developed a few questions authors should consider when doing autoethnography:

1 How is your experience pertinent to others besides yourself? Yes, autoethnography is personal. You had an experience. So did we. Why should anyone care? Excellent autoethnographies move beyond oneself by elucidating our relationships with others and show how cultural principles, products, and practices infuse our experiences.
2 How does your autoethnography connect to existing research? We receive submissions that never mention autoethnography or discern how extant research informs a manuscript's topic. What ideas and arguments have other writers and researchers made about your topic? Tell us. And then tell us how your experiences align with, or diverge from, these ideas and arguments.
3 How is your autoethnography pertinent to theory? Implicit and explicit theoretical traditions inform many autoethnographic projects—make these traditions explicit for readers. What theoretical concerns does your manuscript address?

4 How is your autoethnography pertinent to policy, whether international, national, local, or organizational? What is the moral of your story, the lessons readers should learn from your words? For example, how does your autoethnography of bullying change practices at school or the workplace? How can your autoethnography be used to challenge ageist and ableist microaggressions? How can your autoethnography assist in changing anti-trans laws in your community? At its best, autoethnography looks to create change, promote emancipation, and make life more relatable, livable, and humane.[29]

The so-what dilemma wasn't just a challenge for COVID-19 submissions. Many submissions we reject also do not answer the so-what question. Authors share experiences without much explanation and seem to assume the mere reporting of an experience is sufficient for good autoethnography. (We elaborate on the use of personal experience in Chapter 3.) In the process of rejecting manuscripts, we also encountered some erroneous assumptions about what autoethnography is and our (in)ability to assess it.

NARRATIVES-UNDER-ANALYSIS AND NARRATIVE ANALYSIS

One important factor in assessing autoethnography is how the researcher understands and uses narratives. Narrative inquiry is an expansive area of research across the humanities and social sciences that developed out of the desire for a more humane, less abstract, and justice-oriented way to do research.[30] Scholars from a diversity of disciplines study narratives, including folktales,[31] national and local myths,[32] historical and life chronologies,[33] television and movie narratives,[34] oral histories,[35] narratives of philosophical ideas,[36] and academic disciplines.[37] However, these folks often conduct narrative inquiry in different ways[38] and often distinguish between *narratives-under-analysis* and *narrative analysis.*[39] Although these terms may seem similar, the difference between *narratives-under-analysis* and *narrative analysis* is fundamental philosophically.[40]

Researchers doing *narratives-under-analysis* treat stories as objects and datum.[41] These researchers break down stories into various parts. They deconstruct stories to discover generalities and create typologies. They seek out themes and leitmotifs within and across stories. At its most extreme, these researchers take a positivist approach to understanding narratives.[42] Rather than thinking *with* stories, they think *about* stories.[43] It is necessary to do *narratives-under-analysis* work to critically assess how stories are used to "oppress, dominate, and subjugate"[44] rather than emancipate people from the auspices of cultural, organizational, and relational power and control.[45] But most autoethnographies, at least what we consider to be the good ones, do not often use a *narratives-under-analysis* frame.

Narrative analysis—what most autoethnographers (should) do—takes a different approach to stories.[46] We read stories "as stories"—think *with* them—and we reflect on "the effect they have on the storyteller, the audience, and our own lives."[47] The parts of the story and how the story compares to other stories aren't the point of *narrative analysis*. Instead, storytelling is a means of being with and making sense of others. The storyteller creates and conveys meanings, observations, and arguments through narrative. As Art Bochner writes,

> When we stay with a story, refusing the impulse to abstract, reacting from the source of our own experience and feelings, we respect the story and the human life it represents, and we enter into personal contact with questions of virtue, of what it means to live well and to do the right thing.[48]

Moreover, "the research product is a story—a case, a biography, a life history, an autobiography, an autoethnography—composed by the researcher to represent the events, characters, and issues that [they have] studied."[49] Autoethnographies aren't just facts, they prioritize meanings, emotions, ethics, and lives.

Let me (Andrew) provide examples of *narratives-under-analysis* and *narrative analysis* from my ethnographic punk rock music research. In "Narrative as an Organizing Process: Identity and Story in a New Nonprofit," I took a *narratives-under-analysis* approach. Consider this excerpt:

> Volunteers switch roles, responsibilities, and tasks. Watching the volunteers' maneuvers through the labyrinth of nightly activities, the Lanc's [a neighborhood art center] organizational processes are impromptu, rather than chaotic. That is the paradox of DIY: it is not "do-it-yourself," but a cooperative, communicative organizational endeavor. The rules at the Lanc are minimal (no smoking indoors, do not enter the back office) giving members an opportunity to slip into roles at different times when they see a need. The Lanc is a continual arena of adjustment and sensemaking, as volunteers move fluidly from position to position.[50]

I used grounded theory to examine organizational narratives and discern the commonalities and differences between these narratives. I analyzed the narratives at macro-, meso-, and micro-levels and assessed how they helped to constitute and maintain the nonprofit organization. I also used the sterile introduction-literature review-methods-results-conclusion formula to represent the work. The article is an example of *narratives-under-analysis*. It's good research, but it isn't autoethnography.

In contrast, "Never Mind the Scholar, Here's the Old Punk: Identity, Community, and the Aging Music Fan"—which is based on the same ethnographic research—is a *narrative analysis*. Although I included a brief literature review and conclusion, most of the article is written as a narrative. Here's an excerpt:

> The man jumps backwards away from me, turns around and runs down the dark street. I am standing on a corner in St. Louis in front of The Lanc cooling off. Sullen—a four-member punk band—finished a set. They were good. Good and loud. It is hot inside. Sweltering. I look around. The red brick buildings across the street are boarded up and closed like the eyes of a sleeping giant. The dark park

> nearby is quiet. The only bright spot is the glimmering [Anheuser]-Busch sign floating on the horizon, hovering over the park.[51]

I wrote the *narrative analysis* following Goodall's recommendation that "from story emerges theory."[52] I wrote what Krizek calls a "fictional literary account" that "allows my readers to meet my cultural participants…in the voice, emotional textures, and the multi-layered immediacy in the participants' own experiences."[53] Rather than taking a *narratives-under-analysis* approach, I wrote a *narrative analysis*, and the themes I engaged are part of the story itself. *Narrative analysis* is how we understand the purpose for and work of autoethnography.

WHEN YOU GET FEEDBACK

We recognize receiving negative feedback on our work does not feel good. We don't like it either. We also don't like writing rejection letters, but we must—we won't support just any text, especially one of poor quality. However, we try to be as kind and supportive as possible when writing these letters. We offer advice about what's missing, what needs fixing, and where the author might send their manuscript if it is not a good fit for the journal.

Nevertheless, after receiving our feedback on their autoethnographies, some authors respond, sometimes angrily, with the following kinds of comments:

a My committee liked my project, so I know it is good; or my paper was accepted for presentation at a conference and the audience liked it; or my best friend said the manuscript was a great read.
b Assessment can exclude and silence authors.
c You can't critique *my* experience! Or the reviewers don't share the same identities and experiences and cannot understand what it means to be me.

We understand and even empathize with authors when their research is rejected. However, when we read these responses, we assume the authors have not read much about research generally and autoethnography specifically. We often reply noting the following:

a Folks you know personally tend to be nice and supportive to "save face" in public (an instance of impression management); it is difficult to offer honest and constructive feedback when others are present.
b Yes, but by not having standards, we risk endorsing poor ideas and arguments. We also do not believe we can live without or outside of assessment. (We are *homo assessors.*)
c We/reviewers often don't critique a person's experience but rather their *representation* of the experience; focusing on the representation allows us to avoid relativistic assumptions and arguments that only we can know what we know.

Allow us to expand on each.

People I Know Liked It

One challenge we receive when offering feedback on a manuscript is the naïve "My committee/audience at a panel/friends/family liked my work." Committees, live audiences, family, and best friends might prefer supporting and celebrating you and may not be as honest as they want to be. Remember impression management? We know parents who think their newborn is the most beautiful newborn ever. Even though the rest of us know that is a silly claim, we likely won't say so, at least not in front of the parents. Your friends, family, and committee members might not be telling you the truth about your work. Your dissertation committee didn't ask for any revisions for your dissertation? Yes, your work may be stellar. But the committee may also not want to work with you anymore, or they might realize there isn't enough time for you to complete sufficient revisions and still graduate. Further, we have met several faculty members who tell nearly every doctoral student they should turn their dissertation into a book. Yet behind closed doors, away from the student, these faculty say they only say this to be nice and make the student feel good. Possibly a well-intended philosophy, but one that can create unrealistic expectations for the student.

Assessment becomes increasingly stringent depending on publication outlet. Class papers are not journal articles. Theses and dissertations are not books. Journal articles and books are different kinds of texts with different audiences and therefore have different criteria for assessment. If we sent a paper we wrote in elementary school to an academic journal, it would be rejected outright. It would not be close to meeting the journal's standards for quality. Performances are a different medium altogether. If you've ever thought, "The book version was better than the movie version," you recognize the medium changes the content and thus one's assessment of the content. (And movies can never be books; both are different representational media with different possibilities and limitations.) Writers also often fall in love with their wordsmithing, overlooking the flaws, errors, and problematic aspects of their work. Seeking feedback from a trusted other or external reviewers can help to "murder your darlings,"[54] as well as determine if you have a work that engages the auto, ethno, and graphy.

Assessment Can Exclude/Silence Authors

The second argument we encounter regarding assessment, specifically rejection, is that it can exclude/silence authors. This argument treats negative assessment as equivalent to censorship. It's not. In the United States, censorship is an idea based upon First Amendment rights in the Constitution that the government cannot silence you as you critique it. Readers, editors, and publishers are not the government. Although it may be trendy to suggest that there is a "marketplace of ideas" and all ideas should be treated equally, this is not true—or rather, not a world we want to support.[55] We're sure you know someone who has a plethora of nonsensical ideas, and we know plenty of people who make cruel arguments.

Further, Art Bochner acknowledged the silenced-voices argument more than two decades ago when he noted that yes, criteria can create the conditions for conformity and "compliance with our own conventions." He also noted that having criteria is necessary to "so that we can imagine and create new and better ways of living in this world."[56] Doing a mass prohibition of creative, experimental, new, and original, as well as underground, underrepresented, unvoiced, and critical autoethnographic work is not in the best interests of autoethnography as a method, orientation, or way of life.[57] Assessment is the heart of the paradox that "Scholarship, with its emphasis on acceptable forms and format, is conservative, yet its purpose is to generate the new, the innovative, and the inventive."[58] Simply because we do not write autoethnographic poetry or write and perform ethnodramas doesn't mean we do not appreciate those artistic forms. Doing so would not allow us to "imagine and create new and better ways of living."

We recognize criteria can cultivate elitism and construct barriers to entry, and we try to understand criteria as a guide for authors and assessors and as ways for people to do this work successfully. Again, we live in a world of assessment: who gets admitted to our programs, who are our best and worst students, who doesn't get hired or fired. We do our best to be as inclusive as possible, to acknowledge, challenge, and tear down some of these constraints, yet in tearing them down, new constraints emerge. We live our lives in constraints; we cannot wholly act as we may wish, or else we risk severe negative assessments.

There's an applicable metaphor from organizational communication that will help clarify our meaning of this point: "balancing creativity and constraint."[59] At work, you are allowed various communicative freedoms. Time to talk with your peers about non-work topics around the water cooler. Joking at the coffee pot in the morning. You are certainly free to offer critiques and ideas that will make work more efficient and productive. However, there are constraints as well. Racist, sexist, ageist, ableist, transphobic, homophobic, or xenophobic jokes are likely to get you sent to the human resources department. You can't tell your boss they're a blundering, blabbering idiot. You *can*, but you likely won't have a job. Your communicative activity at work needs to fall within the boundaries of creativity and constraint for it to be welcomed and appreciated. The same goes for writing autoethnography.

Can assessment silence someone's story? Yes. Yet how do we determine what is good and bad? Does everything get published? How much do we care about making sense and for whom we make sense? Assessment is necessary to refine, and even prohibit, bad practices and arguments. For example, unless there is a compelling reason to do so, we will not publish manuscripts that use the generic "he" or that espouse racist, sexist, ageist, ableist, transphobic, homophobic, or xenophobic ideas. We would have issues with manuscripts claiming the earth is flat or denying the Holocaust. Given the use of personal experience, we caution writers against offering hasty generalizations, and sometimes we must attend to the potential harm and legal issues a manuscript might inflict on the author or others implicated by the author's account.

You Can't Critique MY Experience

This is the argument we most encounter against assessment: "It's autoethnography and it's my experience and you can't offer feedback on my experience; it happened to me, not you." We understand the impetus for this reaction but find the logic flawed. As authors, we recognize that writing is a personal experience; as autoethnographers, we recognize writing as an extremely personal experience. In response, we often distinguish between assessing the person and assessing the person's *representation* of their experience; we are not interested in assessing the experience itself (as if we could—we aren't them and we weren't there!) but rather the description of the experience. Does an author's story ring true? Is the manuscript filled with concrete details and thick description? Does the author engage extant research? Does the author's use of literary devices work? Is the manuscript academically sound and a good read? Does the author tell us what they will do and then do it? Is the manuscript impactful?[60]

We might assess an author's interpretation of their experience, or the language they use, or the arguments they make from their experience. We might assess how the experiences connect or if they are unclear. Such critique might involve how they arrange or frame their experiences or which experiences they share. Their characters' so-called "dialogue" might be a badly written monologue. Sometimes writers just don't provide enough information and inadequately convey the point of their story.

With these questions, notice that we try not to assess the author but rather the author's manuscript. This is a distinction that goes back so far that even Voltaire wrote about it: "In every author let us distinguish the man [sic] from his works."[61] When feedback is offered on an autoethnography, we try to emphasize the critique isn't about their actual life but rather how they have portrayed an experience from their life.[62] Granted, occasionally we might assess a person and their life based on the information they share—we provide an example of this at the end of Chapter 3—but we try to stay as close to the text itself.

PUBLISHED AUTOETHNOGRAPHY

Assessment can be a tricky and contested endeavor, but we do it and we do it often. When we participate in situations in which assessment matters—a class paper or presentation, a thesis or dissertation defense, pursuing publication, seeking tenure and/or promotion, or, again, as Pelias astutely observed, across much of our waking lives—then we need to have explicit discussions about how assessment happens. Knowing how assessment can happen allows us to better prepare for situations comprised of assessment (that is, nearly every situation).

Assessing autoethnography is also a necessary and important endeavor as well-crafted texts have a better chance of being read, used, cited, purchased, and shared. If we are committed to social justice, then we must create coherent and compelling texts; sloppy and indecipherable texts may be misunderstood and disregarded and used as examples of what not to do as a writer/researcher/autoethnographer. If our ideas and arguments don't make sense, then how can we expect others to care about them, share them, and use them for change?

We recognize the impossibility of pleasing every reviewer or reader, as well as the inability to create a perfect text. But we should recognize the control we have over the craft of our texts, care about the texts we craft, and realize that, once we publish a text and put it into the world, we lose interpretive control over it; readers will assess it and us. (We will discuss such assessment in greater detail in Chapter 3 and the Conclusion.) Further, the permanency of print—a characteristic of most publications—doesn't allow us to edit the text later. We can control how we craft the original text, and we should do our best to make it is as good as it can possibly be.

NOTES

1 See Charlotte Bloch, *Passion and Paranoia: Emotions and the Culture of Emotion in Academia* (London: Routledge, 2016); Jeffrey R. Di Leo, "The Paranoid Imperative: Affect, Emotion, and Neoliberal Academe," *Symploke* 29, no. 1 (2021), 163–178, https://doi.org/10.1353/sym.2021.0009.

2 Ronald J. Pelias, "The Critical Life," *Communication Education* 49, no. 3 (2000), 220–228, https://doi.org/10.1080/03634520009379210.

3 Ronald J. Pelias, "The Critical Life." David Foster Wallace makes a similar observation: "Day to day I have to make all sorts of choices about what is good and important and fun, and then I have to live with the forfeiture of all the other options those choices foreclose." David Foster Wallace, *A Supposedly Fun Thing I'll Never Do again* (New York: Little, Brown and Company, 1997), 267.

4 We have revised this paragraph from Adams and Herrmann, "Good Autoethnography," 1.

5 We attribute this bias toward, and celebration of, reading and writing to the rise and exaltation of literacy. See Walter J. Ong, *The Technologizing of the Word* (New York: Methuen, 1982).

6 I (Tony) taught at Northeastern Illinois University (NEIU) for nine years (2008–2017). NEIU was (is) a designated "Hispanic Serving Institution" (HSI) located in Chicago, Illinois (USA). Many students spoke Spanish as their first language. Several faculty were proud to teach at an HSI, yet would only allow instruction in English. Some faculty were even criticized for speaking Spanish with students. I was shocked, and saddened, by the English bias at such a diverse HSI, but I also recognize this issue is systemic: outside of specific language majors and departments, many higher education institutions within the United States require instruction in English.

7 H. L. Goodall, Jr., *Casing a Promised Land: The Autobiography of an Organizational Detective as Cultural Ethnographer* (Carbondale: Southern Illinois University Press, 1994).

8 As McKerrow writes, "privileging civil discourse as a solution to human problems carries with it the promise of what might be called the tyranny of civility. Civil behavior may be more than politeness, but in its execution it may also serve to mask very real differences in power relations. In a word, civility may perpetuate servitude"; "...merely getting along is woefully inadequate as a response to social issues." Raymie E. McKerrow, "Coloring Outside the Tines: The Limits of Civility," *Vital Speeches of the Day* 67 (2001), 279–280. Also see Audre Lorde's brilliant speech/essay, "The Uses of Anger," *Women's Studies Quarterly* 9, no. 3 (1981), 7–10.

9 Erving Goffman, *The Presentation of Self in Everyday Life* (New York: Doubleday, 1956).

10 Mark R. Leary, *Impression Management and Interpersonal Behaviors* (Madison, WI: Brown & Benchmark, 1995), 2.

11 John Durham Peters, *Speaking into the Air: A History of the Idea of Communication* (Chicago, IL: University of Chicago Press), 131. Some folks claim to be "open books," "honest

and direct, always and everywhere" and claim to not care about "what other people think." Yet these claims contribute to cultivating an impression of "the rebel." These claims are also impossible to live in practice, at least without consequence. If you are the rebel who thinks you share everything, then open a social media account and publicly post the usernames and passwords to your bank information, the names and contact information of those who have slighted you, and every insecurity and ailment you have experienced. If you would hesitate to share such information publicly, if you want to keep some information private, then you know and do impression management.

12 Walter Fisher, "Narration as a Human Communication Paradigm: The Case of Public Moral Argument," *Communications Monographs* 51, no. 1 (1984), 1–22, https://doi.org/10.1080/03637758409390180. Many scholars have described the ways we live in/with/as story. See, for example, much of Art Bochner's work: Bochner, *Coming to Narrative*; Bochner, "Narrative's Virtue's"; Bochner, "It's about Time"; Arthur P. Bochner, "Perspectives on Inquiry II: Theories and Stories," in *Handbook of Interpersonal Communication*, eds., Mark L. Knapp and Gerald R. Miller (Thousand Oaks, CA: Sage, 1994), 21–41; and Arthur P. Bochner, "Perspectives on Inquiry III: The Moral of Stories," in *Handbook of Interpersonal Communication*, eds., Mark L. Knapp and John A. Daly (Thousand Oaks, CA: Sage, 2002), 73–101.

13 Hans-Georg Gadamer offers a similar perspective on prejudice. In attempting to reclaim prejudice from its negative connotation, Gadamer notes "all understanding inevitably involves some prejudice" (270); "the human intellect is too weak to manage without prejudices" (273); and prejudices serve as "conditions of understanding" (277). Hans-Georg Gadamer, *Truth and Method*, 2nd ed., trans., Joel Weinsheimer and Donald G. Marshall (New York: Continuum, 2000). We thank Jay Brower for reminding us about Gadamer's work.

14 Tony has written about framing: Tony E. Adams, "Frames of Homosexuality: Comparing *Los Angeles Times'* Coverage of California's Proposition 6 (1978) and Proposition 8 (2008)," *Sexuality & Culture* 17 (2013), 213–228, https://doi.org/10.1007/s12119-012-9145-2. See also Robert M. Entman, "Framing: Toward Clarification of a Fractured Paradigm," *Journal of Communication* 43 (1993), 51–58, https://doi.org/10.1111/j.1460-2466.1993.tb01304.x; Robert M. Entman, "Media Framing Biases and Political Power: Explaining Slant in News of Campaign 2008," *Journalism* 11, no. 4 (2010), 389–408, https://doi.org/10.1177/1464884910367587; Maxwell McCombs and Salma I. Ghanem, "The Convergence of Agenda Setting and Framing," in *Framing Public Life*, eds., Stephen D. Reese, Oscar H. Gandy, Jr., and August E. Grant (Mahwah, NJ: Lawrence Erlbaum, 2001), 67–81. M. E. McCombs and Donald L. Shaw, "The Agenda-Setting Function of Mass Media," *The Public Opinion Quarterly*, 36 no. 2 (1972), 176–187, https://doi.org/10.1086/267990.

15 Michael Billig, *Learn to Write Badly: How to Succeed in the Social Sciences* (Cambridge: Cambridge University Press, 2013). Arthur Bochner has applied Billig's arguments to autoethnography. See Arthur P. Bochner and Carolyn Ellis, *Evocative Autoethnography: Writing Lives and Telling Stories* (New York: Routledge, 2016), 78–79. We thank Art for recommending Billig's work.

16 We know of two articles that have been removed from a journal's website *after* they were published: Karl Andersson, "I Am Not Alone—We Are All Alone: Using Masturbation as an Ethnographic Method in Research on *Shota* Subculture in Japan," *Qualitative Research* 22 (2022), https://doi.org/10.1177/14687941221096600.

17 Anne Lamott, *Bird by Bird: Some Instructions on Writing and Life* (New York: Anchor, 1995), 20.

18 There are exceptions to this rule. One of Andrew's former colleagues is an expert rigger, one of the best in the world. Rigging is the art and craft of hanging—generally with rope—equipment and people during a theatre production. If not done correctly, people can die. Because rigging is such a niche area of expertise and would never make a publisher much profit, they publish on demand: Delbert A. Hall, *Rigging Math Made Simple* (Johnson City, TN: Spring Knoll Press, 2013).

19 Adams and Herrmann, "Good Autoethnography."

20 Michael Quinn Patton, *Qualitative Research and Evaluation Methods*, 3rd ed. (Thousand Oaks, CA: Sage, 2002), 542.

21 Kenneth J. Gergen, "Pursuing Excellence in Qualitative Inquiry," *Qualitative Psychology* 1, no. 1 (2014), 49, https://doi.org/10.1037/qup0000002.

22 Poulos, *Essentials of Autoethnography*, 75.

23 H. L. Goodall, Jr., *Writing Qualitative Inquiry: Self, Stories, and Academic Life* (Walnut Creek, CA: Left Coast Press, 2008), 42.

24 Several researchers have written about the importance of, and criteria for, assessing autoethnography. See Keith Berry, "Implicated Audience Member Seeks Understanding: Reexamining the 'Gift' of Autoethnography," *International Journal of Qualitative Methods* 5, no. 3 (2006), 94–108, https://doi.org/10.1177/160940690600500309; Keith Berry, "Autoethnography," in *The Cambridge Handbook of Identity*, eds., Michael Bamberg, Carolin Demuth, and Meike Watzlawik (Cambridge: Cambridge University Press, 2022), 324–344; Carolyn Ellis, "Creating Criteria: An Ethnographic Short Story," *Qualitative Inquiry* 6, no. 2 (2000), 273–277, https://doi.org/10.1177/107780040000600210; Carolyn Ellis, *The Ethnographic I: A Methodological Novel about Autoethnography* (Walnut Creek, CA: AltaMira, 2004), 249–268; Ragan Fox, "Recalling Emotional Recall: Reflecting on the Methodological Significance of Affective Memory in Autoethnography," *Text and Performance Quarterly* 41, no. 1–2 (2021), 61–80, https://doi.org/10.1080/10462937.2021.1915497; Gingrich-Philbrook, "Autoethnography's Family Values"; Craig Gingrich-Philbrook, "Evaluating (Evaluations of) Autoethnography," in *Handbook of Autoethnography*, eds., Stacy Holman Jones, Tony E. Adams, and Carolyn Ellis (Walnut Creek, CA: Left Coast Press, 2013), 609–626; Alec Grant, "Autoethnography," in *Critical Qualitative Health Research: Exploring Philosophies, Politics and Practices*, ed., Kay Aranda (New York: Routledge, 2020), 159–176; Alec Grant and Susan Young, "Troubling Tolichism in Several Voices: Resisting Epistemic Violence in Creative Analytical and Critical Autoethnographic Practice," *Journal of Autoethnography* 3 no. 1 (2022), 103–117, https://doi.org/10.1525/joae.2022.3.1.103; Sherick Hughes, Julie L. Pennington, and Sara Makris, "Translating Autoethnography across the AERA Standards: Toward Understanding Autoethnographic Scholarship as Empirical Research," *Educational Researcher* 41, no. 6 (2012), 209–219, https://doi.org/10.3102/0013189X12442983; Ronald J. Pelias, "Writing into Position: Strategies for Composition and Evaluation," in *The SAGE Handbook of Qualitative Research*, 4th ed., eds., Norman K. Denzin and Yvonna S. Lincoln (Thousand Oaks, CA: Sage, 2011), 659–668; Laurel Richardson, "Evaluating Ethnography," *Qualitative Inquiry* 6, no. 2 (June 2000), 253–255, https://doi.org/10.1177/107780040000600207; Robert Schroeder, "Evaluative Criteria for Autoethnographic Research: Who's to Judge?," in *The Self as Subject: Autoethnographic Research into Identity, Culture, and Academic Librarianship*, eds., Anne-Marie Deitering and Robert Schroeder (Chicago, IL: ACRL Publications, 2017), 315–346; Nigel P. Short and Alec Grant, "Burnard (2007): Autoethnography or a Realist Account?," *Journal of Psychiatric and Mental Health Nursing* 16, no. 2 (2009), 196–198, https://doi.org/10.1111/j.1365-2850.2008.01348.x; Andrew C. Sparkes,

"Autoethnography and Narratives of Self: Reflections on Criteria in Action," *Sociology of Sport Journal* 17, no. 1 (2000), 21–43, https://doi.org/10.1123/ssj.17.1.21; Andrew C. Sparkes, "Creating Criteria for Evaluating Autoethnography: Pedagogical Possibilities and Problems with Lists," in *International Perspectives on Autoethnographic Research and Practice*, eds., Lydia Turner, Nigel P. Short, Alec Grant, and Tony E. Adams (New York: Routledge, 2018), 256–267; Andrew C. Sparkes, "Autoethnography: Accept, Revise, Reject? An Evaluative Self Reflects," *Qualitative Research in Sport, Exercise and Health* 12, no. 2 (2020), 289–302, https://doi.org/10.1080/2159676X.2020.1732453; Andrew C. Sparkes, "When Judgment Calls: Making Sense of Criteria for Evaluating Different Forms of Autoethnography," in *Handbook of Autoethnography*, 2nd ed., eds., Tony E. Adams, Stacy Holman Jones, and Carolyn Ellis (New York: Routledge, 2022), 263–276.

25 Tony E. Adams, Stacy Holman Jones, and Carolyn Ellis, "Making Sense and Taking Action: Creating a Caring Community of Autoethnographers," in *Handbook of Autoethnography*, 2nd ed., eds., Tony E. Adams, Stacy Holman Jones, and Carolyn Ellis (New York: Routledge, 2022), 5–6.

26 Andrea Braithwaite, "From Brand to Genre: The Hallmark Movie," *Television & New Media* 24, no. 5 (2023), 488–498, https://doi.org/10.1177/15274764231171070.

27 Cited in Herrmann and Adams, "Autoethnography and the 'So What' Question," 3.

28 G. Thomas Couser, *Recovering Bodies: Illness, Disability, and Life Writing* (Madison: University of Wisconsin Press, 1997), 70.

29 The so-what section revised from Herrmann and Adams, "Autoethnography and the 'So What' Question."

30 Bochner and Herrmann, "Practicing Narrative Inquiry II."

31 Italo Calvino, *Italian Folktales* (Boston, MA: Houghton Mifflin Harcourt, 2013).

32 Kyle Longley, Jeremy Mayer, Michael Schaller, and John W. Sloan, *Deconstructing Reagan: Conservative Mythology and America's Fortieth President* (New York: Routledge, 2015). James F. McCloy and Ray Miller, Jr., *The Jersey Devil* (Wilmington, DE: Middle Atlantic Press, 1976).

33 Stephen Crites, "The Narrative Quality of Experience," *Journal of the American Academy of Religion* 39, no. 3 (1971), 291–311, http://www.jstor.org/stable/1461066. Paul Ricoeur, *History and Truth*, trans., Charles A. Kelbley (Evanston, IL: Northwestern University Press, 1965).

34 David Bordwell, *The Way Hollywood Tells It: Story and Style in Modern Movies* (Berkeley: University of California Press, 2006). Stephanie L. Young and Art Herbig, "'I Am Also a We': Exploring Queer Worldmaking in Sense8," *QED: A Journal in GLBTQ Worldmaking* 7, no. 2 (2020), 69–93, https://www.muse.jhu.edu/article/773400.

35 Donald A. Ritchie, *Doing Oral History* (Oxford: Oxford University Press, 2014).

36 Charles Guignon, "The History of Being," in Hubert L. Dreyfus and Mark A. Wrathall, eds., *A Companion to Heidegger* (Oxford: Blackwell, 2005), 392–406.

37 William F. Eadie, *When Communication Became a Discipline* (Lanham, MD: Rowman & Littlefield, 2021).

38 Donald E. Polkinghorne, *Narrative Knowing and the Human Sciences* (Albany: State University of New York Press, 1988).

39 Bochner and Herrmann, 2020. Brett Smith, "Narrative Analysis," in Adrian Coyle and Evantia Lyons, *Analysing Qualitative Data in Psychology* 2 (2016), 202–221.

40 Bochner and Herrmann, "Practicing Narrative Inquiry II."

41 Adams and Herrmann, "Good Autoethnography." Brett Smith and Javier Monforte, "Stories, New Materialism and Pluralism: Understanding, Practising and Pushing the

Boundaries of Narrative Analysis," *Methods in Psychology* 2 (2020), https://doi.org/10.1016/j.metip.2020.100016.

42 Andrew Abbott, "From Causes to Events: Notes on Narrative Positivism," *Sociological Methods & Research* 20, no. 4 (1992), 428–455, https://doi.org/10.1177/0049124192020004002.

43 The thinking-with vs. thinking-about distinction with narratives is the essence of Fisher's concept of *homo narrans*: as storytelling beings, we make sense of and relate to each other via stories. Fisher, "Narration as a Human Communication Paradigm."

Many others have made a similar argument about narratives. Again, see Art Bochner's work, especially *Coming to Narrative*. Kenneth Burke argues that stories can serve as "equipment for living"; Arthur Frank calls narrative the "self's medium of being"; and Charles Guignon writes, "we are the stories we enact." Robert Coles calls stories "tools" for managing life, tools that "not only keep us company, but admonish us, point us in new directions, or give us the courage to stay a given course." Laurel Richardson notes, "people make sense of their lives through the stories that are available to them, and they attempt to fit their lives into the available stories." Brody describes stories as things we "try on" and "wear": "Narrative allows us to try on future behavior much as we can try on different suits of clothes before buying one of them. The point of the analogy is that clothing which may look ideally suited for us on the rack may look very different when we try it on and look in the mirror." Kenneth Burke, *The Philosophy of Literary Form: Studies in Symbolic Action*, 3rd ed. (Berkeley: University of California Press, 1974), 67; Arthur W. Frank, *The Wounded Storyteller* (Chicago, IL: University of Chicago Press, 1995), 53; Charles Guignon, "Identity, History, Tradition," in *The Blackwell Companion to Hermeneutics*, eds., Niall Keane and Chris Lawn (New York: John Wiley & Sons, 2016), 141; Robert Coles, *The Call of Stories: Teaching and the Moral Imagination* (Boston, MA: Houghton Mifflin, 1989), 159. See also Laurel Richardson, "Narrative and Sociology," *Journal of Contemporary Ethnography* 19, no. 1 (1990), 129, https://doi.org/10.1177/089124190019001006; Howard Brody, *Stories of Sickness*, 2nd ed. (Oxford: Oxford University Press, 2002); Jerome Bruner, "Life as Narrative," *Social Research* 54, no. 11 (1986), 11–32, https://www.jstor.org/stable/40970444; and Kanwarjeet Singh, Jane Southcott, and Damien Lyons, "Walking the Doors—To Be to Become: An Autoethnography of Diasporic Beings and Multiple Becomings," *Journal of Autoethnography* 3, no. 1 (2021), 19–37, https://doi.org/10.1525/joae.2022.3.1.19.

44 Andrew F. Herrmann, "The Historical and Hysterical Narratives of Organization and Autoethnography," in *The Routledge International Handbook of Organizational Autoethnography*, ed., Andrew F. Herrmann (New York: Routledge, 2020), 24.

45 Robin M. Boylorn, "'Keep Remembering': Racialized Memory at The Lynching Memorial," *Journal of Autoethnography* 2 no. 1 (2021), 83–87, https://doi.org/10.1525/joae.2021.2.1.83.

46 Bochner and Herrmann, 2020.

47 Andrew F. Herrmann and Kristen DiFate, "Introduction to the Special Issue: The New Ethnography: Goodall, Trujillo, and the Necessity of Storytelling," *Storytelling, Self, Society* 10, no. 1 (2014), 4.

48 Arthur P. Bochner, "Narrative's Virtues," *Qualitative Inquiry* 7, no. 2 (2001), 132, https://doi.org/10.1177/107780040100700201.

49 Bochner and Herrmann, "Practicing Narrative Inquiry II," 294.

50 Herrmann, "Narrative as an Organizing Process," 252.

51 Herrmann, "Never Mind the Scholar," 157.

52 H. L. Goodall, personal communication, March 17, 2010.

53 Robert L. Krizek, "Lessons: What the Hell Are We Teaching the Next Generation Anyway?," in *Fiction and Social Research: By Ice or Fire*, eds., Anna Banks and Stephen Banks (Walnut Creek, CA: AltaMira, 1998), 94.
54 Arthur Quiller-Coach, *On the Art of Writing* (New York: G. P. Putnam's Sons, 1916), 216.
55 Kevin Johnson, "At Stake in the Rules of Communication is Democratic Life Itself: Does 'The Marketplace of Ideas' Matter Anymore?," *Communication and Democracy* 56, no. 2 (2022), 205–209, https://doi.org/10.1080/27671127.2022.2141740; Thomas W. Joo, "The Worst Test of Truth: The Marketplace of Ideas as Faulty Metaphor," *Tulane Law Review* 89, no. 2 (2014), 383.
56 Bochner, "Criteria against Ourselves," 269.
57 Adapted from Herrmann, "The Future of Autoethnographic Criteria."
58 Krizek, "Lessons."
59 Eric M. Eisenberg, H. Lloyd Goodall, Angela Trethewey, and Marianne LeGreco, *Organizational Communication: Balancing Creativity and Constraint* (Boston, MA: Bedford/St. Martin's, 2016).
60 Adapted from Herrmann, "The Future of Autoethnographic Criteria" and Adams, "Autoethnographic Responsibilities."
61 Voltaire, *A Philosophical Dictionary* (1764), https://archive.org/details/aphilosophicald03voltgoog/page/n247/mode/2up.
62 Bochner, *Coming to* Narrative; Nicholas L. Holt, "Representation, Legitimation, and Autoethnography: An Autoethnographic Writing Story," *International Journal of Qualitative Methods* 2, no. 1 (2003), 18–28, https://doi.org/10.1177/160940690300200102.

CHAPTER 2

The "Graphy" of Autoethnography

The Craft of Writing (about Oneself)

A beautiful but sweltering summer day in Peoria, Illinois (USA). We sit across from each other in a mostly empty Irish pub. Andrew takes a sip of his Smithwick's. "I've been thinking of the chart that you showed me. The one you use in your autoethnography courses".

"Students seem to find it helpful," Tony says. "It helps me too. I have been revising it for more than a decade. It shows how I visualize the path from the 'auto' to the 'ethno' and the 'graphy.'"

"What if we reversed the path for this book?" Andrew asks. "What if we started with the graphy?"

"Say more…" Tony says, retrieving the pocket notebook he often carries.

"When we are doing our editorial work for the journal," Andrew continues, "we seem to talk about the writing more than anything else. We discuss the boring prose and lack of compelling stories. We wonder why so many autoethnographic manuscripts try to follow the sterile introduction-literature review-method-findings-discussion-conclusion format."

"Yes!" Tony says, "and the lack of Geertzian 'thick description.' Thick description is a, if not the, hallmark of good ethnography."

"Ready for another beer?" the server asks.

"Absolutely," Andrew replies, then continues.

"I tell my autoethnography students to 'storify' their personal experiences. I tell them to think about their favorite scenes in their favorite films, television shows, and novels. What about those scenes capture and enrapture them? When doing autoethnography, details matter, as does the quality of the writing. I tell them to write their work similar to how their favorite scenes portray life."

"That's a brilliant approach. Yes, Let's start with the graphy, with writing and representation. I too have been encouraging folks to prioritize story first, do the theorization and analysis later. Many folks neglect the art, the craft, of assembling characters into characters, words into situations and onto pages. They merely share experience without

DOI: 10.4324/9781003281771-3

conveying the meaning of the experience. Autoethnography is one of the few methods that includes "graphy" as a core component; we do not do interview-graphy, phenomenology-graphy, or case study-graphy research. Folks wanting to do autoethnography need to take graphy seriously."

And that's how we arrived here, to this chapter, and why we placed this chapter before the auto and the ethno.

THE PROBLEM: (POOR) ACADEMIC WRITING

When starting a new job, here's something you might be interested in knowing:

> In serial socialization experienced organizational members serve as role models for the newcomer. In contrast, disjunctive socialization occurs when there are no role models for the newcomer to emulate. Finally, socialization can be investiture or divestiture, that is, socialization either values the personal characteristics of the newcomer, or attempts to remake the newcomer in the organization's image.[1]

Read that again. Or don't. Andrew doesn't ever want to read it again—and he wrote it for his dissertation. We use this example because it falls under the auspices of standard academic writing. There are times when this type of writing is necessary, e.g., writing for other experts on a specific topic where no translation into everyday parlance is needed. However, as our advisor Art Bochner asked after reading Andrew's literature review, "Is all organizational socialization research this boring?" Unfortunately, much of it is.

Many qualitative researchers—yes, many—struggle with writing and/or treat writing as secondary to the research process. Yet beyond introductory writing coursework in college, few scholars take courses in writing, especially creative writing. Fewer than that get to take courses in narrative or storytelling or autoethnography. Even fewer are self-taught. This makes some sense—as undergraduates, master students, doctoral students, and teachers, we are trained as researchers to make sure we *get the research right*. Getting the research right is important. But we do not spend much time learning *how* to write or represent (graphy) our research.

Several scholars have expressed this concern. "I have a confession to make," Laurel Richardson writes.

> For thirty years, I have yawned my way through numerous supposedly exemplary qualitative studies. Countless numbers of texts have I abandoned half-read, half-scanned. I'll order a new book with great anticipation—the topic is one I'm interested in, the author is someone I want to read—only to find the text boring.[2]

"Can something be done?" Richardson asks. She responds by calling us to better attend to "writing as a method of inquiry."[3]

In "The Critical Life," Pelias describes his reaction to receiving one of the communication discipline's primary journals, *Communication Monographs*

> You see five articles, most by more than one author, on topics of interest to you but located in a paradigmatic logic you find less than convincing. You read the abstracts and shake your head, not because you are confused by the content, but because you cannot understand how the scientific model continues to thrive in the discipline given the number of arguments that show why the heart needs to accompany the head ... You place the issue on a stack of material you plan to read. During the next several months, you will keep skipping over it until you finally place it on your bookshelf alongside other unread *Monographs*.[4]

In *Evocative Autoethnography*, Bochner and Ellis ask:

> Are published social science articles a good read? Do you look forward to reading empirical research monographs? Do you keep social science journals and research papers by your bedside to browse at night?[5]

Bochner and Ellis then synthesize common criticisms of academic writing: excessive jargon, boring and "tortuous" prose, and how many projects and texts—projects and texts that take so much time and effort to complete—are "not worth the time and effort" to read.[6] "It seems foolish, at best, narcissistic and wholly self-absorbed, at worst," Richardson remarks, "to spend months or years doing research that ends up not being read and not making a difference to anything but the author's career."[7]

Fledderus characterizes academic writing as "esoteric," "impenetrable," and "elite"; Mykhalovskiy describes "the university" as an "insular" and "isolated" institution of intellectuals who produce books and articles only to be read "by a handful of other academics"; and as anthropologist Ruth Behar notes a "huge fear of good writing in anthropology."[8]And as mentioned in the previous chapter, Billig's book, *Learn to Write Badly: How to Succeed in the Social Sciences*, offers a stinging but necessary critique of academic writing.

"Our tasks as scholars in general and ethnographers in particular is to write sentences that fairly represent the realities we have experienced," Bud Goodall writes. "It is also to make the reading of that reality accessible to others who have not seen it and who must rely on our guidance to share it."[9] Bad writing does not entice and engage readers. Simple as that.

Andrew's excerpt on organizational socialization isn't merely boring. It is also inaccessible to a wider audience. This is a problem.

> If we as professors need our dictionaries, thesaurus, and encyclopedias open with us as we struggle through a piece of scholarship, how many people outside the academy are going to read it, even if they are extremely interested in the topic? Basically none.[10]

Several scholars offer suggestions for making qualitative research more accessible. In "Making Qualitative Research Reports Less Boring," Darrel Caulley encourages qualitative researchers to incorporate techniques of creative nonfiction in their work—develop scenes, foreground concrete and realistic details, use active voice, create conversation, and prioritize rhythm in the writing.

In the 1998 book, *Fiction and Social Research*, Banks and Banks encouraged researchers to learn and use techniques of fiction to represent their work; Tierney calls qualitative researchers to create texts "more in relation to fiction and storytelling"; in *The Ethnographic I*, Ellis includes the chapter, "Writing a Methodological Novel: Thinking Like an Ethnographer, Writing Like a Novelist"; and in a section about "ethnographic fiction" in *Ethnography: A Way of Seeing*, Wolcott notes, "the writer of ethnographic fiction *is* a dedicated storyteller."[11] Scholars such as Patricia Leavy have led the way with such a call.[12] Some disciplinary organizations even try to create outlets to translate esoteric research into more accessible prose. For instance, the National Communication Association publishes *Communication Currents* to explain "scholarly information in straightforward language geared for broad audiences,"[13] and the American Sociological Association publishes *Contexts*, a "quarterly magazine that makes cutting-edge social research accessible to general readers."[14]

As Art Bochner once asked, "How many people do you want to read your work—5, 500, or 5000?" More? How you answer this question should determine not only how you craft your texts but also how much time you spend crafting them. We sometimes joke that academic writing is so jargon-filled and poorly written that we write for "The International Journal of Two Readers."[15] We want more people to read our work. Autoethnography can help us do that.

*

When graphy is used as a suffix, it suggests the art and practice of engaging and creating certain representations. Cartography: the art and science of map-making; photography: the art and science of capturing and processing images; musicography: the art of writing music; and choreography: the art of staging movement and dance.

For us, autoethnography is comprised of not one but two kinds of graphy. First is the graphy associated with autobio-graphy, the art of writing (about) one's life. Here the emphasis is on personal experience, the "I," the self-reflective writer who produces a text, the subject and the object of research. (We'll discuss the auto in Chapter 3.)

The second graphy is the graphy of ethno-graphy, the art and science of representing cultural principles, practices, and products. The ethno emphasizes looking outward, observing the world around us, and representing that world by producing concrete and compelling thick descriptions. Further, when understood as a research method, ethnography is one of the few methods that includes -graphy as a core component. We don't do survey-graphy or textual-analysis-graphy research. If a manuscript claims to be ethnography, but the author hasn't demonstrated much care for the graphy, then they aren't doing nor making good ethnography.

Assembled, we have auto-ethno-graphy, the art and science of representing one's life in relation to cultural principles, practices, and products. If a researcher claims to do autoethnography but hasn't demonstrated any care for the graphy, then they aren't doing nor making good autoethnography. If they craft an esoteric, sterile, and boring text—a sin for serious autobiographers *and* ethnographers—then they are not doing (good) autoethnography.[16]

If we want to do good autoethnography, we cannot treat writing as an afterthought, a tangential, secondary, after-the-fact act. We cannot just do research and then "write it up." For autoethnography, graphy is not separate from the research process. Graphy *is* the research process. You need to work the graphy—writing, editing, and rewriting over and over—until you have an autoethnography (product).

By the way, Andrew wrote about organizational socialization again, but this time from a first-person perspective:

> I started the new position today! Officially, I am the 'Information Technology Coordinator for the College of Arts and Sciences.' That won't fit on the business card. I'll be working for the college and working with ITS [Information Technology Services]. I met with the Associate Dean Laura, and the Academic IT Director Sam. My job, as described in my interviews, will be to coordinate activities and projects between the College and ITS, and working on faculty development. I am looking forward to this. My office is embedded in a building that houses the Department of Communication. On the campus tour a professor says, 'You'll find this place runs as slow as the Byzantine Empire with twice the paperwork.' I'll change that. I'm very efficient. I'm proactive.[17]

Which of Andrew's two excerpts would you rather continue to read?

A SOLUTION: GOOD (AUTOETHNOGRAPHIC) WRITING

Art Bochner supervised our dissertations, and Carolyn Ellis served on our dissertation committees. We took multiple courses with each, and in each course, they foregrounded the craft of writing and representation. Art and Carolyn have spent decades doing and writing about autoethnography, and although they may not have coined the term "autoethnography," they are the primary scholars to explicitly describe autoethnography as a method—what it is *and* how to do it.[18] Art and Carolyn are the most prominent and most cited autoethnographers, and many books about autoethnography begin with their work. We are grateful for being able to work with them.

In our graduate programs, we learned that to do good autoethnography, one must learn how to do good ethnography *and* good autobiography (and affiliated forms of life writing). To learn about ethnography, we read Geertz's *The Interpretation of Cultures*, John Van Maanen's *Tales of the Field*, Laurel Richardson's *Fields of Play: Constructing an Academic Life*, Robin Clair's *Expressions of Ethnography: Novel Approaches to Qualitative Methods*, Soyini Madison's *Critical Ethnography: Methods, Ethics, and Performance*, Ruth Behar's *The Vulnerable Observer*, Harry Wolcott's *Ethnography: A Way of Seeing*, and Bud Goodall's *Writing the New Ethnography*. To learn autobiography and life writing, we read Anne Lamott's *Bird by Bird*, Stephen King's *On Writing*, Judith Barrington's

Writing the Memoir: From Truth to Art, Dorothy Allison's *Two or Three Things I Know for Sure*, Ron Pelias's *Methodology of the Heart*, Norman Denzin's *Interpretive Biography* [which 20+ years later became *Interpretive Autoethnography*], Robert Coles' *The Call of Stories*, and Arthur Frank's *The Wounded Storyteller*. We also read works by Hunter Thompson, bell hooks, Dwight Conquergood, Joan Didion, Audre Lorde, Tim O'Brien, David Foster Wallace, Susan Sontag, Philip Lopate, Gloria Anzaldúa, Nick Trujillo, and John Berger. These authors care about craft and know how to tell good stories about oneself in cultural contexts. They were our early autoethnographic muses.

Although texts explicitly about autoethnography were still limited in 2001–2008, the years we were in our graduate programs, we also read the few works close to, or solely about, autoethnography: Bochner and Ellis' classic chapter, "Autoethnography, Personal Narrative, Reflexivity: Researcher as Subject," Ellis's *Final Negotiations* and *The Ethnographic I: A Methodological Novel about Autoethnography*, Ellis and Flaherty's *Investigating Subjectivity: Research on Lived Experience*, Deborah Reed-Danahay's *Auto/ethnography: Rewriting the Self and the Social*, Norman Denzin's *Performance Ethnography* [which later became *Performance Autoethnography*], Ellis and Bochner's *Composing Ethnography: Alternative Forms of Qualitative Writing* and *Ethnographically Speaking: Autoethnography, Literature, and Aesthetics*, as well as several books in Bochner and Ellis' first book series, *Ethnographic Alternatives* (which included Banks and Banks' *Fiction and Social Research* and Goodall's *Writing the New Ethnography*). We read more works by Pelias and Goodall, and new works by Carol Rambo, Stacy Holman Jones, Bryant Keith Alexander, Barbara Jago, and Lisa Tillmann.

Across these works, authors prioritize the craft of writing and representation. They demonstrate thick description and show how to create compelling accounts of cultural life.

*

Autobiographers and life writers care about the craft of writing—writing is an essential facet of the genre, and a good autobiographer must take storytelling seriously. We didn't need to be convinced of this—before our graduate programs, we knew what autobiography was and that one had to be a good writer to do it well. Yet we didn't know anything about ethnography—we had to learn about it, and as we did, we learned that, like autobiographers, ethnographers also had to be good writers to do ethnography well. For example, Geertz writes in *The Interpretation of Cultures*

> From one point of view, that of the textbook, doing ethnography is establishing rapport, selecting informants, transcribing texts, taking genealogies, mapping fields, keeping a diary, and so on. But it is not these things, techniques, and received procedures that define the enterprise. *What defines it is the kind of intellectual effort it is: an elaborate venture in, to borrow a notion from Gilbert Ryle, "thick description."*[19]

We also read Van Maanen's 1988 *Tales of the Field: On Writing Ethnography*, a classic and still timely book about the craft of writing-up ethnographic fieldwork. Van Maanen categorized ethnographic accounts in three primary ways: realistic tales, confessional tales, and impressionistic tales. In realist tales, the most traditional form to represent ethnography, Van Maanen noted the importance of concrete details and extensive description. "[W]hile there are no particularly evocative or stylistic features" of the realist tale, he writes, "part of its effect no doubt turns on the flow, tempo, and form of the writing."[20] Confessional tales are intimate, self-reflective, and "highly personalized" accounts of the ethnographer *as* fieldworker.[21] And impressionistic tales offer readers a "'you-are-there' feel."

> The author must not give away the ending before it is time. A degree of tension must be allowed to build and then be released. Contextual descriptions must be condensed yet rich enough to carry the reader along. Artistic nerve is required of the teller … A general audience unfamiliar with the studied scene can judge the tale only on the basis of its plausibility or believability, not on the basis of accuracy or representativeness … The audience cannot be concerned with the story's correctness, since they were not there and cannot know if it is correct. The standards are largely those of interest (does it attract?), coherence (does it hang together?), and fidelity (does it seem true?).[22]

"[T]he main obligation of the impressionist," Van Maanen argues,

> is to keep the audience alert and interested. Unusual phrasings, fresh allusions, rich language, cognitive and emotional stimulation, puns, and quick jolts to the imagination are all characteristic of the good tale … It is no surprise that some of the best ethnographic writing is done when impressionist tales are told.[23]

Note Van Maanen's assessment—impressionist tales are some of the *best* ethnographic writing; contrarily, some of the worst ethnographic writing isn't impressionistic.

Although Van Maanen focuses on realist, confessional, and impressionistic tales, he also introduces other forms of ethnographic tales, e.g., "critical tales," "advocacy tales," and "literary tales." Literary tales rely on techniques of fiction. They

> combine a reporter's sense of what is noteworthy (newsworthy) with a novelist's sense of narration, dense characterization, dramatic plots, flashbacks (and flashforwards) and alternative points of view are illustrative techniques.[24]

In our graduate programs, we learned about autoethnography via these works and authors. We quickly realized that if we wanted to succeed with our courses, dissertations, and careers, and if we wanted to be good autoethnographers, then we had to take writing and representation seriously—or risk being assessed as not serious about our learning and work.

*

Most of the manuscripts we reject at the *Journal of Autoethnography* and our affiliated book series stem from an author's inability to write. These authors seem to treat writing as secondary or insignificant. And the issue isn't just with folks who have been trained in rigid, social scientific ways to represent their work. Many interpretive qualitative researchers also overlook the necessity of the graphy when writing a first autoethnography. That is why we prioritize graphy here, early in this book. If you want to do good autoethnography, you must care about craft. Good ethnographies and autobiographies—and thus autoethnographies—are compelling, insightful, and concrete; rarely are they boring.[25] If you submit a boring manuscript to us, don't be surprised by the feedback you receive not only from us but also from reviewers.

*

Autoethnographers must take graphy seriously; graphy is important for both ethnography and autobiography. Even if you understand the auto as only about personal experience, and not necessarily the auto of autobiography, that's fine—but ethnography is still there, and good ethnographies, even realist ethnographies, are well-written and compelling and demonstrate a steadfast commitment to thick description.

Recent books about ethnography also emphasize the importance of craft. For example, in both editions of *Writing Ethnography*, Jessica Smartt Gullion[26] describes the importance of storytelling for ethnographers, characteristics of good stories, vulnerability and reflexivity, narrative voice, caring about audiences, showing and telling, character development, and writing as inquiry. And as Wolcott notes in *Ethnography Lessons*, "because some ethnographies are well written and therefore more satisfying, they are the ones we read."[27]

LET'S START AT THE BEGINNING: FUNDAMENTALS OF WRITING

The song "Do-Re-Mi" (*The Sound of Music*) offers a clever and catchy way to learn primary music notes, the tools for making songs. Once we learn these notes, we can then create different songs. We can experiment with time and tempo, rests and refrains, melodies and motifs. Although "Do-Re-Mi" foregrounds the making of music, the song opens by comparing the song-making process to learning how to read: Folks learning English often begin by learning A–B–C.

To begin assessing the graphy of autoethnography, let's begin here, with the structure and assemblage of characters (letters, spaces, punctuation) into coherent fragments (words, sentences, paragraphs) in a particular language. When we review manuscripts written in English and an author misspells "autoethnography" without explanation (e.g., "autoethnografy")—if the author assembles letters in an incorrect way based on the shared and standard rules for spelling a term—then we might evaluate the author's proficiency with English, their care for their manuscript, and their knowledge of "autoethnography." If the author misspells a term repeatedly and without explanation, then we might question their commitment to doing their work and assess their work as subpar, of low quality, not worthy of our time and attention.

At the *Journal of Autoethnography*, some folks have submitted manuscripts using "auto-ethnography," "auto ethnography," "[auto]ethnography," and "auto/ethnography" (we even had one manuscript use three of the four spellings!). When this occurs, we expect an explanation for the hyphen ("-"), the space (" "), the brackets ("[ ]"), and the forward slash ("/"), especially since the author deviates from how the term is spelled at the journal. There may be good reasons for spelling autoethnography in these ways, but if there are no explanations, then we expect the author to match how the very journal with which they're submitting the work spells the term—that would help facilitate our understanding. Readers might wonder about the different spellings too. If the author does not offer an explanation, we may again question their commitment to their work and their knowledge of autoethnography, and we may assess their work as subpar, of low quality, not worthy of our time and attention.

We can expand assessment to the level of the sentence: If someone writes, "Method autoethnografy favorite me," we may not understand the author's argument(s) and wonder about the author's ability to use English to adequately portray their work.[28] The misspelling of a key term and the inclusion of an incomprehensible sentence might motivate additional assessments of a writer's project and, consequently, their character—whether they are serious about the manuscript and if they are a lazy writer. Further, careless authors do not effectively convey their experiences and ideas; if we cannot understand an author's text and if it takes too much time and effort to decipher what we think they intend to say, we might misunderstand the work or consider it to be inadequate. If we serve as reviewers for the manuscript, we wouldn't recommend it for publication, share it with others, use it in our classes, or promote it on social media. We might even use the manuscript as an example of bad autoethnography. Although we expect a few errors in any manuscript—we still find errors in our published work—an abundance of errors can suggest a carelessness in craft and an author's apathy and inadequacy about their observations and arguments. If they don't care about their words and ideas, why should we?

We can expand from the sentence to the structure of a manuscript. Given the emphasis on craft and storytelling, autoethnographies rarely use a traditional introduction-literature review-method-findings-analysis-conclusion formula. This formula isn't inherently bad or incorrect but can restrict the ability to create a compelling read—a necessity for serious ethnographers, autobiographers, and autoethnographers. Consider the "exemplary autoethnographies" we've included in both editions of the *Handbook of Autoethnography*.[29] None of the exemplars follow such a format. Additionally, together, we have edited more than a dozen books and special journal issues about autoethnography and we have never included a chapter structured in such a formulaic way. Most of the books published in the *Writing Lives* book series or the articles published in the *Journal of Autoethnography* also do not follow this formula. Indeed, there are exceptions—the formula isn't inherently bad—but trying to represent an autoethnography using the formula is akin to expecting novels and other creative works to follow the formula. Does *One Hundred Years of Solitude* include a literature review? Does *The Little Prince* have a methods section? What are the findings of *The Color Purple*? These are inappropriate, even silly expectations to have of such texts.

We can assess the claims an author makes about autoethnography. We have reviewed manuscripts in which authors make statements such as "autoethnographers strive for generalization and objectivity" or "autoethnography is a new research method." The first claim goes against a core premise of autoethnography, a method that prioritizes and celebrates particularization and subjectivity; the second claim not only disregards projects that have formally used autoethnography in the past 40+ years, but also centuries-old projects that, while not formally called "autoethnography," portrayed intersections between self and society. By making such erroneous claims, we would question the author's knowledge of autoethnography and ability to do credible autoethnographic research. Indeed, autoethnography might be new to a topic, situation, or discipline, but to broadly refer to autoethnography as new is erroneous.

We do not want to quantify or establish a threshold of errors with writing—dear reader, that's up to you—we all have thresholds regarding how many errors are tolerable, and what we should do if we cannot, or if it takes too long, to decipher and understand a text. As *homo assessors*, we assume we all have these thresholds, but we don't talk about them too much, as doing so can feel insensitive and threatening. "Mediocre writing," Andrew Sparkes writes, "is likely to lead to the presentation of a mediocre autoethnography that then leads to a rejection."[30] And that's one of our core arguments: The more cumbersome a text is for readers, the fewer readers you'll have, the fewer readers who will understand what you're trying to convey, the fewer readers to share your insights and ideas with others. Take pride in your work—seek feedback from trusted sources, care about craft and about crafting a compelling story.

READING TO BECOME A BETTER WRITER

If a lot of academic writing is boring and unreadable, that also means it is practically useless to broader audiences; we don't write at a fifth grade reading level, as Tony learned to do with news reporting. And if academic writing is practically useless to broader audiences, then how can we create the conditions necessary to use our work to promote the positive change we want to see in our relationships, workplaces, and communities? We can't. Many autoethnographers, especially critical autoethnographers, want to reach larger audiences; they do not want their work to be lost. One way not to get lost is to focus on the graphy—how we write and represent our experiences.

Unlike the Goddess Athena, who was created fully formed, no one comes to autoethnography as a fully formed writer. Writing is a process of becoming and requires consistent practice. Our life histories in the introduction illustrate how we did this. We still practice by writing most every day, and we view our works, including this book, as works-in-progress. We came to be autoethnographers through certain practices and habits. First, we read. Second, we write. And third, we had/have superb mentors. Let's consider our first practice.

To write well, you need to read. This is not a new idea. "If you want to be a writer," Stephen King says, "you must do two things above all others: read a lot and write a lot. There's no way around these two things that I'm aware of, no shortcut."[31] However, learning to write autoethnography goes beyond the required reading in a class. An autoethnography is not just a sterile research article. It needs to be a compelling read too. It needs to entice the reader, invite them into the text. Autoethnography thus draws on many facets of literature: flashbacks and flashforwards, perspective changes, vignettes, stream of consciousness, poems, short stories, climaxes, resolutions, dreams, asides, monologues, conversations, denouements, and codas. It makes sense why Tierney writes, "I remind my students that if they want to read good writing and think about how to construct their own texts then they should read novels, not social science."[32] Yet Tierney expresses concern that academics "trained to write as social scientists are not able to simply transform our writing to another genre with much success." It takes training to write good autoethnography, and if you aren't willing to commit to the training and the craft, then autoethnography may not be good for you. And that's okay: just choose a method that doesn't emphasize graphy the way autoethnography does.

To quote Stephen King again, the point is: "If you don't have time to read, you don't have the time (or the tools) to write. Simple as that."[33] Reading is fundamental to writing.

Besides learning the tools and the craft of writing good narratives, reading fiction has other beneficial effects. Fiction can increase your empathy, the ability to observe and share the feelings of others, understand their point of view.[34] As Bal and colleagues write,

> Often when someone reads a fictional story, identification with the characters in the story and emotional involvement in the story causes the reader to sympathize with the characters, and perhaps even experience the events in the story as if the reader experiences the events [themselves]. Consequently, the reader practices being empathic while reading a fictional story.[35]

Reading fiction also increases social cognition, how people understand social interactions, and it can make us better people.[36]

Yet reading is only half of King's statement: "read a lot and write a lot." Write a lot. As Carolyn reminds us, this means putting our butts in chairs in front of screens and notebooks. Dedicate time to write. Find time to write without distraction. Yes, writing is a luxury—we may not have Woolf's privileged room of one's own[37]—but it is worth considering how much writing matters to you and what distractions you might have. Do you spend hours binging television, playing games, or scrolling on social media? You must determine how writing and autoethnography matter to you.

This doesn't mean we have to be isolated in silence. We have written together while listening to 80s radio. Andrew has a fondness and affinity for funk when he writes because he gets "in a groove." Andrew identifies as a night writer. You'll find him starting to write around midnight and ending near dawn. He also writes in coffee shops and appreciates the ambient noise. Tony identifies as an 8–12 writer: Ideally, he enjoys writing in the morning, 8 am–12 pm, and again in the evening, 8 pm–12 am. Yet he often has a more realistic schedule: he might write from 9:30 am to 10:30 am and then 10:30 pm to 11:30 pm. Somedays he will only write one sentence, possibly a paragraph, in between meetings, and sometimes even during meetings. (Hint: Tony may appear as though he is taking notes; but he might be writing, especially if the meeting is boring.) Somedays he will write at his local queer bar—not on busy days and nights, but rather Mondays, Tuesdays, and Thursdays during happy hour. Sometimes he takes notes on napkins or his phone.

In May 2006, we, along with Sara Dykins Callahan, interviewed Norman Denzin for Carolyn Ellis's Advanced Qualitative Methods graduate course. During the interview, Andrew asked Denzin, "How do you write so much? I walked into the book exhibit and there's your handbook and another handbook and then your self-authored works and multiple chapters and all those journals ..."

"Every morning," Norman replied.

"How long?" Andrew asked.

"4-5 hours," Norman said. "If you do that five days a week, the writing will add up. You just have to free up the time. I stay at home. Nobody bothers you, you have nobody interrupting you. I try to stay focused for a few hours and then do other things the rest of the day."[38]

Good writing is a difficult task. Each word matters. Every choice is meaningful. Andrew gave the history chapter he wrote for the *Routledge International Handbook of Organizational Autoethnography* the title "The Historical and Hysterical Narratives of Organization and Autoethnography." You may have already identified the error. He strived for alliteration, and a bit of irony, but after it was published, he realized he should have used "hilarious" instead of "hysterical" because the latter invokes a terrible history of violence against women. One word makes a difference. "Whether it's a vignette of a single page or an epic trilogy like *The Lord of the Rings*, the work is always accomplished one word at a time."[39]

A LESSON FROM ANDREW'S AUTOETHNOGRAPHY COURSE

When I (Andrew) mentor students first learning to do autoethnography, I use a specific term to help them craft their experiences: "Storify." This term combines Bud Goodall's two rules for using evocative language: show, don't tell; and "Describe before you evaluate or analyze."[40] Goodall describes this second rule as "'show me the data.' Readers like to reach their own conclusions rather than having the meaning summed for them. Rich descriptions of scenes, details about characters and events—all of these are data in a story."[41]

Often a student will write something in a draft that piques my interest, a kernel to expand upon, some gem that has been skimmed or a skirted interaction.

> "That's interesting," I'll say, "Now storify it."
> "Go deeper here. Storify it."
> "I want more details. Storify this."

When I use this term, students look at me quizzically, "What do you mean?"

"I want you to think of your favorite novel," I say. "The genre doesn't matter. Romance. Fantasy. Science Fiction. Detective fiction. Horror. Absurdist comedy. It doesn't matter if your favorite novel is Judy Blume's *Are You There God? It's Me, Margaret*, Octavia Butler's *Kindred*, Albert Camus' *The Plague*, Bonnie Garmus' *Lessons in Chemistry*, or J. R. R. Tolkien's *Lord of the Rings*. Now think of your favorite scene from that novel."

I wait a few moments and then call on a student.

"Stacey, what's your favorite novel?"

"Raven Leilani's *Luster: A Novel*," she replies.[42]

"I've never heard of it," I say, "which is good because I have no preconceptions. Now tell me about your favorite scene."

"It's a bit embarrassing," she says. "The book has a lot of sex in it. The main character, Edie, is scandalous."

"That's ok," I say, "Do you have a favorite scene?"

"Yes. Edie is the narrator. She's lusty and funny and insecure. Her mind is constantly racing, and she describes what she's thinking before she has sex, during sex, after sex. She also describes the complications of being the third person in an open heterosexual marriage. There's a scene in the car with Eric, the guy in the open marriage. Edie and Eric attended a firework show and it began to rain. Soaking wet, Eric takes off his shirt, and smiles in a way that, and I quote, 'makes me want to sit on his face.'"

A few students giggle.

"There's more to the scene than mere sex!" Stacy laughs.

"I'm sure there is," I say. "What makes the scene memorable for you?"

"The descriptions. Leilani doesn't just say 'wet' like I did. Her description of Eric's smile is so vivid I can imagine it, feel it. She doesn't just describe; she helps us feel the description."

"*That's* what I mean when I say 'storify' an experience," I say. "I want you to provide details about what happens. Offer rich descriptions of the scene, the setting, the emotions, the characters. Sufficient details make the best scenes."

*

Let's begin with a few examples from fiction. Consider this sentence describing a person entering a tunnel: "It's darker in there than he thought, and as he walked in, it got darker until it got dark." It tells us, but it doesn't show us. It doesn't offer rich descriptions and doesn't give us a great scene. It's not *storified.*

Here's the actual scene. We will provide more context later, after you read it.

> It was much blacker inside than he had imagined it would be. At first the opening behind him cast dim white light ahead and he could see yet more cars, jammed bumper to bumper (*it must have been bad, dying here* he thought, as claustrophobia wrapped its stealthy banana fingers lovingly around his head and began to first caress and then to squeeze his temples, *it must have been really bad, it must have been*

> *fucking horrible*), and the greenish-white tiles that dressed the upward-curving walls. He could see the pedestrian railing to his right, stretching dimly ahead. On his left, at thirty- or forty-foot intervals, were big support pillars. A sign advised him DO NOT CHANGE LANES. There were dark fluorescents embedded in the tunnel's roof, and the blank glass eyes of closed-circuit TV cameras. And as he negotiated the first, slow banked curve, bearing gently to the right, the light grew dimmer until all he could see were muted flashes of chrome. After that the light simply ceased to exist at all.[43]

A few observations: First, there's only one character. There's no dialogue, no interaction. Simply one character alone with himself, his thoughts, and his surroundings. Second, note the depth to the description. The writing doesn't just tell you what the character sees, it shows you what he sees. Adjectives—there aren't just tiles, the tiles are greenish-white. There aren't just broken TV cameras, the cameras are blank glass eyes. And ever so slowly, the light dims and dims until it's black. This is the kind of rich detail that gives you a "feeling."

The scene is from one of Andrew's favorite books, Stephen King's *The Stand*. There has been a global pandemic and 95% of the world's population is dead, and Larry, a main character, tries to get out of New York City through the Lincoln Tunnel. Granted, most of us are not going to write a 1,200-page tome about the survivors of the apocalypse. The point is that this kind of rich description, this kind of detail, makes scenes memorable.

Although not fiction, good ethnographic, autobiographic, and autoethnographic writing, must have this rich description. Such deep descriptive writing can be attuned to the outer world, like in the excerpt above. The writing puts you in the scene. You can imagine it, visualize it. It's detailed, *storified*. Consider this autoethnographic description:

> My arms are in front of me, bent at the elbows, held close to my body, hands curled, but not clenched. I get hit from behind and I swing around. There are body parts everywhere zooming in and out my field of vision: chests, heads, arms, and legs. My body is getting hit repeatedly from all sides. Something hard hits my leg. A boot maybe? It doesn't hurt. I am ecstatic. Another hit from the side, and I ram into the chest of the guy with liberty spikes, who shoves me away. My body flails backwards. The back of my calves hit something that feels both hard and soft. I am falling backwards over Adrianna. My butt hits the hard tile floor hard. Jarring. Before I register the sting, a hand reaches out from above. I reach out as the hand grips my forearm. I am lifted quickly from the floor and bounce hard into another body and am immediately hit in the back by yet another. I spin and get slammed into in the front and back simultaneously. I gyrate to the right, and smack into a short young man. I feel the press of his arms shove me in the back. The music stops.[44]

This kind of rich description transports readers into a mosh pit at a punk rock show. You don't have to be in the apocalypse or in a mosh pit to understand what's happening. You don't have to be a horse or a spider on a farm, the pilot of the *Millennium Falcon*, or a cynical private detective, to be transported into the worlds of *Animal Farm*, *Charlotte's Web*, *Star Wars*, or Sam Spade. The rich description immerses readers into the story.

The rich description can be focused on our outer world and what's going on around us. It can also be attuned to one's inner world, the world of our personal thoughts and emotions.

> When it happens for the first time, I am leaning over the bathtub with a portable shower hose rinsing the soap from my hair. At first, I think my ears must be stopped up. Perhaps the pressure from the shower hose is too great or maybe I have some hard wax in my ears. I shake my head like a dog after a bath, but I still hear the low buzzing sounds. I bend my head in one direction, then the other, gently tapping my wrists against each ear. The sounds persist.[45]

Here, Art Bochner describes the first time he noticed his tinnitus. As far as "action" goes, not much happens externally—simply a man at the sink. Art mostly describes his inner world: what he thinks, how he feels, his attempts at making sense. He does not tell us, "This is unnerving." Rather, he describes the setting and the seriousness of his thoughts, trying to determine the cause of the inexplicable sound, and how to get rid of it.

Robin Boylorn offers a brilliant example of how autoethnographers can use inner dialogue. Boylorn, a Black woman, describes a moment when an unfamiliar White woman speaks to her in a grocery store in Alabama (USA). Boylorn first tells readers that the unexpected-yet-polite interaction surprised her, as she had concerns about White Alabamians being visibly racist and segregated, not friendly and polite. Boylorn then describes telling the woman that she recently relocated to Alabama, and the woman asking, "Well, what are you going to do here, teach?" Using inner dialogue, Boylorn reflects on the woman's question:

> I am caught off guard by her immediate and accurate assessment of my profession, especially since I do not look like a teacher standing before her in a tank top and sweat pants, my hair camouflaged beneath a head scarf and driver's cap, not likely looking a day over twenty-one.
>
> "Yes, actually," I say, still surprised at her guess. "How could you have possibly known that?"
>
> "You talk so well," she says smiling. And while I know she means this as a compliment, I can't help but consider her assumption that as a Black woman, perhaps "talking well," or as my family often said, "talking proper or White," somehow distinguished me from the other Black women she encounters on a daily basis, including the [Black] woman behind the deli counter, from whom she held her words.
>
> "My mother used to correct my English all the time," the woman explains, perhaps reading the confusion on my face. Though her latter words somewhat softened the sentiment, I can't shake the potential innuendo embedded in her words. Is she simply not used to encountering an educated Black person? Am I one of those educated Negroes she has heard about?
>
> "Thank you," is all I know to say.[46]

In this example, Boylorn offers succinct, yet powerful, inner dialogue to show how she made sense of the brief interaction. She offers private reactions, for readers, that a camera or recorder could never capture,[47] and she provides access to "hard-to-get-at dimensions of social life"[48]—that is, a fleeting interaction infused with race and racist assumptions among strangers in a grocery store.[49]

Or consider this excerpt that describes one person's struggle with the "Them" in his own psychotic episodes

> I go on like this for weeks. After my wife leaves for work every morning, I close all the blinds around me. I set out a row of cups on the kitchen counter for my protection when they barge through the door. I search for the cameras in the room. I taunt them with faces and foul imagery. I play my guitar loudly in corners to send them shockwaves of noise and hatred. I use every moment to fight against the spies. I await their eventual collapse into the physical world. I will win this, but this spectacular victory never comes, as the intensities build higher and higher in my mind. I keep the blinds closed but put away the weapons before my wife returns home. I take baths to ease the psychosis. I drink sedating teas. Each bath I draw, there is no empty silence. I hear birds chirp. That is Them. I hear children's voices. That is Them. I hear cars accelerate at the intersection. That is Them. Every noise affects me, digging into my guts and piercing what is left of my life. There are razors on the side of the bathtub. I look at them, and they move. The voices tell me to kill myself, and I fight for my life.[50]

I (Andrew) also tell my students to storify in their experiences when we discuss dialogue. Consider this sentence: "I was frustrated and had an argument with my sister." Even if we knew the context, the following sentence doesn't read much better: "After sitting at the train station for an hour, I was irritated. When my sister arrived, I started an argument with her." Dialogue is a place where a writer can show us, rather than tell, what is happening.

> "What the hell took you so long?" I ask, sliding into the passenger seat.
>
> "I fell asleep," she says.
>
> "You fell asleep?"
>
> "Yeah."
>
> "I've been waiting for an hour, freezing in the bitter wind. And you were asleep?"
>
> "I'm sorry."
>
> "You're sorry. Great. I tried calling you several times."
>
> "I forgot to charge my phone."
>
> "You're still careless and selfish, just like you were as a kid. Head in the clouds, useless on the ground."

Maybe not the best dialogue, but an example of how to show the situation rather than merely tell readers about it. I can now further refine the dialogue and storify it.[51]

Freeman describes thick description as "the ability to create a rich, contextualized description of an event to increase verisimilitude and transferability of the findings."[52]

That's the kind of description we expect of autoethnography. Yet there is a second aspect to thick description. Noting that it is not just enough to describe, Geertz simultaneously emphasizes *interpretation*. Connecting ethnographic details to extant cultural theory is part of writing thick description. As Geertz wrote, using the sexist and once common generic "he"

> that man is an animal suspended in webs of significance he himself has spun…I take culture to be those webs, and the analysis of it to be therefore not an experimental science in search of law but an interpretative one in search of meaning.[53]

But how do we connect our words and experiences to those webs of significance? We'll discuss that technique, a part of the ethno, in Chapter 4.

AESTHETIC DECISIONS

We receive many manuscripts with an abundance of unexplained textual flourishings: italics, underlining, boldface, various indents and spacings, different colored and sized fonts, images, poems, and drawings. "This text is an aesthetic mess," we often say.

Why did the author indent this sentence more than the next sentence?

Why did the author use a different typeface for this sentence?

Why did the author left align this sentence?

And right align this sentence?

And center align this sentence?

Why did the author use smaller font here?

And larger font here?

Why did the author boldface **these words**, capitalize THESE WORDS, italicize *these words*, and strikethrough ~~these words?~~
Why did the author include an image? And a poem? And a drawing?

Attempting to be cute and creative, some authors manipulate form so much they create difficult to decipher texts; their unexplained manipulations distract and detract from the purpose, content, and focus of the manuscript.

*

Nearly two decades ago, Craig Gingrich-Philbrook described how autoethnographic texts "disappoint, annoy, and outrage [him], particularly when their trumpeted 'literary qualities' seem amateur—at best—and reductive and anti-intellectual at worst."[54] He challenged autoethnographers to be more deliberate with their textual flourishes: do not offer empty pledges regarding craft, or use italics randomly and incessantly, or use poetry without any knowledge of "metapoetic discourse" (e.g., some authors use "line breaks" for "'looks' than to mark breath or cognitive rhythmic patterns").[55]

We agree with Gingrich-Philbrook and wish more autoethnographers would follow his advice. Every aesthetic choice should have a reason for being used and readers need to know these reasons for the text to make good sense. Unfortunately, some authors believe their text has "aesthetic merit"[56]—an important criterion for autoethnographic texts—by merely diverging from one-inch margins and 12-point font. Unless form is itself an argument, form should not distract and detract from content.[57]

As readers, if we encounter an unfamiliar term, we can use a dictionary to decipher its meaning. But if we encounter an unfamiliar form, we do not have a resource to decipher its meaning—we do not have a dictionary to define the meanings of italics, underlining, boldface, indents and spacings, different colored and sized fonts, images, poems, and drawings. We can consult with Strunk and White's *Elements of Style*, the *Publication Manual of the American Psychological Association*, and podcasts like Mignon Fogarty's *Grammar Girl* for insights about some meanings of punctuation, capitalization, italics, and spacing, but if an author manipulates form *without explanation*, they risk creating an indecipherable and confusing text. Unless you are trained as a graphic artist, we suggest keeping textual flourishes to a minimum; embrace the K.I.S.S. acronym: Keep It Simple Silly.[58]

Here's an example—a paragraph describing Tony's visit to his father's house and entering his former bedroom for the first time in more than a decade:

> Time hasn't touched the space: swimming ribbons from 1987 still decorate the wall; with exception of the comforter, the bed is the same; the desk with remnants of grade school—pencils, broken crayons, stickers, scented erasers; a wood box filled with once-loved stuffed animal toys—a sock monkey, two Cabbage Patch kids ("Brendon" and "Veronica"), and Teddy Ruxpin, a 1980s "talking bear" who moves its mouth with the playing of a cassette tape. I approach the large bookcase and see autographed baseballs, an altered *Golf* magazine cover on which my face graces the cover, and five father–son golf trophies.

Now consider this version:

Time

hasn't touched

the

space: **swimming** ribbons

from 1987 **still decorate the wall**; with <u>exception of</u>
<u>the</u> comforter,

the bed is

the same; the desk

with

remnants of **grade** school—pencils,
broken

crayons,

stickers,

scented erasers; a wood box filled with

once-loved stuffed animal toys—*a sock monkey,*

two Cabbage Patch kids

("Brendon" and

"Veronica"),

and Teddy Ruxpin, a 1980s "talking bear" *who moves its mouth*
with **the playing** of

a **cassette tape**.

I approach **the large bookcase** and see

autographed baseballs,

an altered *Golf* magazine cover on which

my

face graces the cover, and five father–son

golf trophies.

The same content with some significant adjustments to form. These adjustments can affect if and how readers access and understand the content. Which version do you prefer? We prefer the first version for accessibility. Form doesn't distract and detract from the content. With the second version, we have many questions: why the erratic spacing, the line breaks, the smaller and larger and different fonts, the boldface, the underlining, and the italics? Do I have a reason for using for these textual flourishes? Maybe I try to portray the experience as a child might, erratic and non-sensical, but I should tell readers that I am doing this, especially if I do so throughout the entire manuscript. Even if I did try to portray the experience as a child, I should also recognize how cumbersome the text might be for readers—not only to read but to understand. How much effort do you put into reading/deciphering/translating a text?

We receive many manuscripts that resemble the second version, and we find it difficult to make sense of the content. The abundant unexplained textual flourishes make the text difficult to read—and so we don't.

We assume that if an author wants to make their work public and have others access and understand their work, then the author must help facilitate such understanding as much as possible. If an author strays from the standards of typical print, we encourage them to explain their aesthetic decisions—tell us about these decisions, offer something akin to an "artist's statement" to help readers understand the form. Plenty of autoethnographers do this.

For example, we receive manuscripts that claim to be "layered accounts" but do not engage or demonstrate an understanding what layered accounts are or how Carol Rambo, the originator of the form, described them:

> The layered account is a narrative form designed to loosely represent to, as well as produce for, the reader, a continuous dialectic of experience, emerging from the multitude of reflexive voices that simultaneously produce and interpret a text.[59]

With layered accounts, Rambo uses three asterisks (* * *) to denote different scenes and perspectives on an issue. In one of her first works about layered accounts, Rambo writes: "Let these three asterisks denote a shift to a different temporal/spatial/attitudinal realm."[60] In another article, Rambo again uses asterisks to "denote a shift to a different temporal/spatial/attitudinal realm."[61] By using a layered account and its affiliated asterisks, Rambo uses a form we couldn't find in a dictionary. As such, she tries to help readers understand her use of form. An author who uses a layered account and its affiliated asterisks should understand how Rambo described using them; a layered account isn't just a random form, and the three asterisks aren't random characters.

Ragan Fox's "DiЯty" opens with this sentence: "Haphazard capitalization and letter direction: a 6-year-old's penmanship. 'Я' is synecdoche for me, broken, DiЯty and unlike other kids."[62] Here, Fox describes why he used the backwards "Я." Fox further portrays recall and memory like the character Carol Anne in *Poltergeist*, a character caught behind the unnerving static of a blank television screen. Fox tells readers he uses these forms to represent "memory's fragmentation" the "partiality" of his perspective. Fox *tells readers* this. He also demonstrates how form itself can be an argument.

In *An Autoethnography of African American Motherhood*, Ferdinand has a chapter called "strikethrough," which merges form and content, e.g., [racist term]. Ferdinand uses strikethrough to impede the legibility of printed racist terms and to demonstrate the frustration and inability to strikethrough these terms in everyday interaction; strikethrough is a stylistic technique and an argument. In the abstract to the chapter, Ferdinand notes,

> The chapter introduces the concept of strikethrough and explores its benefits to eliminating racist terminologies and in correcting events, including racially motivated ones, like the alarming number of Black women and girls killed in police-involved encounters.[63]

Ferdinand *tells us* how and why she uses strikethrough; as readers, we do not have to guess why some words are ~~struck-through~~.

In "Performative Writing as Scholarship," Ron Pelias uses three forms to represent his ideas. These forms also serve as arguments. Pelias uses the abstract to the article similar to an artist's statement and offers some insights about the form of the text and thus how to read it

> The article, divided into three sections, argues for the methodological power of performative writing. Part 1 borrows from the literary tradition by offering an apology on behalf of performative writing as it links the poetic and the performative. Part 2 continues the argument by structuring its claims in the form of a logical proof. Part 3 completes the case by offering a short story of how performative writing has functioned within the academy. The essay enacts the performative writing method as it calls for its use.

In "For Father and Son: An Ethnodrama with No Catharsis," Pelias uses facets of the dramatic form—e.g., "genre," "plot," "characters," "scenes"—to frame the relationship he has with his son. Pelias engages each of these forms to discern what is, what isn't, and what if. For example, for "genre," he describes how the relationship could be understood as mystery, futurist, farce, melodrama, tragedy, comedy, and absurdist drama. Form *and* content serve a purpose, and Pelias *tell readers* this.

In *Staring at the Park*, Jane Speedy uses form and content to portray how life after a stroke might feel. Speedy deliberately writes against certain, clear, and coherent "stroke survivor's narratives"—narratives with tidy endings that, as she demonstrates, can irresponsibly "leave out any disjunctions within the world."[64] Instead, Speedy shows how a stroke, and post-stroke life, can be characterized by chaos, incoherence, and repetition. Speedy also shows the purpose and power of poetry, especially how poetry allowed her to present, represent, and understand the experience of a stroke. She offers brilliant ruminations about the "economy and amplification" of poetry, including how poetry could capture "fragments of conversation as people passed by my hospital bed," as well as offer "shorter, cleaner and sharper excursions into other worlds than either novels, which were too long, or learned medical papers about strokes, which were too boring."[65] Speedy tells us the decisions she makes about form, and as readers, we are not left to wonder why the text is repetitive or poetic.[66]

These authors describe how they use form and show how content and form work together. They provide guidance about how to understand their aesthetic decisions. We do not suggest eliminating textual flourishings from texts, and we do not advocate a rigid threshold regarding sufficient and effective artistry one should include in a text. If an author uses an abundance of aesthetic techniques, these techniques should be used deliberately. These techniques may also have to be explained for readers. If not, authors should recognize that these techniques can distract and detract from readers' ability to understand the work. Isn't a point of making our work public to have readers access and understand our work? If you create a cumbersome text, don't be surprised if readers don't care about it or that it isn't assessed favorably. K.I.S.S.

LANGUAGE MATTERS

In *Narrating the Closet: An Autoethnography of Same-Sex Attraction*, I (Tony) described nuances of disclosing same-sex attraction, an act often referred to as "coming out (of the closet)." I described experiences of sexuality before, during, and after coming out, as well as demonstrated how the coming out process often never ends as every new audience makes for a new time to disclose.

I am proud of this book—I worked on it for nearly a decade. It began when I began to come out (2001). I wrote parts of it during my master's program (2001–2004) and more during my doctoral program (2004–2008) where it became my dissertation. To the day I submitted the final page proofs (2011), I strived to describe accurate and inclusive relationships between sex, gender, and sexuality and demonstrate how these relationships informed the coming out process.

Although I then identified as a gay man and used the lesbian, gay, bisexual, and queer (LGBQ) acronym throughout, I knew these terms were limited. LGBQ didn't fully capture the coming out experiences of everyone who wasn't heterosexual—I knew plenty of men who enjoyed having sex with men but who didn't identify as gay, bi, or queer and who hid such sex from others to avoid consequences (impression management). In striving for accuracy and inclusivity, I thus decided to use "same-sex attraction" as much as possible, including in the title of the book.

I also didn't include "trans," "transgender," or "transexual" throughout much of the book. I focused on disclosures of non-heterosexual sexual orientations, not disclosures of gender identity, and I didn't want to conflate coming out as trans with coming out as LGBQ. (Such a conflation was/is common in research about sexual orientation.) LGBQ and T identities can go together—there are overlapping experiences of sex, gender, and sexuality—but for a project focused on disclosing sexual orientation, I didn't (and still don't) consider trans a sexual orientation; a person who is trans can also be heterosexual, gay, bisexual, queer, etc.

Given the limitations of the LGBQ acronym and the emphasis on sexual orientation, I then had to determine if I was discussing same-*sex* attraction or same-*gender* attraction. I chose same-sex attraction solely because of legal uses of sex, not gender. My driver's license, passport, and birth certificate all used sex, not gender, and in the United States, at that time of writing, same-*sex* marriage was prohibited—two people couldn't get married if their birth certificates or government-issued identifications indicated the same sex, whereas same-gender couples could get married if their legal documents indicated different sexes; different sexes could indicate a heterosexual union and thus allow for a legal consummation.[67]

As a communication scholar, I recognize and respect the consequentiality of language: We uses words to complement or criticize others, lift them up or tear them down, and generate reactions, e.g., yelling "fire" in a crowded place, saying "I love you" on a first date, sharing suicidal ideations, and making promises. When we go public with our words, when we use certain words about and around others, we convey meanings, induce impressions, and indicate our commitments and values. I care a lot about the language I use, and although I had a firm grasp of the terminology regarding sex, gender, and sexuality when I submitted *Narrating the Closet*, I knew such terminology would change and possibly change quickly. Further, given the permanency of print, I knew it would be impossible to revise the text once published.

Knowing what I know now, I can identify several transphobic aspects of the text.

I used the "she/he" binary throughout the book. "Cisgender" and the singular "they" would have helped, but neither were in widespread use—not an excuse or justification, I just didn't know these words. Within the United States, same-sex marriage would soon be legalized (2015)—an act that released some pressure about who could enter a contractual union. Legal documents that once enforced rigid definitions of sex have slowly accommodated variations of gender, and I would now use "same-gender attraction" instead of "same-sex attraction" in the title. I learned about these transphobic aspects by following discourses about sex, gender, and sexuality, and because readers have called attention to the transphobic terminology. I recognize what is accurate and inclusive at one time may not be accurate and inclusive at another time. However, as a writer I hold myself accountable for the words that I use and used, and I try to do better.[68]

I have been asked to revise and update *Narrating the Closet* and I have thought about doing so. But I have encountered another problem related to terminology and how to best conceptualize coming out. In the book, I focused on revealing same-sex attraction and reactions to coming out as LGBQ. Now, and thankfully, the terminology of sex, gender, and sexuality has become increasingly nuanced and fragmented, and I am less certain about how to represent coming out. For instance, what does "lesbian," "gay," or "bisexual" mean for someone who identifies as non-binary or genderqueer—identities that dodge, disavow, or transcend rigid female and male identities? How does coming out happen for someone who identifies as allosexual, ceterosexual, asexual, or monosexual?

Further, I once identified as a "gay man" and I wrote the book from the experience as a gay [cis]man, but what happens to those past experiences if I no longer identify in such a way? I now identify as more queer, pansexual, and demisexual. Does the work, and the experiences I convey in the work, change because of these new identifications? Although there are still problems disclosing LGBQ identities, these identities have also evolved swiftly, and I do not feel I can accurately capture the evolution. I could explore what it means to come out as not-heterosexual, but such framing would position heterosexuality as the norm by which other sexual orientations are understood and assessed.

I might update *Narrating the Closet* one day, but I would need a lot of time and help. I want it to be as accurate and inclusive as possible. I am not striving for perfection, but the terminology, and thus the focus of the project, feels overwhelming. I do not want to publish a work that I know could harm the very people and communities I claim, care for, and represent.

*

We can assess an autoethnographic manuscript without assessing the person's life by assessing the language an author uses to describe their experiences. Many style manuals and reference works include sections about appropriate and inclusive language, and language that has been, or is becoming, problematic. For example, I (Tony) use the latest version of the chapter, "Bias-free Language Guidelines," from the *Publication Manual of the American Psychological Association* (APA) manual in *every* course I teach, not as a definitive rulebook but to encourage students to be mindful about the terms they use. The chapter includes sections about inclusive terminology to use when describing age, ability, sexuality, gender, sex, race, ethnicity, and national origin such as avoiding the generic "he" (e.g., "mankind," "policeman," "man's purpose in life"), being as specific as possible when discussing race, ethnicity, and national origin, using "sexual orientation" instead of "sexual preference" or "homosexuality," and, with dis/ability, when to use person-first or identity-first language. "Just as you have learned to check what you write for spelling, grammar, and wordiness," the APA states, "practice reading your work for preconceptions about groups of people."[69]

With the *Journal of Autoethnography* and our book series, we do our best to make sure that every manuscript uses accurate and inclusive language. This means identifying and refusing disparaging language, challenging seemingly innocent but problematic colloquial expressions, finding alternate terms for terms with troublesome etymologies (e.g., "slave"/"master"), using the inclusive singular "they" when possible, specifying regions (e.g., not allowing "America" to pass as synonymous with the "United States *of* America"), and being mindful of how authors describe their participants and/or persons implicated in their work. (Yes, we still receive manuscripts using the generic "he.") We do not want to silence an author, and authors may have a compelling reason to refuse such changes, we only ask that they are transparent about their reasoning and that their reasoning is grounded in respect, accuracy, and experience rather than tradition, ignorance, or hate.[70]

If an author submitted a manuscript using antiquated and potentially offensive terms without sufficient justification, we would assess the manuscript as inadequate (and, depending on the severity of the offense, might assess the author as bigoted). Note that this assessment isn't about the author's experience, but rather with how the author chooses to represent their experience. If an author still wants to use these terms, then they can do so in their private writings or they can find another publication outlet. Write whatever you'd like in your private journals, but if you pursue publication, we encourage you to take great care in the terms you use and how you describe your experiences. (We will focus on framing in the next chapter.)

Naively neglecting terminology is an easy and unnecessary way to harm your credibility as a writer and a researcher. If you think terminology is neutral and unimportant, then don't be surprised by readers who criticize your work because of troubled terminology. The words one uses or doesn't use can generate impressions about the author, as a person, and how much they care about others and their work. Engage in good impression management and be mindful of the language you use to describe your and others' experiences.

NARRATIVE PROBABILITY AND NARRATIVE FIDELITY

You have crafted the text and have a good working draft. You've created characters and maybe some dialogue. You have used narrative voice, tension, and form strategically, and you have explained these decisions for readers. Now you should assess how well the story hangs together, if its internal components make sense, and whether the story is believable, lifelike, and could resonate with readers' experiences.

Walter Fisher, the narrative theorist who designated us *homo narrans*, described two ways to assess the quality of narratives: "narrative probability," an assessment of whether a story is coherent and could have happened the way the author describes; and "narrative fidelity," an assessment of whether a story resonates—"rings true"—with our lives.[71] Simply put, good narratives demonstrate both; bad narratives do not. Although the author must attend to making sure their story is coherent and lifelike, we can also use these criteria to assess the value and viability of a narrative. As Fisher argues, if a story meets the "tests" of narrative probability and narrative fidelity, readers will more likely accept the story and incorporate it into their lives.[72]

Sometimes we encounter a narrative that feels disjointed and incoherent—it is missing details and the characters are flat; it lacks narrative probability. Sometimes we might assess as work as being too embellished, too grand, and wonder if the experiences ever really happened; it lacks narrative fidelity. Tony has this reaction to much of David Sedaris' life writing—although his stories are coherent, they feel too big and unrealistic. I do not believe some of the tales happened, at least as Sedaris describes them; they feel severely embellished. We have also had this reaction to some autoethnographers—they tell such grand tales about their life we think they're lying. They would have to be 150+ years old to live through all the situations they describe, not their early 30s. To borrow some terminology from Harry Frankfurt, these authors, to us, feel like "fakers," "phonies," and "bullshitters."[73]

As autoethnographers interested in the symbiotic dance of self and culture, we must be mindful of the ways in which our stories—especially our characters, descriptions, dialogue, interpretations, and conclusions—illustrate narrative probability and narrative fidelity. Even though our stories can and do change with time, space, and context, even though memory is fluid and fallible and revision is always possible,[74] we must, to the best of our ability, create probable, trustworthy, and resonant autoethnographic tales.[75]

*

Just as one can't be recognized as a nurse, musician, lawyer, therapist, or potter without sufficient credentials and demonstrated commitment—these callings and careers require immense time, skill, and practice—one cannot be recognized as a serious autoethnographer if they do not recognize techniques for doing good autoethnography. One component of doing good autoethnography means caring about the time, skill, and practice necessary for good autoethnographic writing and representation. If not, one will likely do autoethnography poorly.

We also do not want to suggest that our writing is perfect, that everyone enjoys our work, and that we don't make any errors. Our writing isn't perfect and not everyone likes it. Yet we constantly practice, challenge ourselves, and understand reading and writing as essential for doing good autoethnography. We hope others will do so too. If one expects to acquire autoethnographic skills without any effort, then they should not be surprised if their work isn't published, purchased, understood, shared, and cited; as Wolcott notes, "Myriad completed ethnographies languish on the shelves because no one finds them interesting enough to read."[76]

NOTES

1 Andrew F. Herrmann, "Narratives and Sensemaking in the New Corporate University: The Socialization of First Year Communication Faculty," PhD diss. (University of South Florida, 2008), http://scholarcommons.usf.edu/etd/291.

2 Laurel Richardson, *Fields of Play: Constructing an Academic Life* (New Brunswick, NJ: Rutgers University Press, 1997), 87.

3 Richardson, *Fields of Play*, 87.
4 Pelias, "The Critical Life," 223.
5 Bochner and Ellis, *Evocative Autoethnography*, 77.
6 Bochner and Ellis, *Evocative Autoethnography*, 78.
7 Richardson, *Fields of Play*, 87.
8 France Fledderus, "Insights and Outlooks: Why Highfalutin Language has to Go," *Discourses in Music*, 4, no. 2 (2003), http://library.music.utoronto.ca/discourses-in-music/v4n2io.html; Eric Mykhalovskiy, "Reconsidering Table Talk: Critical Thoughts on the Relationship between Sociology, Autobiography and Self-indulgence," *Qualitative Sociology*, 19 (1996), 131–151, https://doi.org/10.1007/BF02393251;Ruth Behar, "Ethnography in a Time of Blurred Genres," *Anthropology and Humanism* 32, no. 2 (2007), 153, https://doi.org/10.1525/ahu.2007.32.2.145.
9 Goodall, Jr., *Casing a Promised Land*, xxiv.
10 Andrew F. Herrmann and Art Herbig, "An Autoethnography of Working, Failing, and Reworking Public Scholarship," in *Popularizing Scholarly Research: Research Methods and Practices*, ed., Patricia Leavy (New York: Oxford University Press, 2021), 104–131.
11 Anna Banks and Stephen P. Banks, eds., *Fiction and Social Research: By Ice or Fire* (Walnut Creek, CA: Sage, 1998); William G. Tierney, "Get Real: Representing Reality," *Qualitative Studies in Education* 15, no. 4 (2002), 385, https://doi.org/10.1080/09518390210145444; Ellis, *The Ethnographic I*, 330–349; Harry F. Wolcott, *Ethnography: A Way of Seeing*, 2nd ed. (Lanham, MD: AltaMira Press, 2008), 205.
12 See Patricia Leavy, *Re/Invention: Methods of Social Fiction* (New York: Guilford, 2023); Patricia Leavy, *Fiction as Research Practice: Short Stories, Novellas, and Novels* (Walnut Creek, CA: Left Coast Press, 2013).
13 https://www.natcom.org/communication-currents.
14 https://journals.sagepub.com/home/CTX.
15 Bob Batchelor, "Creating Public Intellectuals: Popular Culture's Move from the Niche to the Mainstream in the Twenty-first Century," in *Popular Culture in the Twenty-first Century*, eds., Myc Wiatrowski and Cory Barker (Newcastle upon Tyne: Cambridge Scholars Publishing, 2013), 2–15; Andrew F. Herrmann and Art Herbig, "Not Another Pop Culture Series! Studying the World(s) We Occupy," in *Communication Perspectives on Popular Culture*, eds., Andrew F. Herrmann and Art Herbig (Lanham, MD: Rowman & Littlefield, 2016), iii–xiv.
16 Paragraph revised from Adams and Herrmann, "Good Autoethnography," 3–4.
17 Andrew F. Herrmann, "Broken Promises: Psychological Contract Breach, Organizational Exit, and Occupational Change," in *Organizational Autoethnographies: Power and Identity in Our Working Lives*, ed., Andrew Herrmann (New York: Routledge, 2017), 144–162.
18 Indeed, some folks used the term "autoethnography" before Bochner and Ellis, but none of these early works explained autoethnography in detail or how to do autoethnography; with exception of Hayano, these few authors just referenced parts of their work as autoethnographic and didn't say much about what the term meant in practice. See Karl G. Heider, "What Do People Do? Dani Auto-Ethnography," *Journal of Anthropological Research* 31, no. 1 (1975), 3–17, https://www.jstor.org/stable/3629504; Walter Goldschmidt, "Anthropology and the Coming Crisis: An Autoethnographic Appraisal," *American Anthropologist* 79, no. 2 (1977), 294, https://www.jstor.org/stable/673841; David M. Hayano, "Auto-Ethnography: Paradigms, Problems, and Prospects," *Human Organization* 38, no. 1 (1979), 99, https://www.jstor.org/stable/44125560.

19 Clifford Geertz, *The Interpretation of Cultures* (New York: Basic Books, 1977), 6, our emphasis. As an example of thick description, Geertz uses and expands upon Gilbert Ryle's description of "winking":

> Consider, [Ryle] says, two boys rapidly contracting the eyelids of their right eyes. In one, this is an involuntary twitch; in the other, a conspiratorial signal to a friend. The two movements are, as movements, identical; from an I-am-a-camera, "phenomenalistic" observation of them alone, one could not tell which was twitch and which was wink, or indeed whether both or either was twitch or wink. Yet the difference, however unphotographable, between a twitch and a wink is vast; as anyone unfortunate enough to have had the first taken for the second knows. The winker is communicating, and indeed communicating in a quite precise and special way: (1) deliberately, (2) to someone in particular, (3) to impart a particular message, (4) according to a socially established code, and (5) without cognizance of the rest of the company. As Ryle points out, the winker has done two things, contracted his eyelids and winked, while the twitcher has done only one, contracted his eye lids. Contracting your eyelids on purpose when there exists a public code in which so doing counts as a conspiratorial signal is winking. That's all there is to it: a speck of behavior, a fleck of culture, and voila!—a gesture.
>
> That, however, is just the beginning. Suppose, [Ryle] continues, there is a third boy, who, "to give malicious amusement to his cronies," parodies the first boy's wink, as amateurish, clumsy, obvious, and so on. He, of course, does this in the same way the second boy winked and the first twitched: by contracting his right eyelids. Only this boy is neither winking nor twitching, he is parodying someone else's, as he takes it, laughable, attempt at winking. Here, too, a socially established code exists (he will "wink" laboriously, overobviously, perhaps adding a grimace—the usual artifices of the clown); and so also does a message. Only now it is not conspiracy but ridicule that is in the air. If the others think he is actually winking, his whole project misfires as completely, though with somewhat different results, as if they think he is twitching. One can go further: uncertain of his mimicking abilities, the would-be satirist may practice at home before the mirror, in which case he is not twitching, winking, or parodying, but rehearsing; though so far as what a camera, a radical behaviorist, or a believer in protocol sentences would record he is just rapidly contracting his right eyelids like all the others. Complexities are possible, if not practically without end, at least logically so. The original winker might, for example, actually have been fake-winking, say, to mislead outsiders into imagining there was a conspiracy afoot when there in fact was not, in which case our descriptions of what the parodist is parodying and the rehearser rehearsing of course shift accordingly.

See Gilbert Ryle, "The Thinking of Thoughts: What Is 'Le Penseur' Doing?," in *Collected Essays 1929-1968*, vol. 2, ed., Julian Tanney (London: Hutchinson, 1971), 494–510.

20 Van Maanen, *Tales of the Field*, 66.

21 Van Maanen, *Tales of the Field*, 73.

22 Van Maanen, *Tales of the Field*, 105.

23 Van Maanen, *Tales of the Field*, 106.

24 Van Maanen, *Tales of the Field*, 132.

25 Carolyn writes, "At the risk of oversimplifying, I want the two sides of my brain to be engaged simultaneously or for the text to call forth one side and then the other, back and forth, until

thinking and feeling merge. I want to be immersed in the flow of the story, lost in time and space, not wanting to come to the end (as in a good novel), and afterwards unable to stop thinking about or feeling what I've experienced." Ellis, "Creating Criteria," 273.

26 Jessica Smartt Gullion, *Writing Ethnography*, 2nd ed. (Lieden: Brill, 2022).

27 Harry F. Wolcott, *Ethnography Lessons: A Primer* (Walnut Creek, CA: Left Coast Press, 2010), 110.

28 We recognize that being able to read and write in English is privilege, and those who can't read and write in English will have a difficult time excelling in English-dominated contexts. And with the imperialism of English, that can include many settings. Many journals, especially those assessed as "top journals," are likely published in English. As autoethnographers, we have referred to this as an aspect of "narrative privilege"—of being able to excel in certain contexts based on a designated skill. See Tony E. Adams, "A Review of Narrative Ethics," *Qualitative Inquiry* 14, no. 2 (2008), 175–194, https://journals.sagepub.com/doi/10.1177/1077800407304417. We write and publish in English and English is our primary/only language. We can excel in many contexts without much attention or difficulty. Our question here is how much effort would you make to read a work riddled with errors or written in an unfamiliar language? Will you read a book that takes hours to process a few pages? Possibly. We just want to stress the importance of create accessible texts—the more errors, the more cumbersome a text will be for readers.

29 Holman Jones et al., *Handbook of Autoethnography*; Adams et al., *Handbook of Autoethnography*, 2nd ed.

30 Sparkes, "Autoethnography: Accept, Revise, Reject?"

31 Stephen King, *On Writing: A Memoir of the Craft* (New York: Pocket Books, 2000), 145.

32 Tierney, "Get Real," 390.

33 King, *On Writing*, 156.

34 See Leavy, *Fiction as Research Practice*; Raymond A. Mar, Keith Oatley, Jacob Hirsh, Jennifer Dela Paz, and Jordan B. Peterson, "Bookworms Versus Nerds: Exposure to Fiction versus Non-fiction, Divergent Associations with Social Ability, and the Simulation of Fictional Social Worlds," *Journal of Research in Personality* 40, no. 5 (2006), 694–712, https://doi.org/10.1016/j.jrp.2005.08.002.

35 P. Matthijs Bal and Martijn Veltkamp, "How Does Fiction Reading Influence Empathy? An Experimental Investigation on the Role of Emotional Transportation," *PloS One* 8, no. 1 (2013), e55341, https://journals.plos.org/plosone/article?id=10.1371/journal.pone.0055341.

36 David Dodell-Feder and Diana I. Tamir, "Fiction Reading Has a Small Positive Impact on Social Cognition: A Meta-Analysis," *Journal of Experimental Psychology: General* 147, no. 11 (2018), 1713–1727, https://doi.org/10.1037/xge0000395; Jessica E. Black and Jennifer L. Barnes, "Fiction and Morality: Investigating the Associations between Reading Exposure, Empathy, Morality, and Moral Judgment," *Psychology of Popular Media* 10, no. 2 (2021), 149; Lynne Tirrell, "Storytelling and Moral Agency," *The Journal of Aesthetics and Art Criticism* 48, no. 2 (1990), 115–126, https://doi.org/10.2307/430901.

37 In response to a woman's magazine that deemed poetry a "less 'rigorous' or 'serious' art form" than prose, Audre Lorde describes the inherent biases and privileges built into media use and assessment. Poetry is often devalued, Lorde notes, because it is the most "economical" art form, a medium that "requires the least physical labor, the least material" and a form that can be "done between shifts, in the hospital pantry, on the subway, and on scraps of surplus paper … A room of one's own may be a necessity for writing prose, but so are reams of paper, a typewriter, and plenty of time." Lorde also suggests poetry has functioned as the "major voice of poor, working class, and Colored women," discursively marginalized populations. And this

connection between a medium (poetry) and its users contributes to the medium's devaluation. See Audre Lorde, *Sister Outsider* (Berkeley, CA: The Crossing Press, 1984), 116. Paragraph revised from Adams et al., *Autoethnography*, 15.

38 Andrew F. Herrmann, Tony E. Adams, and Sara B. Dykins Callahan, "Pursuing, Practicing, and Portraying Qualitative Research: An Interview with Norman K. Denzin," *Qualitative Inquiry* (2023), https://doi.org/10.1177/10778004231202939.

39 King, *On Writing*, 156.

40 Goodall, Jr., *Writing Qualitative Inquiry*, 30.

41 Goodall, Jr., *Writing Qualitative Inquiry*, 30.

42 Raven Leilani, *Luster: A Novel* (New York: Farrar, Straus and Giroux, 2020).

43 Stephen King, *The Stand: The Complete and Uncut Edition* (New York: Doubleday, 1990), 315.

44 Herrmann, "Never Mind the Scholar."

45 Bochner, "Autoethnography as a Way of Life."

46 Robin M. Boylorn, "Gray or for Colored Girls Who Are Tired of Chasing Rainbows: Race and Reflexivity," *Cultural Studies ⇔ Critical Methodologies* 11, no. 2 (2011), 182, https://doi.org/10.1177/1532708611401336.

47 Mary Karr, *The Art of Memoir* (New York: Harper Perennial, 2015).

48 Patricia Leavy, "Fiction and the Feminist Academic Novel," *Qualitative Inquiry* 18, no. 6 (2012), 517.

49 This discussion of Boylorn's experience is adapted from Tony E. Adams and Stacy Holman Jones, "The Art of Autoethnography," *Handbook of Arts-Based Research*, ed., Patricia Leavy (New York: The Guilford Press, 2018), 151.

50 Matthew S. Johnston, "Through Madness and Back Again: An Autoethnography of Psychosis," *Journal of Autoethnography* 1, no. 2 (2020), 137–155, https://doi.org/10.1525/joae.2020.1.2.137.

51 Bochner and Ellis offer keen advice for writing dialogue: "Think about dialogue in the movies. It moves the action forward. It's crisp and sounds realistic. Good screenwriters realize that actual conversations between people tend to be humdrum and monotonous when precisely reproduced. So they eliminate the vocal pauses (ums and ahs), repetitions, and incomplete expressions of actual speech." Bochner and Ellis, *Evocative Autoethnography*, 115.

52 Melissa Freeman, "The Hermeneutical Aesthetics of Thick Description," *Qualitative Inquiry* 20, no. 6 (2014), 827.

53 Geertz, *The Interpretation of Cultures*, 5.

54 Gingrich-Philbrook, "Autoethnography's Family Values," 301. Also see Gingrich-Philbrook's response to his earlier article: Gingrich-Philbrook, "Evaluating (Evaluations of) Autoethnography."

55 Gingrich-Philbrook, "Autoethnography's Family Values," 308.

56 Laurel Richardson, "Evaluating Ethnography," *Qualitative Inquiry* 6, no. 2 (2000), 254, https://doi.org/10.1177/107780040000600207.

57 As media scholar Joshua Meyrowitz writes, media producers "generally want audiences to be aware of content elements, but not to be aware of grammar elements." Grammar elements comprise the aesthetics of form, e.g., the texture and thickness of paper for print media, camera angles, frames, and shots for visual media. Joshua Meyrowitz, "Multiple Media Literacies," *Journal of Communication* 48, no. 1 (1998), 100–102, https://doi.org/10.1111/j.1460-2466.1998.tb02740.x.

58 K.I.S.S. becomes more necessary if an author engages additional representational media alongside printed/written text. As mentioned in the Introduction, we are focused primarily on assessing writing. Autoethnographers who engage different representational media—music, video, drawing—wade into additional expectations for assessment: What counts as a good song, or a good video, or a good drawing? Assuming your song, or video, or drawing is good just because you made it can convey ignorance and arrogance.
59 Rambo Ronai, "The Reflexive Self through Narrative"; Rambo Ronai, "Multiple Reflections of Child Sex Abuse."
60 Rambo Ronai, "The Reflexive Self through Narrative," 102.
61 Rambo Ronai, "Multiple Reflections of Child Sex Abuse," 397.
62 Ragan Fox, "DiЯty," *Text and Performance Quarterly* 39, no. 3 (2019), 250, https://doi.org/10.1080/10462937.2019.1643906.
63 Renata Ferdinand, *An Autoethnography of African American Motherhood: Things I Tell My Daughter* (New York: Routledge, 2022), 49–68, https://doi.org/10.4324/9780367822897.
64 Jane Speedy, *Staring at the Park: A Poetic Autoethnography* (Walnut Creek, CA: Routledge, 2015), 27.
65 Speedy, *Staring at the Park*, 13.
66 This paragraph about Speedy's book has been revised from Tony E. Adams, "Review: Jane Speedy (2015). Staring at the Park: A Poetic Autoethnographic Inquiry," *Forum Qualitative Sozialforschung Forum: Qualitative Social Research* 16, no. 3 (2015), https://doi.org/10.17169/fqs-16.3.2416.
67 See Julie A. Greenberg, "When Is a Man a Man, and When Is a Woman a Woman?," *Florida Law Review* 52, no. 4 (2000), 745–768; Julie A. Greenberg, *Intersexuality and the Law* (New York: New York University Press, 2012); Joanne Meyerowitz, *How Sex Changed: A History of Transsexuality in the United States* (Cambridge, MA: Harvard University Press, 2002).
68 In *Revision*, Carolyn Ellis describes new relationships we can have to our past autoethnographic work. How we feel about our work at the time of publication may not reflect how we feel about the work at a later time. And that's ok, even common. We call writers to do their best now and solicit sincere and trusted feedback about their projects. We view our past work as works-in-progress and know we will feel different about a project days, months, and years after it has been published.
69 American Psychological Association, "Bias-Free Language Guidelines," in *Publication Manual of the American Psychological Association* (Washington, DC: American Psychological Association, 2020), 131.
70 Revised from Herrmann and Adams, "Learning to Be Editors," 3.
71 Walter Fisher, "Narration as a Human Communication Paradigm," 8.
72 Adams et al., *Autoethnography*, 99.
73 Harry G. Frankfurt, *On Truth* (New York: Random House, 2010), 3–4.
74 See Mark Freeman, *Hindsight: The Promise and Peril of Looking Back* (New York: Oxford University Press, 2010); Ellis, *Revision*.
75 Paragraph revised from Adams et al., *Autoethnography*, 95.
76 Wolcott, *Ethnography Lessons*, 111.

CHAPTER 3

The "Auto" of Autoethnography

Narrating the Self and Assessing the I

Let's begin with a low-tech activity. Locate a pen and paper, or open a blank note file or Google doc. Record everything you're doing at every moment of the day. Every thought, observation, feeling, and move you make, every email and text you write, every story you read, every thought, observation, feeling, and move you make while writing and reading these emails, texts, and stories. Record the background noises and your physical location, and the media you use and avoid. Also make sure to record relevant names, times, and dates. Then try to record what is happening behind you, around you, and on your street, city, and country. Do your best to record everything, everywhere, and all at once.[1]

Now do this as long as you can, though attention, ability, sleep, aging, and eventual death will complicate how long you can do so. You'll have to stop sometime, and when you stop, you'll miss recording facets of experience that you might later remember as meaningful. You can't always know what is meaningful in the moment and what is not, and you may not realize the significance of an experience for days, months, or years. What did you select to (not) record? What details couldn't you capture quickly? Which thoughts interrupted your focus?

And did you notice the word "meaningful"? That's an important word for autoethnography. Autoethnographers don't just record and report experience. They make sense—meaning—of their experience and try to convey this meaning for others. Yet recording and reporting every single thought, feeling, and act is not only impossible but also, well, boring. Further, the recording probably wouldn't result in a report that would be purchased, read, understood, enjoyed, shared, cited, and engaged by others (audiences).

For example, allow me (Tony) to tell you about a typical morning: I prefer to wake at 9 am. I first determine if my husband is sleeping next to me or if he is in the house or at the gym. I then look at my iPhone to read the texts and emails sent throughout the night. I might then check social media accounts or possibly watch a video on YouTube.

DOI: 10.4324/9781003281771-4

When motivated, I leave the bed and start my coffee, pour a glass of water, use the bathroom, and move to my desktop computer where I will respond to emails and texts until I finish my coffee and water. Depending on my mood, I often play music—if I'm content, I might play dance or 1980s ballads; if I'm anxious or grumpy, chill or classical tunes help. If time permits, I might get a second cup of coffee and/or water, continue with my messages, prepare for a course, or write. Once I finish my coffee and water, I take a shower, eat a snack, and return to my computer for another hour or two. I engage in this process most days. I could continue with this account. Interesting? Novel? Should I post this account on social media? Would you use my description in your classes, cite it in your next project, or share it with friends and colleagues? I sense probably not—the account is, well, boring. And it isn't autoethnography…yet. I need to have a reason, a purpose, for sharing these experiences.

I need to make the account meaningful.

I need to discern the significance of these experiences *and* offer a reason for sharing the experiences. I could return to the account and explore how technology infuses my life, how I feel beholden to it—how attached I am to my iPhone and computer, how much time I spend with texts, emails, and social media, and the number of hours I spend stimulated by screens, words, sounds, and images. I might even interrogate my resources and privileges that allow me to live in these ways, particularly my physical abilities to move, see, hear, and read, as well as my access to time, technology, food, drink, a room of one's own, and reliable shelter.

I might connect the experiences to others and/or existing research (ethno) and make them more interesting (graphy). Maybe I will interview folks about their everyday attachments to technology. Maybe I will explore what scholars (e.g., Marshall McLuhan, Sherry Turkle, Andrew Herrmann) have written about media usage or what scholars (e.g., Peggy McIntosh, Devon Carbado, Keith Berry) have written about social privilege.[2] Maybe I will work to craft my experience in compelling ways—introduce dialogue, experiment with narrative voice, identify a problem or pose a question, and create dilemmas readers will want to solve. Maybe I will use Ron Pelias's article, "The Critical Life," or Carolyn Ellis's tribute article to Pelias, "The Emotional Life," as models for the project[3]; I might even call it "The Digital Life," if I foreground technology, or "The Privileged Life," if I interrogate the resources that allow me to live comfortably.

These explorations might become the seeds for an autoethnographic project, but if I want to share such work with others (e.g., teachers, professors, friends, colleagues, members of my dissertation committee, journal and book editors), I need to do much more work. First, the work needs more focus. I still haven't shared everything about my typical morning—such an attempt would prove futile—and I must determine what information is (not) relevant for the specific project. If I'm writing about our incessant attachments to technology, or the privileges inherent in my everyday life, I need to stay focused on the specified topic. I shouldn't include information that isn't relevant to these topics, e.g., where my parents live, the bullying I experienced in high school, my favorite restaurant.

Notice even in this chapter opening, I start small and create two possible projects. I stay focused on how I might use my experiences for an autoethnographic project, and I hope that you, reader, will notice a way to begin an autoethnographic project and to assess an autoethnographic project. Some projects cover too many topics in a very short space, with authors struggling to include too much unrelated information or failing to explain the meaningfulness of the experiences they share. We may think everyone wants to hear all the details of our lives. But they don't—there isn't enough time to do so, and taking one's time to read about the details of others' lives might impede how we live our lives and how we spend our time doing and relating the tasks that bring us joy. If we stay focused and offer reasons for sharing an experience, then we have a better chance of creating a report that would be read, understood, enjoyed, purchased, shared, cited, and engaged by others.

In this chapter, we focus on assessing the auto of autoethnography by offering insights into the kinds of personal experiences one might use in an autoethnographic project, as well as how to analyze and represent these experiences. Assessing the auto of autoethnography also invokes a meta-aspect of *homo assessory*: with autoethnography, not only do we assess which experiences matter but also, via self-reflexivity, assess how we/others understand and represent these experiences and how we/they portray and convey their meaning and significance; we evaluate our experiences *and* evaluate how we evaluate our experiences.

ASSESSING PERSONAL EXPERIENCE

Generally, ethnographers illustrate and interrogate cultural principles, products, and practices and use thick description to represent and facilitate understanding of these phenomena. Generally, autobiographers (and life writers) story and share certain experiences to offer insights about how these experiences might look and feel, create a record of the past, and espouse lessons for living. Autoethnographers merge these goals of ethnography and autobiography by storying and sharing their experiences to promote understanding of various facets of cultural life.

Thus, for a manuscript to be autoethnographic, the explicit use and engagement with the author's experience is essential. That's the essence of auto, as auto refers to self/oneself. The author must be present in the text, at the very least to offer insights about their positionality and connection to the topics they represent.

As we noted in the introduction, sometimes we've had authors claim a manuscript was autoethnographic solely because it/they used the personal experiences of others. We find this claim unfounded and silly as it would make any study that treats others' experiences as data "autoethnographic." Biographies are not autobiographies, and methods (e.g., surveys, interviews, focus groups, oral histories) used to gather and analyze others' experiences are valuable, but they're not inherently autoethnographic. Sometimes we will receive a 30-page manuscript that only includes 1–2 pages of the author's experience. Although we do not quantify the amount of personal experience one must use in autoethnography, unless the manuscript offers a methodological discussion about autoethnography, the limited sharing of such experience is insufficient for autoethnography.

With autoethnography, we expect the author's experience to be prioritized—used, engaged, reflected on, and analyzed throughout a project. Indeed, others' experiences may be included in a project (ethno), but the author's experiences and reflections should be present throughout a manuscript. And they should use their experiences and reflections to offer interesting insights about social research and/or social life.[4] If the author's self isn't fully present, used, engaged, and analyzed, then one isn't doing good autoethnography.

There are hundreds, even thousands, of books by ethnographers, autobiographers and life writers, and autoethnographers about how to best use and represent—and thus assess—personal experience. For example, in writing about assessing ethnographic research, Laurel Richardson expects authors to offer "adequate self awareness," as well as "embodied" and "credible" accounts of "lived experience."[5]

In *The Ethnographic I*, Carolyn Ellis provides "guidelines for personal writing papers"—guidelines that can serve as assessment criteria. Ellis encourages autoethnographers to provide complex and "detailed descriptions," write "concretely" and "evocatively," and use "dramatic tension and character development."[6] Ellis also offers advice for "editing personal narratives."[7]

With autoethnography, Art Bochner expects a vulnerable and honest "tale of two selves"—a "believable journey" from who the author was to who they perceive to be now, a "life course reimagined or transformed by crisis."[8]

In *Writing the Personal: Getting Your Stories onto the Page*, Sandra Faulkner and Sheila Squillante identify several questions to consider when using and sharing personal experience.[9] Who is your audience? Who might your experience implicate? What structure works best to represent these experiences? And what is the purpose of your project? (This last question resembles the "So what?" question we should ask of any autoethnography.)

Which experiences work best for autoethnography? How much should you share? How might others assess such self-representation? These questions guide our focus. We begin with one kind of text we don't like: the life chronology.

THE DREADED LIFE CHRONOLOGY

We review many manuscripts authors claim to be autoethnography but merely include a myriad of disparate personal experiences; the authors write in a "this happened, and this happened, and this happened" style without much focus or narrative coherence. We refer to these manuscripts as "life chronologies," unfocused and boring representations of personal experience. They are the most common type of manuscript we reject.

With life chronologies, the author doesn't demonstrate the connection between or discern the meaningfulness of their experiences; in form and content, they resemble Tony's opening account of a typical morning and the opening autobiographical accounts we used in the introduction to this book. Sometimes authors describe their everyday thoughts and feelings and actions and reactions without a stated purpose. Sometimes authors focus on few unrelated events. Sometimes authors try to describe a multitude of life experiences, something like

> At five, my grandfather bought me a dog. At seven, I learned how to add, subtract, multiply, and divide. My mother was abusive; her mother was abusive, too. My father enjoyed baseball. In high school, I had a terrible car accident. In college I majored in education. When I graduated, my cousin was diagnosed with cancer. At 30, my best friend joined the military. At 40, I married and moved to a different country. At 50, I divorced, and moved back to my original country. I enjoy peaches, parsley, and potatoes.

These manuscripts struggle with thick description and focus. They also fail to answer the So-what? question for good autoethnography: What is the point, the purpose, of sharing these details? How do they connect? And why should readers care?

If someone wants to use autoethnography to study domestic abuse, then every experience they share should relate to domestic abuse. If the relationships between the experiences aren't evident, the author must explain the relationships for readers. They also shouldn't share unrelated experiences, e.g., their experiences playing volleyball, learning a language, or combating climate change. If an author writes about racist microaggressions, they shouldn't write about their favorite food, and if they write about grieving the loss of a loved one, they shouldn't describe dreams of becoming a professional poker player. If an experience doesn't directly relate to a specific topic, don't include it. Do not write about disparate topics in one project; stay focused and strive for coherence. K.I.S.S.

Notice that we do not assess the actual experiences used in a life chronology—we don't dispute their accuracy or meaningfulness for the author. Instead, we assess which experiences are used and how they are represented. Save meaningful but unrelated experiences for other projects—that's where the author can write about volleyball, language acquisition, climate change, their favorite foods, and playing poker, just not all at once. To do good autoethnography, personal experiences must be selected, shared, and analyzed deliberately and with focus. Only then can authors offer informed insights about the meaningfulness of these experiences, what the experiences suggest about cultural life, and why we should care.[10]

WHICH PERSONAL EXPERIENCES?

We began this chapter by demonstrating the impossibility of being able to record every detail of our lives. Yet for projects that require the use of personal experience, what do we record and report? We value autoethnography because we recognize and appreciate the epistemic potential of personal experience: these experiences can generate invaluable insights about social life, insights often impossible to acquire through other methods. But which experiences make for good autoethnography, and how can we use these experiences?

Given our years of doing, reviewing, and editing autoethnography, we have discerned several interrelated categories of autoethnographic projects. These projects demonstrate the kinds of experiences that work well for autoethnography. Although these are not the only ways to categorize autoethnographic projects, if you do a project that doesn't fit into one of these categories, make sure to have a focus and purpose and that autoethnography is the best method to use. For us, these projects easily and effectively address the So-what question we ask of autoethnography: they have a focus and a purpose and, unlike life chronologies, foreground certain kinds of experiences. When people ask, "why autoethnography?" we respond by describing these kinds of projects. These projects illustrate reasons to use autoethnography.

Demonstrate Insider Knowledge

For decades, ethnographers have debated the benefits and consequences of being insiders and outsiders to the communities they study. The method of participant observation—of taking part in a community but distancing oneself enough to credibly observe it—is a hallmark of ethnographic practice. Being close but not too close to the folks we study, finding ways to establish trust with others, and then exiting the field post-research are often taken-for-granted principles of ethnography. (We will discuss ethnography in Chapter 4.)

For autoethnographers, the relationship between insiders and outsiders is fluid. Given the use of personal experience, autoethnographers embrace and celebrate an "epistemology of insiderness"[11]: they describe situations we couldn't fully know and feel without direct experience, and they generate knowledge that outsiders would not be able to easily know or acquire. Our embodied experiences matter; they can teach us much about cultural life.

For example, Pelias shows how personal experience allows him to "function as an insider, an ethnographer who uses his privileged position to uncover the familiar, to understand what a given experience might say about the human condition."[12] In discussing her use of personal experience and memoir, Ann Cvetkovich noted, "I wanted to capture how depression feels—the everyday sensations that don't immediately connect to any larger diagnosis or explanatory framework."[13] Using autoethnography to explore how he performed "multiple characters" on the popular reality television series *Big Brother*, Ragan Fox explains,

> Other research methods would not provide immediate, ongoing, and in situ access to the *Big Brother* house, nor would CBS likely permit non-affiliated investigators to enter the show's immediate contexts (e.g., soundstage, casting interviews, and sequester house).[14]

And Lisa Tillmann wrote, "I can show you a view [of living with an eating disorder] no physician or therapist can, because, in the midst of an otherwise 'normal' life, I experience how a bulimic *lives* and *feels*."[15] Autoethnographies offer highly personal accounts of private situations (e.g., living with depression) in difficult-to-access places (e.g., a physician's office) and often for extended periods of time (e.g., the run of a show, a lifetime of [not] eating).[16]

We do not suggest such intimate, insider knowledge is better or more complete than an outsider's account—just different. Outsiders can perceive taken-for-granted acts and beliefs or distinguish patterns that community members may not notice. Yet an insider can talk about the everyday feelings and negotiations of an identity or experience, as well as intentions and motivations that might otherwise be unavailable or inaccessible to unfamiliar observers.[17] Insider and outsider perspectives both have value.[18]

Repeated I Unique Experiences

Sometimes autoethnographers identify interesting, and sometimes unnerving, patterns of behavior. Consider microaggressions, the

> everyday verbal, nonverbal, and environmental slights, snubs, or insults, whether intentional or unintentional, which communicate hostile, derogatory, or negative messages to target persons based solely upon their marginalized group membership.[19]

Microaggressions are difficult to observe and record *as they occur*—we don't know when they might occur, and they can inflict pain when they do. Microaggressions are difficult to challenge as well, not only because we can't plan for and are pained by them but also because the aggressor may feel as though they are acting appropriately and with good intentions. To challenge microaggressions, the target/victim must quickly process an unexpected, jarring, and seemingly innocent act, call attention to the act, and inform the aggressor why they hurt.

When I (Tony) teach workshops about research methods, I assess the benefits and limitations of using various methods to study certain topics such as microaggressions. For example, I ask: What kinds of information (data) might we (not) acquire through interviews and surveys about microaggressions? How can we use textual analysis and phenomenology to study microaggressions? What can we learn from our direct experiences with microaggressions?

Once when I asked these questions in a workshop, a monolingual (English) Mexican woman shared a recent experience with microaggressions. A few days prior, she felt ill and went to the hospital. Upon entering, the person at the intake desk began speaking to her in Spanish.

> "I don't speak Spanish," the woman replied.
> When she met the nurse, the nurse began speaking to her in Spanish.
> "I don't speak Spanish," she replied.
> When she met with the doctor, he began speaking to her in Spanish.
> "I don't speak Spanish," she replied.

Within a few hours, an (un)expected pattern of behavior emerged—a pattern that, while familiar to the woman, would have been difficult to observe with advance planning.

Individually, the employees may have been well-intended with their question—they wanted to connect with the patient and provide the best care for her. If this kind of encounter happened one time, or even a few times, it may not be memorable or meaningful. But these kinds of encounters didn't happen just one time. The woman described how such questioning happens most days in many contexts. "I'm tired of people asking if I speak Spanish," she said. "It's exhausting having to correct their erroneous assumptions. And when I do correct them, they become upset and I come across as confrontational." Although the woman didn't necessarily fault each individual, she was unnerved by the accumulation of these experiences and the assumptions many others make about her. These are also experiences and assumptions that neither of us, as White cismen, have ever experienced, and probably won't—living in the United States, we have the privilege of not having to worry about others in everyday settings tangling us in their erroneous assumptions about the language we speak; most folks assume we speak English, and we do, and we do not have to devote time, energy, and attention to correcting their assumption.

By identifying problematic patterns of behavior, autoethnographers can promote understanding of these patterns and work to remedy them.[20] In this example, readers may better understand what microaggressions are and how and when they occur. Readers may also, hopefully, reflect on if/how they may perpetuate such patterns, rethink their assumptions they have about others, and consider how their seemingly innocent thoughts and actions can hurt.

Repeated experiences are good topics for autoethnography. Unique, fleeting, and one-time experiences can work too. In *Interpretive Biography* (first published in 1989 and reissued in 2013 as *Interpretive Autoethnography*), Norman Denzin described how "epiphanies" make for good autoethnographic projects. Denzin describes epiphanies as "significant, turning-point moments,"[21] "often moments of crisis" that "alter the fundamental meaning structures in a person's life."[22] An epiphany "reframes, reparadigms, renarrates the past."[23] We often do not tend to know when or how epiphanies will occur, but when they do, they can demarcate a time before and after an event, e.g., the sudden death of a partner, parent, sibling, or child,[24] a new realization about past sexual abuse,[25] intimate and jarring disclosures or medical diagnoses, revelations of long-held secrets.[26] Epiphanies are also difficult to observe and record as they happen—hence, the need for, and importance of, direct, personal experience. Autoethnographies that interrogate epiphanic moments can make excellent case-study type publications.

Cultural Identities ↔ Social Privileges

Sometimes when I (Tony) teach autoethnography, I use an assignment that asks students to reflect on their (lack of) social privileges.[27] I first ask students to read four chapters: Peggy McIntosh's "White Privilege and Male Privilege," Devon Carbado's "Privilege," and Keith Berry's "Things I Don't Have to Do" and "Things I Must Still Do."[28]

In these chapters, McIntosh, Carbado, and Berry use their experiences to describe how race, gender, and/or sexuality informs mundane social interaction. Each author develops a list of social privileges and subsequent disadvantages that stem from claiming, or being perceived to be, people of particular races, genders, and sexualities. Using the form and content of these readings as models, I ask students to identify five privileges they feel they have related to an identity they claim, and then to identify five disadvantages they feel they encounter because of an identity. This simple assignment often generates profound responses and productive conversations about identities in interaction, as well as how and where we experience privilege and disadvantage. Note that this assignment also asks students to demonstrate insider knowledge and identify repeated patterns of privilege and disadvantage.

As White, middle-class, monolingual cismen living in the United States, we will never know how it feels to live as a Black woman or how women feel when cismen take away their reproductive rights, or the struggle of asexuality, or the dilemmas faced by a desi butch, or what it means to be an Amazigh woman; we need writers like Robin Boylorn, Cassidy Ellis, Adam Key, Naveen Minai, and Mounia Mnouer to describe these experiences and tell these stories.[29] This isn't an appeal to relativism, but rather an observation that when we move through cultural contexts some of us can escape the oppression of "unwanted attention" and some of us can't.[30] We can imagine and speculate how such attention feels, but we also need others to use their experiences to tell and show us.[31] These kinds of projects can make for good autoethnography.

Writing Alongside/Against Research and Representation

Have you encountered a song, television series, or film that matched, or didn't match, your experiences? Have you read an article or a book that promoted progressive, or oppressive, ideas and arguments? Have you ever witnessed an (un)flattering representation of a group? If so, then you may have a start to an autoethnographic project.

Some autoethnographers use their experiences to write alongside certain texts and/or show how their experiences resemble or are informed by these texts.[32] Conversely, some autoethnographers use their experiences to write against certain texts, especially those that do not match their experiences or that, from their perspective, espouse harmful messages.[33] Some autoethnographers may praise, or take issue with, the representation of certain groups, especially groups with which they have direct, insider experience. And some autoethnographers may study topics that are mis-studied or under-studied.

For example, Carol Rambo used autoethnography to write about her experiences as a child living with a "mentally retarded" mother, as "the literature has ignored the lived experience of children of mentally retarded parents."[34] Zibricky used autoethnography to provide insider knowledge about raising a child with autism. Informed by feminism and disability studies, she noted, "Little is known about mothers raising disabled children."[35] Zibricky used her "lived experience" to offer insights about the "culture of motherhood" and to write against harmful "longstanding beliefs of a patriarchal society where mothers are expected to be held responsible for the moral regulation of their children" and to be "expert mothers at all times to their dependent children."[36] Shelly Carter used autoethnography to juxtapose general trends and sterile facts about domestic abuse with her direct experiences of abuse including the particularities of how abuse might look, as well as how difficult it might be to leave an abusive relationship.[37] And across much of her work, Sandra Faulkner writes against faulty assumptions about family and common misconceptions of parenting, specifically motherhood.[38] These writers not only offer insider accounts of historical misrepresentation, mental impairment, autism, abuse, motherhood, and parenting but also use their experiences to write against research that erroneously represents or neglects these experiences.[39]

Ahmet Atay makes a similar call about social media use—an understudied area ripe for autoethnographic work. Atay suggests autoethnographers can approach social media in three distinct ways.[40] First, much like autoethnography IRL (in real life), we can use autoethnography to explore "our cultural identities and experiences" with cyber cultures and online communities.[41] Second, we can use autoethnography to study digital immersion where the "writers identify with their avatars, images, or digital depictions."[42] Third, Atay reminds us that we are already involved in digital life writing through our social media use.[43] The "fragmented, digitalized, and patched-together vignettes" that we "display on digital platforms" are worthy of autoethnographic investigation.[44] For example, Jimmie Manning wrote about how he got catfished while looking for companionship online.[45] Rima Wilkes, through what she terms "dialogic autoethnography," examined her positionalities related to age, gender, and sexuality while attempting to date online.[46] Tasha Dunn and Ben Myers detailed the trials and tribulations of maintaining the secrecy of their relationship online and their attempts to maintain IRL and social media boundaries for their relationship.[47] And Andrew described he and his fellow scholars use their experiences with social media define and refine the concept of "polymedia."[48]

By sharing our experiences to complement or challenge existing research and representation, we learn the benefits and limitations of certain texts, reasons to celebrate or improve them, and possible new projects to pursue.

Illustrate sensemaking Processes

Some researchers use autoethnography to offer insights into sense-making processes, especially about experiences that generate confusion and discomfort. "I tend to write about experiences that knock me for a loop and challenge the construction of meaning I have put together for myself," Carolyn Ellis notes. "I write when my world falls apart or the meaning I have constructed for myself is in danger of doing so."[49] Tami Spry makes a similar observation: "After years of moving through pain with pen and paper," she writes, "asking the nurse for these tools in the morning after losing our son in childbirth was the only thing I could make my body do."[50] These authors embody Richardson's conceptualization of writing-as-inquiry by working—writing—through the confusion and discomfort for themselves and readers (audiences). Doing so can allow us all to imagine ways of navigating similar circumstances.

For example, autoethnographers have described how they make sense of living with an aural or visual impairment;[51] the grief and trauma of losing a pet, child, parent, sibling, or partner;[52] experiences with health care and conditions;[53] navigating the academic job market;[54] and maneuvering everyday life as with marginalized identities.[55] We need writers to tell us about their intimate experiences with these topics to help us better understand issues such as the able-bodied biases of everyday life, living with grief, seeking treatment, finding employment, managing stigma, becoming resilient, and the benefits and barriers of being assessed as certain kinds of people. Such stories have the potential to teach us how to recognize oppressive cultural principles, practices, and products; check our own relationship to these phenomena; and devise more peaceful, passionate, and productive ways of getting along together.[56]

Although writing can be a cathartic process, autoethnographers do not write only for themselves. If they did, why pursue publication? By attempting to make sense of their struggles, these autoethnographers write for others and encourage readers to bear witness to their experiences. They also give readers "equipment for living,"[57] narrative accounts to *live with* (*narrative analysis*) rather than merely *think about* (*narratives-under-analysis*) should they encounter similar circumstances.[58]

Reflections on Research Practice

As qualitative social researchers generally, and autoethnographers specifically, we are the research instrument, the "primary instrument of data collection and interpretation."[59] *We* decide what we want to research. *We* determine the field and sites to study. *We* bring our body to the fields and sites, which can affect how people react to and interact with us. *We* decide which experiences and information to (not) share, and *we* decide the language to use to frame these experiences and information. *We* bring our body, emotions, values, beliefs, attitudes, and knowledge to our projects.

As autoethnographers, we often reflect on and share how we act as the research instrument. We reflect on the nuances of the act and craft of research and representation. We identify ethical conundrums, missteps, and breakthroughs; offer ideas about how to better work with people; and describe how we involve, or not involve, community members in our projects.[60] For example, Carolyn Ellis has written about the relational ethics of (mis)representing intimate others in our work and sharing our work with community members; Kathleen Blee offers reflections on her important but exhausting work with members of the Ku Klux Klan; and García-Iglesias's describes the "erotic arousal" that can occur during an interview.[61] Sharing such information is not a weakness. Instead, to the best of our ability, many autoethnographers believe that by being transparent about the decisions and failures we make in research projects can facilitate trust and credibility with readers. Sharing these experiences can also allow us to discern better practices for doing social research and who we want to be as writers/researchers.

*

These are not the only kinds of projects autoethnographers do, nor do we intend for these categories to be rigid or prescriptive. We imagine there are a multiple of autoethnographic projects that wouldn't fit these categories. Yet these are the kinds of autoethnographic projects we often encounter, do ourselves, and which easily demonstrate the strengths of and reasons for using autoethnography. These projects also help autoethnographers respond to the So-what question and expectation for good autoethnography. So what? Why does sharing your experience matter? Sharing it can inspire new techniques for research. Sharing it can illustrate the problems and possibilities of existing research and representation. Sharing it can illustrate problematic patterns of behavior or make sense of life-changing events. Sharing it can offer lessons about social life that may be difficult to acquire through other methods. We hope these categories will help authors and readers better understand ways they can use autoethnography in their work as well as justify that work to others who might not be familiar with autoethnography.

Thus far, we have discussed the use of personal experiences in a manuscript. Figuring out which self/selves to include and which experiences to share. Next, we discuss ways to assess the *representation* of personal experience—the zone where the auto and the graphy intersect.

ASSESSING THE *REPRESENTATION* OF PERSONAL EXPERIENCE

In the previous chapter, we discussed being mindful of the terminology we use in our manuscripts. Language matters, and how we frame situations can generate specific impressions and reactions. As such, we can assess the language an author uses to represent their experiences and arguments. Doing so allows us to assess the content of an autoethnography without assessing a person's life.

For example, at the *Journal of Autoethnography*, we do not accept manuscripts that are defensive about, or apologize for, using autoethnography. The journal exists to recognize and celebrate autoethnography; authors should not be defensive about the method for the journal. We also caution against manuscripts that characterize autoethnography as a "new" or "emerging method." Autoethnography might be new to a particular topic, situation, or discipline, but to argue generally that autoethnography is a new orientation to research is wholly inaccurate and suggests an author hasn't read much about autoethnography. Formally, folks have been doing autoethnography for decades; informally, folks have been doing autoethnographic projects for centuries, though they may not have been called "autoethnographies."

Further, we can assess autoethnography based on faulty arguments. In many of those early rejected COVID manuscripts we mentioned in Chapter 1, some authors argued COVID would end soon, in a month or two, and claimed to have made full sense of pandemic life. These manuscripts made bold predictions about the future, how life would feel after COVID. Yet authors rarely acknowledged that we were all still living through the twists and turns of the pandemic; they claimed to have COVID figured out, but there was (is) still much to learn.

Art Bochner often reminds us that it is difficult to make sense of an experience, especially a traumatic one, as we live through it—we are too close to the experience. Instead, Bochner suggests, autoethnographers work best with hindsight, after we have distance from the experiences we describe.[62] As Kierkegaard wrote, "It is quite true what Philosophy says: that Life must be understood backwards. But that makes one forget the other saying: that it must be lived—forwards."[63] Even at the time of this writing, more than four years later, we're still living with COVID; a lot of meaning has been made, but there's still a lot of meaning to make.

We can assess the content of an autoethnography in other ways too.

Fault and Framing

One of our first classes in the doctoral program at USF was Art Bochner's Narrative Inquiry (Fall 2004). For the final assignment, we had to write and present a family story. I (Tony) decided to write about the troubled relationship I had with my biological father, someone who, at the time, I hated. I understood my father as cruel, and I didn't want contact with him.

I told Art about my final project. I described how my father hurt me with his words and deeds. I shared a long list of harms he committed against me.

"He quit talking to me when I came out as queer. He abused my mother. He forced me to play golf and baseball." I told Art. "He yelled at me for crying. He criticized me for being weak and passive. He didn't spend time with me."

"Your list is a good start for the project," Art said. "I also have a question: How might *you* have hurt your father with *your* words and deeds?"

Intriguing and insulting question, I thought.

"You blame your father for the pain he inflicted," Art continued. "This blame may be warranted. But you have framed yourself as a passive and innocent participant in the relationship. Sometimes the problems in a relationship are made together, by both people."[64]

I reflected on Art's remark for weeks. I realized that I wasn't merely a passive and innocent participant in the relationship. I had my list of the ways my father hurt me with his words and deeds, but I could also create a list of how I may have hurt him with my words and deeds: I lied to my father—I said his deceased mother knew about my queerness, but she didn't know; I hated him for abusing my mother, but I don't think he knew I knew he abused my mother; I often faked my ability to play golf and baseball, sports that he loved; sometimes I cried to make him angry, or to get his attention; and although he didn't want to spend time with me, I didn't want to spend time with him.

I finished the course successfully, and my final project was accepted for presentation at the first International Congress of Qualitative Inquiry (ICQI) in 2005. After ICQI, I submitted my paper for possible publication in *Qualitative Inquiry*. The paper was accepted,[65] and as I finalized it for publication, I felt slightly guilty about how I represented my father and our relationship, not because I wrote about him without telling him, but because he didn't have any input about what I said about him/us. Given his limited reading and writing abilities and inability to access and use a computer, I also realized that he wouldn't have the skills or chance to be able to reply to my account; I could portray him however I desired, and he could not respond.[66]

Art taught me many lessons about interpersonal and familial relationships. He taught me about the privilege and power we have as writers and, when writing about others, to be cautious about how we fault and frame them in our work. People are complex, and sometimes, though hopefully not too often, we all mess up and perform acts that adversely affect others. We try to act in commendable ways, but sometimes we get stressed, overwhelmed, and angry, and we say and do unfortunate things. "Make your characters complex, not simply all bad or all good" Carolyn Ellis writes.[67] Sheila Squillante notes,

> I tell my students, 'no angels, no devils' in memoir or in life. We are all complicated and deeply flawed and villainizing or canonizing is not only silly; it's reductive and disrespectful of the person or the relationship we're writing about.[68]

Even the "worst" humans are not "monsters," Gerrard and McNaughton argue. "[I]f they are monsters, then so too are we, at least potentially—there's a recurring streak of evil in the human blueprint."[69] We do not suggest fault is never justified, especially in situations of abuse, violence, and terrorism; wrongdoers should be held accountable for their bad acts. But outside of such severe situations, everyday relational life is much more nuanced and complicated.

*

I (Andrew) encountered a similar quandary around the same time. The question I pondered was "*Should* I tell this story?" Let me tell a story.

> I'm sitting in a conference room at the second ICQI (2006). As a presenter, I'm located at the table in the front of the room. Three presenters are scheduled before me. I'm supposed to present "Home is Where the Heart Was: A Family's Stories of Foreclosure" a project I worked on in Carolyn Ellis' Autoethnography class (Spring 2005). However, as I listen to the other presenters, I begin to question my presentation.
>
> Should I present this project? I think it is important. It's evocative and offers some unique insights about families, family silences, homes, and houses. However, the project not only contains my experiences but also those I have gathered from other family members. Their stories implicate other people too. I'm wary. Why am I having an ethical dilemma minutes before I am supposed to present?
>
> My turn arrives and I present a different project altogether. I called it "Reflexivity, Narrative and Ethical Undecidability: On Not Presenting 'Home Is Where the Heart Was.'"[70] I described the ethical dilemma of telling personal narratives that I wasn't sure we should present. After the presentation Bob Krizek said, "Just because you can collect a story, doesn't mean you have to tell it."

You may have a story, but do you have to tell it?[71] You don't want to be told "You talk too damn much and too damn much of it is about you."[72] Is the time right? Is it ethical? What is your threshold for (not) faulting others? Although important questions, we don't have easy, definitive answers. We only encourage you to consider these questions, be mindful of how we represent others, share and justify the ethical decisions we make with readers, and recognize how we might be assessed on if/how we fault and frame others and what we (don't) share.

*

These experiences taught us some critical lessons about doing and assessing autoethnography, especially how and what we (don't) write. Consider a manuscript about an author's 30 consecutive, unsuccessful, and exhausting attempts at dating. The person could share one, or a few, of their bad experiences—and they might blame one, or a few, of the prospects for the failed dates. But what if the author blames all 30 prospects for the failed affairs and offers no reflection on their role in and contribution to the affairs?

Indeed, the 30 prospects may have been terrible, but, as a reader, I would question the author's perspective, credibility, and lack of self-reflection. I would also question the accuracy of the manuscript—30 consecutive bad dates where only the other person was bad seems unrealistic, embellished; the others can't be the sole cause of the failed dates, the author needs to take some responsibility too—people make relational problems together.

We can have bad relationships—we've had plenty of them—but to fault *only* and *all* the others for *relational* problems isn't realistic. And probably unhealthy. The author faulting only and all their exes for failed encounters is an unreliable narrator. It isn't that the author doesn't tell the truth—how others failed them might be *their* truth. "Rather an unreliable narrator is one who tells lies, conceals information, misjudges with respect to the narrative audience."[73] An unreliable narrator has lost their credibility.[74]

We could replace "dating prospects" with "students." At the journal, we occasionally receive articles about an author's work with students. Sometimes these articles describe an author's failures with instruction, note how terrible current students are, and solely fault students for the author's instructional failures. Moderate failures and a few bad students and classes over one's career are expected. But an author who faults students, and only the students, for their failures as an instructor is an unreliable narrator.[75] An interviewee for Andrew's dissertation about faculty narratives of sense-making and socialization described how he could not connect with his students and faulted them for the inability to connect. During the interview, he seemed oblivious to deriding students constantly, calling them "prissy" "stuck-up" "pieces of shit," and "little fucks."[76] The interviewee's report was too one-sided and uncomplicated, and the instructor took no responsibility for his faults and failures.

Again, sometimes fault is justified, but autoethnographies riddled with one-sided charges of fault in which the author doesn't take responsibility for their actions, reactions, and interactions, limitations of their sensemaking, and the ways that they too may have contributed to conflict feel suspect. Such tales can feel too certain, unbelievable, and not credible; they lack narrative probability and narrative fidelity. Being accountable and offering multiple perspectives don't extinguish fault, and others do affect and impede how we live—again, we are *homo assessors* and *homo socius*. But a manuscript that merely faults and complains is not a convincing account; we expect authors to offer complicated analyses of their experiences and ways that they too should/could have lived differently. If they can't offer a complicated tale, then they should explain why they can't do so; as Geertz writes, "To be a convincing 'I-witness,' one must, so it seems, first become a convincing 'I.'"[77]

Truth, Memory, and Working the Past

The film *Big Fish* portrays how stories can build or harm relationships, serve as sense-making devices in a person's life, and constitute a person's—and a family's—identity.[78] The film is an ideal text to illustrate questions about the accuracy of our stories, especially differences between historical truth, the "factual" aspects of an experience, and narrative truth, the meaning and significance of an experience. (Barrington refers to these truths as "factual truths" and "emotional truths."[79]) *Big Fish* also portrays questions about and frustrations with narrative probability and narrative fidelity.

Big Fish opens with Ed Bloom, the father, telling an often-shared story about the origin of his marriage and the birth of Will Bloom, his son. Frustrated with Ed for telling this story at Will's wedding, Will criticizes Ed and refuses contact with him for three years. They resume contact when Will learns that Ed has been diagnosed with terminal cancer.

Although we learn that Ed conveyed facts through his stories, the film pivots upon Will's frustration with not knowing many facts about his father, Will's quick dismissal of his father's stories as fictional, and Will's refusal to discern the truths in Ed's storied experiences.

In one scene, Will asks Ed about the historical truth of Ed's stories. "The thing about icebergs is you only see 10%, the other 90% is below the water where you can't see it," Will says. "That's what it is with you, dad. I'm only seeing this little bit that sticks above the water…I have no idea who you are because you have never told me a single fact."

"I've told you a thousand facts," Ed replies. "That's what I do. I tell stories."

"You tell lies, dad."

Will struggles with the ability to discern the believability (narrative fidelity), meaning and accuracy (historical truth) of Ed's stories, as well as life lessons Ed learned because of his experiences.

Two additional scenes illustrate the tension between historical truth and narrative truth.

In one scene, Sandra, Ed's wife and Will's mother, gasps when she finds a past letter from Ed.

"What is it?" Will asks.

"It was during the war," she replies. "Your father went missing. They thought he was dead."

"That really happened?" Will asks.

"Not everything your father says is a complete fabrication," she replies.

In another scene near the end of the film, Dr. Bennett, the family doctor, notices the relational distance between Will and Ed.

"Did your father ever tell you about the day you were born?" Dr. Bennett asks.

"Yeah," Will responds, "a thousand times. He caught an uncatchable fish."

"Not that one," Dr. Bennett says. "The real story. Did he ever tell you that?"

"No."

"Well, your mother came in about three in the afternoon," Dr. Bennett says.

Her neighbor drove her, on account of your father was on business in Wichita. You were born a week early but there were no complications. It was a perfect delivery. Now, your father was sorry not to be there. But it wasn't the custom for the men to be in the room for deliveries then, so I can't see how it would've been much different had he been there. And that's the real story of how you were born. Not very exciting, is it? And I suppose if I had to choose between the true version and an elaborate one involving a fish and a wedding ring, I might choose the fancy version. But then that's just me.

Will replies, "I kind of liked your version."

By foregrounding the tensions between historical truth and narrative truth, *Big Fish* offers a good example to think about how we shape our experiences into stories. Will initially disregarded the meaning and narrative truth of Ed's stories. However, for Ed, these creative stories conveyed truth, recounted history, and espoused life lessons.[80]

*

As writers who use and represent personal experience, we should recognize various ways to understand "truth" in relation to the work we do and be able to respond to others who inquire about the truthfulness of an account. Norman Denzin distinguishes between "historical truth," truth based on "existing empirical data" (e.g., artifacts, police records); "aesthetic truth," truth based on how well a story aligns with the conventions of writing genres (e.g., autobiography); and "fictional truth," the truth associated with "verisimilitude" and making "believable experiences" for audiences. Denzin views autobiographical works as comprised of all three, "a mixture of fiction and nonfiction" with truths "about life and particular lived experiences."[81]

These versions of truth encapsulate the various truths for autoethnographers: we merge facts and aesthetic techniques to create compelling and believable accounts of social life. "It is not the 'facts' themselves that one tries to redeem through narrative tellings," Bochner says, "but rather an articulation of the significance and meaning of one's experiences."[82]

As we demonstrated in the opening to this chapter, we can't record everything—that is, all historical facts—and, when we write, we make decisions about the experiences we (don't) include, as well as the terms we use to frame and thus interpret these experiences.

We make decisions about the "emphasis, tone, syntax," and "diction" of our writing.[83]

We fictionalize names, situations, and places to protect individuals and organizations; if applicable, Institutional Review Boards (IRBs) may even require us to do so, especially when working with vulnerable populations.

We compress years of experience into a single text, and depending on the focus of our project, we may alter the sequence of these experiences. "I sometimes reorder events to make the narrative work," Barrington writes. "I approximate dialogue that I can't recall word for word. I frequently leave out whatever makes the story too complicated for a stranger to grasp."[84]

If we conduct and transcribe an interview, we often do not include the full transcript in our publications, but mere selections from it based on the focus of a project and the arguments we want to advance.[85] (We also expect readers to trust our ability to make these selections.) When we ask others about their lives, we may assume, erroneously, that they are sharing historical truths; we may conveniently forget that their memories are also fallible, affected by time, space, context, and ability.

We reveal some information and conceal other information, and although some may view the omission of information a "lie,"[86] understanding impression management means recognizing the abundance of information we frequently withhold from audiences. "Behind the story I tell is the one I don't," Dorothy Allison writes. "Behind the story you hear is the one I wish I could make you hear."[87]

*

A decade ago, in a workshop I (Tony) taught about interpersonal communication, when discussing how we engage in impression management by altering and omitting information we share with audiences, a woman offered a brilliant example.

The woman had two dogs (fact/historical truth). She described how, if a stranger asks if she has any pets, she will alter her response depending on her swift assessment of the stranger's character. "If I fear they will negatively assess me," she said,

> I will respond with 'Yes, I have two dogs.' But if I perceive the stranger as friendly and open-minded, I'll say, 'Yes, I have two pit bulls.' Unfortunately, pit bulls have a bad reputation, and while I would like to not care about how others assess me and my dogs because of their breed, I also do not have the time, energy, or desire to debate a stranger about the suitability of my beloved pets.

This is one of my favorite examples of impression management, what truth means, and how we can use language to frame a topic for an audience and how such framing can influence others' responses. Did the woman lie? She had two dogs. She merely used language strategically to frame and adapt her response to the perceived audience. (If the woman didn't have two dogs, that would be a lie, and, if we learned this, could affect how we assess her character and credibility.)

Note also that I didn't record the experience as it happened. I didn't know the woman would share the example, and I didn't know I would use the example here, in this book, more than a decade later. I recreated the example to portray the essence of the experience. Did the woman say those exact words in that exact order? Doubtful. But she said something like them. I didn't make up the situation—it happened in one of my workshops—but I also can't confirm the word-for-word accuracy of her remarks (I don't remember her name). But that's not the point—I use the example to convey the kinds of decisions one might undertake when using language and sharing information about one's life. Solely using historical truth to assess the acceptability of an account isn't the only way to assess a narrative. Granted, we shouldn't lie or fabricate information without telling our audience we are doing so, but that's not what the woman did, and that's not what I did by recreating the account.

Unless an autoethnographer classifies a work as "fiction," one shouldn't fabricate their experiences; the experiences should still have roots in historical truth. "One of the rules I use for writing interpretive ethnography," Bud Goodall notes, "is that in the interests of telling a good story it is permissible to omit details that have no bearing on the tale, but it is *not* permissible to make things up."[88] Barrington writes,

> when you name what you write memoir or fiction, you enter into a contract with the reader. You say "this really happened," or you say "this is imaginary." And if you are going to honor that contract, your raw material as a memoirist can only be what you have actually experienced.[89]

Pelias offers a similar argument: "There are certain kinds of contractual obligations you evoke with certain types of genres," he says. "So if you evoke memoir, part of what you're saying is, 'I'm going to tell the truth as I understand it.'"[90]

With autoethnography, we should report, from our perspective, the essence and meaningfulness of what we believe happened; if not, we must tell readers we will fabricate information, or tell readers that we aren't sure about the accuracy of our recollection. We haven't made up any of the experiences we have shared so far; if we did, we should have told you. Yet we also don't claim the experiences are historically accurate. What we believe to be truthful, and what really happened, may be tangled with the nuances of recollection.

*

In my (Tony's) first book, *Narrating the Closet*, I describe a memory about my childhood of being spanked by my father after he found me watching a television program portraying naked men. I was probably seven years old, and I framed the situation an early lesson about the risks of revealing same-sex attraction. I have remembered this vivid and scarring moment for years. When my mother read the book, she told me that no one had ever spanked me. No one. Ever. She claimed she would have never allowed my father to hurt me. I told her I remember my father spanked me multiple times. She disagreed and said that she would not have allowed him to do so. My mother, who I only reference at the beginning of the story—claimed that my experience did not happen and, as my parent, she felt implicated by my account for not protecting me.

I still believe the spanking happened in the way I described. I also recognize my mother does not. But just because she didn't think the spanking happened doesn't make my memory disappear. I still recall being spanked, often, with a leather belt, in the bathroom. I was an only child, and there were few others who could have spanked me—besides my father, mother, grandpa, and grandma, I didn't have regular contact with others outside of school. Maybe my father didn't spank me, but I think (know) someone did, and maybe my mom never knew; I may have been scared to tell her, especially if doing so would have resulted in more beatings. So what? I share this situation here to be transparent with you, reader, and in so doing, add nuance, and hopefully credibility, to my (uncertain) account. Something happened, and I think I know what happened, but maybe I don't. I'm doing the best I can to relay a memory that still feels real and accurate.[91] Even if I could live life backwards and return to the event, I would likely have a different interpretation of it and tell a different story. I was a young and naïve child.

Memories can rearrange events in various and sundry ways. We forget details and recollection can feel fuzzy.[92] In an interview we conducted with Norman Denzin in 2006, he described trying to represent a memory of the past in a present project. "I'm trying to write this scene I remember living from 1958 or 1959," he said.

> It's a dance scene set in my family's dining room. It's a scene from a party my parents had. I hear Pete Fountain playing the clarinet. I see people dressed in 1950s outfits, women with Mimi Eisenhower bangs, and men wearing dark pleated trousers. I'm trying to write a scene that embodies this moment I remember…I was 17. We write in this type of space. We all do it.[93]

Notice that Denzin isn't solely concerned about the historical facts of the experience, but he also doesn't intend to make up information. We narrate past events as we remember them, from the perspective of the present. As we recall and retell, we adopt, edit, and emphasize different aspects of an experience—and we may never fully realize when and how we do so.[94]

Andrew has written three autoethnographies about his relationship with his father.[95] All three are very different. In some places his feelings and memories contradict each other. Did he purposefully lie in the first one, or the second one, or the third one? No. So why the differences? New knowledge, changed attitudes, different theoretical frameworks, the passage of time, and his father's actual death all contributed to the changes. These types of changes make sense because the auto (one's feelings, thoughts, and experiences) is embedded in and combined with the ethno (others' acts and reactions). Just because his positionality changed does not solely make Andrew an unreliable narrator, especially if he is transparent about these changes.

*

The (in)accuracy of memory isn't just an issue for autoethnographers. Any research project—oral history, interviews, focus groups, surveys—designed to ask people about past events must recognize that the information gleaned from such asking would be affected by these folks' perspectives and interpretations at the time of retelling. Just as we can't record every feeling and reaction to every waking moment, others can't either; we rely on memory and retrospection, and the information we share at one time may change at a later time. Incessantly questioning the historical accuracy of a person's memory during the data collection process—that is, telling these others that we first need others to validate their reports of their experiences—would be cruel and condescending. The data collection process would probably end abruptly. Instead, as qualitative social researchers generally, and autoethnographers specifically, we should recognize that, while we care about facts, our goal isn't necessarily to *validate* the facts but rather to convey the essence of meaningful experiences. That's our purpose, and that's how we should be assessed: did we astutely, accurately, and compellingly convey these experiences to the best of our ability?

We can't record and report every thought and thing that happens across life, but we can try to convey formative and significant thoughts and events. If we are going to fictionalize a scene or situation, character or place, tell the reader. But don't make up personal experiences without saying so—as autoethnographers, doing so would be akin to making up data. Identify your questions and struggles and describe the artistic licenses you took with your text. Strive to be as honest as possible while simultaneously recognize the impossibility of full honesty; as Heidegger reminds us, every revealing is a concealing.[96]

ASSESSING THE PERSON

Thus far, we have described various ways to assess autoethnography without assessing the person's life. We've focused on how we can use and represent personal experience in our projects. Most of the time, we believe assessing autoethnography can be accomplished without assessing how a person lived and we can critique autoethnography without necessarily critiquing how the author lived.[97] Yet sometimes, what a person shares about their life can affect assessments of this person's character and credibility. Sometimes such an assessment is appropriate, and sometimes not—it depends on who you ask.

Consider my (Tony) assessment of Shamla McLaurin's five-page article, "Homophobia: An Autoethnographic Story," an article which appeared in a 2003 issue of *The Qualitative Report*, a journal I read frequently and greatly respect.[98] I think about this article often as it pushes me to consider the limits of, and need for, assessing autoethnography. I respect the article for its honesty but, simultaneously, it sickens me; I want to assess this article because to not do so makes me feel like a bystander, complicit in advocating harmful research, and perpetuating troubling autoethnographic practices.

In the article, McLaurin details her "biases and prejudices" against homosexuality, what she calls her "homophobia." She identifies as a "recovering homophobe" and tries to work through the racial, religious, and rural discourse she experienced as a child, particularly discourse that framed homosexuality as an undesirable and unacceptable trait.[99] She describes learning that homosexuality was similar to "crack addiction or a demon possession" and feared associating with gays and lesbians "as if they possessed some sort of contagious disease."[100] She describes befriending Jen, a lesbian, a relationship that encouraged her to question what she learned about the "unusual way of life."[101]

However, because of the relationship, others assumed McLaurin was also a lesbian, which made her feel like a "freak."[102] McLaurin then describes speaking out against homosexuality at "every opportunity."[103] The article concludes with McLaurin claiming more acceptance of homosexuality but still considering it "wrong"[104]; meeting Cindy, another lesbian, and trying to further remedy her homophobia; and how she may "never be able to understand homosexuality" and may thus be a "recovering homophobe" for life. McLaurin even worries that someone might read the article and "mistake [her] for a closet homosexual."[105]

It stings when I read these statements in an academic article. It stings when I finish the article and do not sense much change in McLaurin's homophobia; to me, she has not demonstrated personal growth or provided much catharsis. I try not to expect a happy ending,[106] and I do not expect homophobia to be easily remedied, but I do expect McLaurin to discuss how she has changed; I want that convincing tale-of-two-selves Bochner suggests should be present in good autoethnography.[107] Instead, I worry that McLaurin legitimates homophobia by suggesting that it exists and is difficult, even impossible, to remedy. I leave the essay not sensing that she has much care for anyone who identifies as lesbian, gay, bisexual, or queer (LGBQ).

I also wonder if what McLaurin writes about homosexuality would ever be written and published about other identities. I am not sure it would be acceptable to say one race is not "desirable or acceptable," or calling a religion an "unusual way of life" or an "alternative lifestyle," referring to a disability as a "contagious disease," or suggesting that when a person reaches a certain age, they will become a "freak." I wouldn't let a misogynistic text, a text that justifies xenophobic beliefs, or a text that espouses ableist values, proceed unquestioned. I do not want to rank or compare slights or harms, only offer a sense of why I expect more nuance, even resolution, from McLaurin/the text. I would have a different reaction if McLaurin published her views on a personal website or an opinion/editorial forum; I expect more rigorous insight and analysis from a peer-reviewed article.

Notice how I assess McLaurin's character and credibility based on how she represents her experiences. I do not want to meet her; her words scare me. I know too many people like her, and I do not need to meet another person who I must convince that I, as a queer man, am a worthy person. Further, based on the biographical information included in the article, I assume McLaurin is working in marriage and family therapy, possibly even as a social worker or a therapist. However, after reading this article, I would never seek her out as a therapist, nor would I recommend her to LGBQ persons. Her representation of experience directly affects how I understand her as a person.

Yet I can complicate my assessment of the text. I applaud McLaurin for describing her homophobia, and I do find some hope the article. She writes to explore, and encourage others to explore, "their own biases and prejudices."[108] She offers a brave, vulnerable, and insider account of homophobia; shows how "prejudice can influence thought and behavior";[109] and claims her "close-mindedness."[110] Further, McLaurin published the article in 2003; maybe her views have since changed.

I also think about the times when I too have been homophobic, and I hope that others would forgive my mistakes. Like McLaurin, I once thought gays and lesbians were disgusting; I have called others "faggots" and "queers"; and even when I began identifying as queer, I still would assess others as being "too queer." While "closeted," I would distance myself from, and even deny, my intimate relationships with men. Maybe my strong reaction is what makes the article good, and I suppose I see value in McLaurin's essay; I can't easily assess her without simultaneously assessing myself. But unlike McLaurin, I feel (hope) I have become a better, more compassionate person, learned the errors of my ways. And I would never publish an article describing any hate I still have toward different others.

I acknowledge McLaurin's honesty and feel she should be able to share her story no matter how controversial or offensive it might be, provided she recognizes the risks of doing so. I wonder if, by assessing this article here, in this book, I use my privilege as an author to discount her story and experience. With my research, I try to identify and challenge instances of oppression and I value social justice. McLaurin may not share such a perspective.[111]

Yet McLaurin made her experience public, and I am only one reader of this work. It is an open-access text with her name associated with it. Those are her views, and in knowing her views, I know how to protect myself and queer others—I warn them about her work and her possible work as a therapist. Her credibility is tarnished, and although I cite the article here and thus give her/it attention, I do so to illustrate the nuances of assessing personal experience.

If we received this manuscript at the *Journal of Autoethnography*, we would desk reject it unless McLaurin was willing to add more nuance and use less hateful language. We already reject manuscripts that espouse racist, transphobic, sexist, ageist, ableist, xenophobic, and homophobic assumptions and arguments, as well as texts that advocate harmful arguments and practices. We do not want to read these texts; we do not agree with these texts; and we do not want to spend our limited time supporting hate and cruelty.

*

The autoethnographic mirror can be unflattering. We might see something beautiful. We might see something ugly. This might be the most difficult part of the auto: Recognizing our shortcomings, biases, and fears; wondering if and understanding a reason to share them; and doing our best to acknowledge our frailties.[112] Although the use of personal experience is necessary for autoethnography, the mere use of personal experience does not make a manuscript autoethnographic. What comprises the auto? Focused and knotty tales from and of a complicated, vulnerable, resilient, passionate, and reflexive self. *You* bind the components of auto-ethno-graphy. *Your* body, mind, emotions, thoughts, insecurities, intuitions, identities, beliefs, and values make you a one-of-a-kind research tool. Show and tell readers why we need to experience your life through your senses and from your perspective. Show and tell us why the topics you consider to be meaningful are worthy of our time and attention.

NOTES

1 A reference to the film *Everything Everywhere All at Once*.
2 Marshall McLuhan, *Understanding Media: The Extensions of Man* (Cambridge: MIT Press, 1994); Sherry Turkle, *Alone Together: Why We Expect More from Technology and Less from Each Other* (New York: Basic Books, 2011); Herrmann, "Communicating, Sensemaking, and (Dis)Organizing"; Peggy McIntosh, "White Privilege and Male Privilege: A Personal Account of Coming to See Correspondences through Work in Women's Studies," in *Understanding Diversity: Readings, Cases, and Exercises*, eds., Carol P. Harvey and June Allard (New York: HarperCollins, 1995), 130–139; Devon W. Carbado, "Privilege," in *Black Queer Studies: A Critical Anthology*, eds., E. Patrick Johnson and Mae G. Henderson (Durham, NC: Duke University Press), 190–212; Keith Berry, "Things I Don't Have to Do," in *Living Sexuality: Storying LGBTQ Relationships, Identities, and Desires*, Keith Berry, Cathy M. Gillotti, and Tony E. Adams (Rotterdam: Brill | Sense, 2020), 43–50; Keith Berry, "Things I Must Still Do," in *Living Sexuality: Storying LGBTQ Relationships, Identities, and Desires*, Keith Berry, Cathy M. Gillotti, and Tony E. Adams (Rotterdam: Brill | Sense, 2020), 143–153.
3 Pelias, "The Critical Life"; Carolyn Ellis, "The Emotional Life: Honoring Ronald J. Pelias," *Studies in Symbolic Interaction* 29 (2006), 9–15, https://doi.org/10.1016/S0163-2396(06)29002-1.
4 We revised this paragraph from Adams and Herrmann, "Good Autoethnography," 2.
5 Richardson, "Evaluating Ethnography," 254.
6 Ellis, *The Ethnographic I*, 365–367.
7 Ellis, *The Ethnographic I*, 369–370.
8 Bochner, "Criteria against Ourselves," 270–271.
9 Sandra L. Faulkner and Sheila Squillante, *Writing the Personal: Getting Your Stories onto the Page* (Rotterdam: Sense, 2016).
10 See Herrmann and Adams, "Autoethnography and the 'So What?' Question."
11 Shulamit Reinharz, *Feminist Methods in Social Research* (Oxford: Oxford University Press, 1992), 260.
12 Ronald J. Pelias, *Performance: An Alphabet of Performative Writing* (Walnut Creek, CA: Left Coast Press, 2014), 152.
13 Ann Cvetkovich, *Depression: A Public Feeling* (Durham, NC: Duke University Press, 2012), 79.
14 Ragan Fox, "You Are Not Allowed to Talk about Production: Narratization On (and Off) the Set of CBS's *Big Brother*," *Critical Studies in Media Communication* 30, no. 3 (2013), 194. See also Stephanie Patrick, "Lights, Camera, Silence: How Casting Processes Foster Compliance in Film and Television Performers," *The Popular Culture Studies Journal* 3, no. 2 (2015), 223–244; Amber Johnson, "Confessions of a Video Vixen: My Autocritography of Sexuality, Desire, and Memory," *Text and Performance Quarterly* 34, no. 2 (2014), 182–200, https://doi.org/10.1080/10462937.2013.879991.
15 Lisa M. Tillmann-Healy, "A Secret Life in a Culture of Thinness: Reflections on Body, Food, and Bulimia," in *Composing Ethnography: Alternative Forms of Qualitative Writing*, eds., C. Ellis and A. P. Bochner (Walnut Creek, CA: AltaMira Press, 1996), 80. See also Lisa M. Tillmann, "Revisiting 'Body and Bulimia Revisited,'" in *Handbook of Autoethnography*, 2nd ed., eds., Tony E. Adams, Stacy Holman Jones, and Carolyn Ellis (New York: Routledge, 2022), 431–442.
16 We revised this paragraph from Tony E. Adams and Jimmie Manning, "Autoethnography and Family Research," *Journal of Family Theory and Review* 7 (2015), 357, https://doi.org/10.1111/jftr.12116.

17 Paragraph revised from Carolyn Ellis and Tony E. Adams, "Practicing Autoethnography and Living the Autoethnographic Life," in *The Oxford Handbook of Qualitative Research*, 2nd ed., ed., Patricia Leavy (New York: Oxford University Press, 2020), 371–372.

18 See Shelly Carter, "How Much Subjectivity Is Needed to Understand Our Lives Objectively?," *Qualitative Health Research* 12, no. 9 (2002), 1184–1201, https://doi.org/10.1177/1049732302238244.

19 Derald Wing Sue, "Microaggressions: More Than Just Race," *Psychology Today*, November 17, 2010, https://www.psychologytoday.com/us/blog/microaggressions-in-everyday-life/201011/microaggressions-more-just-race. Also see Derald Wing Sue and Lisa Spanierman, *Microaggressions in Everyday Life*, 2nd ed. (Hoboken, NJ: John Wiley & Sons, Inc., 2020).

20 Many of the chapters in Robin Boylorn and Mark Orbe's *Critical Autoethnography* and Amber Johnson and Lore/tta LeMaster's *Gender Futurity, Intersectional Autoethnography* use autoethnography to study microaggressions. Robin M. Boylorn and Mark P. Orbe, *Critical Autoethnography: Intersecting Cultural Identities in Everyday Life* (New York: Routledge, 2021); Amber Johnson and Lore/tta LeMaster's *Gender Futurity, Intersectional Autoethnography: Embodied Theorizing from the Margins* (New York: Routledge, 2020). See also Burhanettin Keskin, "When 'Even' Is Uneven: 'Inclusion' as Exclusion," *Journal of Autoethnography* 2, no. 4 (2021), 396–404, https://doi.org/10.1525/joae.2021.2.4.396; Ashlee A. Lambert, "'What Are You?' An Autocritography of Language, Stereotypes, and Microaggressions," *Journal of Autoethnography* 2, no. 1 (2021), 13–25, https://doi.org/10.1525/joae.2021.2.1.13; Robin M. Boylorn, "Gray or for Colored Girls Who Are Tired of Chasing Rainbows"; Joelle Cruz, James McDonald, Kirsten Broadfoot, Andy Kai-chun Chuang, and Shiv Ganesh, "'Aliens' in the United States: A Collaborative Autoethnography of Foreign-Born Faculty," *Journal of Management Inquiry* 29, no. 3 (2020), 272–285, https://doi.org/10.1177/1056492618796561; Diane Sabenacio Nititham, "Positionalities of Precarity: An Autoethnography of 'Making It' in the Neoliberal Academy," *Journal of Autoethnography* 3, no. 1 (2022), 38–56, https://doi.org/10.1525/joae.2022.3.1.38. Elizabeth S. Parks, "The Hybrid I/Eye: A Critical Autoethnography of Intersecting Race and Disability Identities," *Journal of Autoethnography* 2, no. 1 (2021), 26–38, https://doi.org/10.1525/joae.2021.2.1.26; Jacob Woods, "A Gay Man in A Hypermasculine Kitchen: An Autoethnographic Account," *Masculinities: A Journal of Identity and Culture* 11 (2019), 98–120, https://dergipark.org.tr/en/pub/mjic/issue/56064/770510.

21 Denzin, *Interpretive Biography*, 22.

22 Denzin, *Interpretive Biography*, 70. See also Matthew G. McDonald, "Epiphanies: An Existential Inquiry," *Existential Analysis* 18, no. 1 (2007), 17–30; Aisha Durham, "Textual Experience: A Relational Reading of Culture," in *Handbook of Autoethnography*, 2nd ed., eds., Tony E. Adams, Stacy Holman Jones, and Carolyn Ellis (New York: Routledge, 2022), 321–328.

23 Herrmann, "Ghosts, Vampires, Zombies, and Us," 334.

24 For example, see Shahd Alshammari, "Narrative Reflections on Losing a Companion Animal: In Memory of Flake," *Journal of Autoethnography* 1, no. 4 (2020), 378–387, https://doi.org/10.1525/joae.2020.1.4.378; Carolyn Ellis, "'There Are Survivors': Telling a Story of Sudden Death," *The Sociological Quarterly* 34, no. 4 (1993), 711–730; Carolyn Ellis, *Final Negotiations: A Story of Love, Loss, and Chronic Illness, Revised and Expanded Edition* (Philadelphia, PA: Temple University Press, 2018); David T. Kottenstette, "Portrait at an Exhibition: An Unlikely Affair with Grief," *Journal of Autoethnography* 1, no. 1 (2020), 29–42, https://doi.org/10.1525/joae.2020.1.1.29; Reinekke Lengelle, *Writing the Self in Bereavement: A Story of Love, Spousal Loss, and Resilience* (New York: Routledge, 2021); Blake Paxton, *At Home with Grief: Continued Bonds with the Deceased* (New York: Routledge, 2018); Laurel

Richardson, *A Story of a Marriage through Dementia and Beyond: Love in a Whirlwind* (New York: Routledge, 2022); Elizabeth Stephens, "Homicide by Police: Coping with Traumatic Death," *Journal of Autoethnography* 1, no. 2 (2020), 111–121, https://doi.org/10.1525/joae.2020.1.2.111; Marcus B. Weaver-Hightower, "Waltzing Matilda: An Autoethnography of a Father's Stillbirth," *Journal of Contemporary Ethnography* 41, no. 4 (2012), 462–491, https://doi.org/10.1177/0891241611429302; Marcus B. Weaver-Hightower, "Analyzing Self and Other in Autoethnography: Telling Secrets about One's Stillborn Child," in *How Qualitative Data Analysis Happens*, eds., Áine Humble and Elise Radina (New York: Routledge, 2019), 3–17. Routledge, 2018.

25 Karen D. Barley, "Life Is Like a Box of Derwents-An Autoethnography Colouring in the Life of Child Sexual Abuse," *The Qualitative Report* 25, no. 2 (2020), 504–524, https://doi.org/10.46743/2160-3715/2020.4155.

26 Goodall, *A Need to Know*.

27 For great discussions of the ways identities can influence social interaction, see Brenda Allen, *Difference Matters*, 3rd ed. (Long Grove, IL: Waveland Press, 2023). See also Danielle M. Stern, "Communication Is…Privilege," in *Communication Is…Perspectives on Theory*, eds., Adam W. Tyma and Autumn P. Edwards (San Diego, CA: Cognella, 2020), 191–202.

28 McIntosh, "White Privilege and Male Privilege"; Carbado, "Privilege"; Berry, "Things I Don't Have to Do"; and Berry, "Things I Must Still Do."

29 Boylorn, "'Keep Remembering'"; Cassidy D. Ellis, "Introduction: Bodies on the Line—Living Reproductive (In)Justice," *Journal of Autoethnography* 4, no. 4 (2023), 538–544, https://doi.org/10.1525/joae.2023.4.4.538. Adam Key, "The Silent A: A Critical Soundtrack of Asexuality," *Journal of Autoethnography* 2, no. 4 (2021), 446–465, https://doi.org/10.1525/joae.2021.2.4.446. Naveen Minai, "Desi Butch (Where the 'Twain Shall Meet): Queer Autoethnography," *Journal of Autoethnography* 3, no. 2 (2022), 160–168, https://doi.org/10.1525/joae.2022.3.2.160. Mounia Mnouer, "A Woman's Journey of Decolonization and Indigenous Amazigh Identity," *Journal of Autoethnography* 4, no. 3 (2023), 348–358, https://doi.org/10.1525/joae.2023.4.3.348.

30 David A. Gerber, "The 'Careers' of People Exhibited in Freak Shows: The Problem of Volition and Valorization," in *Freakery: Cultural Spectacles of the Extraordinary*, ed., Rosemarie Garland Thomson (New York: New York University Press, 1996), 44.

31 "For members of marginalized groups, speaking personally and truthfully about our lives plays a small part in erasing years of invisibility and interpretation by others." Judith Barrington, *Writing the Memoir: From Truth to Art* (Portland, OR: The Eighth Mountain Press), 14. Okely and Callaway's *Anthropology and Autobiography* explores how identities of nationality, age, gender, and personal history influence researchers in the field and as writers. Judith Okely and Helen Callaway, eds., *Anthropology & Autobiography* (New York: Routledge, 1992).

32 See Bernadette Marie Calafell, "Captain Sisko and Me: Reflections of a Fatherless Daughter," *Journal of Autoethnography* 5, no. 2 (2024): 181–195, doi: https://doi.org/10.1525/joae.2024.5.2.181. M. Cuellar, "The Makings of a Boyfriend: Doing Sexuality through Parasocial Relationships," *The Popular Culture Studies Journal* 3, no. 2 (2015), 270–298; Durham, "Textual Experience"; Renata Ferdinand, "Skin Tone and Popular Culture: My Story as a Dark Skinned Black Woman," *The Popular Culture Studies Journal* 3, no. 2 (2015), 324–348; Janice D. Hamlet, "Still Standing, Still Here: Lessons Learned from Mediated Mentors in my Academic Journey," *The Popular Culture Studies Journal* 3, no. 2 (2015), 299–323.

33 See Tasha R. Dunn, *Talking White Trash: Mediated Representations and Lived Experiences of White Working-Class People* (New York: Routledge, 2019); Moana Luri de Almeida, "The

Evil Woodcutter and the Amazon Jungle: What Comics Have Taught Me about the Environment," *The Popular Culture Studies Journal* 3, no. 2 (2015), 386–414.

34 Carol Rambo Ronai, "My Mother Is Mentally Retarded," in *Composing Ethnography: Alternative Forms of Qualitative Writing*, eds., Carolyn Ellis and Arthur P. Bochner (Walnut Creek, CA: AltaMira, 1996), 110; See also "Remixing/Reliving/Revisioning 'My Mother Is Mentally Retarded,'" in *Handbook of Autoethnography*, 2nd ed., eds., Tony E. Adams, Stacy Holman Jones, and Carolyn Ellis (New York: Routledge, 2022), 401–410.

35 C. Dawn Zibricky, "New Knowledge about Motherhood: An Autoethnography on Raising a Disabled Child," *Journal of Family Studies* 20, no. 1 (2014), 40, https://doi.org/10.5172/jfs.2014.20.1.39.

36 Zibricky, "New Knowledge about Motherhood," 41.

37 Carter, "How Much Subjectivity Is Needed."

38 Sandra L. Faulkner, "That Baby Will Cost You (REDUX): The Story of an Intended Ambivalent Pregnancy (and Motherhood)," in *Handbook of Autoethnography*, 2nd ed., eds., Tony E. Adams, Stacy Holman Jones, and Carolyhn Ellis (New York: Routledge, 2022), 443–450.

39 Paragraph revised from Adams and Manning, "Autoethnography and Family Research," 359.

40 Ahmet Atay, "What Is Cyber or Digital Autoethnography?," *International Review of Qualitative Research* 13, no. 3 (2020), 267–279, https://doi.org/10.1177/1940844720934373.

41 Atay, "What Is Cyber or Digital Autoethnography?," 272.

42 Atay, "What Is Cyber or Digital Autoethnography?," 272.

43 Ahmet Atay, "Digital Life Writing: The Failure of a Diasporic, Queer, Blue Tinker Bell," *Interactions: Studies in Communication & Culture* 2 no. 1 (2018), 183–193, https://doi.org/10.1386/iscc.9.2.183_1.

44 Atay, "What Is Cyber or Digital Autoethnography?," 273.

45 Jimmie Manning, "Ipsedixitism, Ipseity, and Ipsilateral Identity: The Fear of Finding Ourselves in the Fissures between Phishing and Catfish," in *Beyond New Media: Discourse and Critique in a Polymediated Age*, eds., Art Herbig, Andrew F. Herrmann, and Adam Tyma (Lanham, MD: Lexington Books, 2015), 83–107.

46 Rima Wilkes, "Dialogic Autoethnography: A Professor Goes Internet Dating and Learns about Positionality," *Journal of Autoethnography* 3, no. 1 (2022), 65–83, https://doi.org/10.1525/joae.2022.3.1.65.

47 Tasha R. Dunn and W. Benjamin Myers, "Contemporary Autoethnography *Is* Digital Autoethnography: A Proposal for Maintaining Methodological Relevance in Changing Times," *Journal of Autoethnography* 1, no. 1 (2020), 43–59, https://doi.org/10.1525/joae.2020.1.1.43.

48 Andrew F. Herrmann, "Communicating, Sensemaking, and (Dis)organizing."

49 Ellis, *The Ethnographic I*, 33.

50 Tami Spry, *Body, Paper, Stage: Writing and Performing Autoethnography* (New York: Routledge, 2011), 36.

51 Alexis Zoe Waters Johnson, "Living in Silence: An Autoethnography of Relating, Coping, and Navigating Daily Challenges with Hearing Impairment," *Journal of Autoethnography* 2, no. 11 (2021), 39–54, https://doi.org/10.1525/joae.2021.2.1.39; Vernon F. Humphrey, "I Can't Be Blind, I Can See," *Journal of Autoethnography* 1, no. 4 (2020), 370–377, https://doi.org/10.1525/joae.2020.1.4.370.

52 Examples of autoethnographers who have written about their experiences with losing a child, parent, or partner include Alshammari, "Narrative Reflections on Losing a Companion Animal"; Carolyn Ellis, "There Are Survivors"; Ellis, *Final Negotiations*; Kottenstette, "Portrait at an Exhibition"; Lengelle, *Writing the Self in Bereavement*; Paxton, *At Home with Grief*;

Richardson, *A Story of a Marriage through Dementia and Beyond*; Stephens, "Homicide by Police"; Weaver-Hightower, "Waltzing Matilda"; Weaver-Hightower, "Analyzing Self and Other in Autoethnography."

53 Examples of autoethnographers who have written about their experiences with health conditions include Patrick Anderson, *Autobiography of a Disease* (New York: Routledge); Bernard J. Brommel, "Sensemaking in the Dialysis Clinic," in *Organizational Autoethnographies: Power and Identity in Our Working Lives*, ed. Andrew F. Herrmann (New York: Routledge, 2017), 87–106; Nicole Defenbaugh, *Dirty Tale: A Narrative Journey of the IBD Body* (Creskill, NJ: Hampton Press, 2011); Speedy, *Staring at the Park.*

54 Andrew F. Herrmann, "'I Know I'm Unlovable' Desperation, Dislocation, Despair, and Discourse on the Academic Job Hunt," *Qualitative Inquiry* 18, no. 3 (2012), 247–255, https://doi.org/10.1177/1077800411431561.

55 See Boylorn and Orbe, *Critical Autoethnography*; Johnson and LeMaster, *Gender Futurity, Intersectional Autoethnography.*

56 Paragraph revised from Adams et al., "Making Sense and Taking Action," 4–5.

57 Burke, *The Philosophy of Literary Form.* Arthur Frank also makes this argument in The Wounded Storyteller.

58 See Coles, *The Call of Stories*; Bochner, "Perspectives on Inquiry III."

59 Forrest Stuart, "Introspection, Positionality, and the Self as Research Instrument: Toward a Model of Abductive Reflexivity," in *Approaches to Ethnography: Analysis and Representation in Participant Observation*, eds., Colin Jerolmack and Shamus Khan (Oxford: Oxford University Press, 2017), 211. "A key part of understanding self as a research tool," Mockler writes, "lies in recognising the links between one's ontological and epistemological positioning and the methods one chooses to employ in the collection of data." Nicole Mockler, "Being Me: In Search of Authenticity," *Creative Spaces for Qualitative Researching: Living Researchi*, eds., Joy Higgs, Angie Titchen, Debbie Horsfall, and Donna Bridges (Rotterdam: Sense, 2011), 160.

60 Katherine Irwin writes about (not) co-authoring with community members: "I assumed that asking study members to coauthor with me would be a way to avoid misrepresenting them. What I found, however, is that setting members did not have the time. Writing with me would mean losing valuable income and advancement in their other projects. While the tattoo community and the dominant academic discourse might have benefited by having multiple perspectives and voices included in what is being written about tattooing, in the end it was important for setting members to make the choice about the personal risks of authorship (or any other research practice and stance). In many cases, the individual deficits of writing against the traditional research canon might be more than setting members want to take on. This is their choice. Also, there is no guarantee that our writing, experimental or traditional, will emancipate and liberate more than it will perpetuate larger power relationships." See Katherine Irwin, "Into the Dark Heart of Ethnography: The Lived Ethics and Inequality of Intimate Field Relationships," *Qualitative Sociology* 29 (2006), 171.

61 Ellis, "Telling Secrets"; Carolyn Ellis, "Emotional and Ethical Quagmires in Returning to the Field," *Journal of Contemporary Ethnography* 24, no. 1 (1995), 68–98, https://doi.org/10.1177/089124195024001003; Kathleen M. Blee, "Studying the Enemy," in *Our Studies, Ourselves: Sociologists' Lives and Work*, eds., Barry Glassner and Rosanna Hertz (New York: Oxford University Press, 2003); Jaime García-Iglesias, "The Maroon Boxer Briefs: Exploring Erotic Reflexivity in Interview Research," *Qualitative Research* 21, no. 5 (2021), 703–718, https://doi.org/10.1177/1468794120927676.

62 See Bochner, *Coming to Narrative.*

63 Søren A. Kierkegaard, *Journals and Papers, 7 Vol* (Bloomington: Indiana University Press, 1967–1978), 111.
64 Arthur P. Bochner, "Response to 'Ethnography in Interpersonal Communication," paper presented at the National Communication Association, Chicago, IL, November 12, 2004. See also Christine E. Kiesinger, "My Father's Shoes: The Therapeutic Value of Narrative Reframing," in *Ethnographically Speaking: Autoethnography, Literature, and Aesthetics*, eds., Arthur P. Bochner and Carolyn Ellis (Walnut Creek, CA: Altamira. 2002), 95–114; Pelias, "For Father and Son."
65 Tony E. Adams, "Seeking Father: Relationally Reframing a Troubled Love Story," *Qualitative Inquiry* 12, no. 4 (2006), 704–723, https://doi.org/10.1177/1077800406288607.
66 Adams, "A Review of Narrative Ethics."
67 Ellis, *The Ethnographic I*, 367.
68 Faulkner and Squillante, *Writing the Personal*, 59.
69 Eve Gerrard and David McNaughton, "Conditional Unconditional Forgiveness," in *The Ethics of Forgiveness: A Collection of Essays*, ed., Christel Fricke (New York: Routledge, 2011), 103.
70 Andrew F. Herrmann, "Reflexivity, Narrative and Ethical Undecidability: On Not Presenting 'Home Is Where the Heart Was,'" paper presented at the Second Annual International Congress of Qualitative Inquiry, Urbana, IL.
71 Keith Berry has some great work about the stories we may not be able to tell. See Keith Berry, "The Consumed Self: Understanding the Stories I Cannot Have," in *Doing Autoethnography*, eds., Sandra L. Pensoneau-Conway, Tony E. Adams, and Derek M. Bolen (Rotterdam: Sense, 2017), 19–27; Keith Berry, "Meditations on the Story I Cannot Write: Reflexivity, Autoethnography, and the Possibilities of Maybe," in *Handbook of Autoethnography*, 2nd ed., eds., Tony E. Adams, Stacy Holman Jones, and Carolyn Ellis (New York: Routledge), 29–40.
72 A line from fictional detective Philip Marlowe, a character in Raymond Chandler, *The Long Goodbye* (New York: Knopf Doubleday, 1988), 25.
73 Peter J. Rabinowitz, "Truth in Fiction: A Reexamination of Audiences," *Critical inquiry* 4, no. 1 (1977), 121–141, https://doi.org/10.1086/447927.
74 Janina Jacke, "Unreliability and Narrator Types. On the Application Area of 'Unreliable Narration,'" *Journal of Literary Theory* 12, no. 1 (2018), 3–28, https://doi.org/10.1515/jlt-2018-0002.
75 Wayne C. Booth, *The Rhetoric of Fiction* (Chicago, IL: University of Chicago Press, 1961).
76 Herrmann, "Narratives and Sensemaking in the New Corporate University."
77 Clifford Geertz, *Works and Lives: The Anthropologist as Author* (Stanford, CA: Stanford University Press, 1988), 79.
78 Tim Burton, *Big Fish* (2003, Columbia Pictures), Film.
79 Barrington, *Writing the Memoir*, 63.
80 This section about *Big Fish* has been revised from Derek M. Bolen and Tony E. Adams, "Narrative Ethics," in *The Routledge International Handbook on Narrative and Life History*, eds., Ivor Goodson, Ari Antikainen, Pat Sikes, and Molly Andrews (New York: Routledge, 2017), 621.
81 Denzin, *Interpretive Biography*, 24. Gutkind also writes, "truth is not a fixed adage, but a concept that shifts under our gaze, multifaceted, determined by whatever self or persona happens to be in charge at the moment." Lee Gutkind, *Keep It Real* (New York: W.W. Norton & Company), 120.
82 Bochner, "Perspectives on Inquiry III," 86.

83 Barrett John Mandel, "The Autobiographer's Art," *Journal of Aesthetics and Art Criticism* 27, no. 2 (1968), 218, https://doi.org/10.2307/428849.
84 Barrington, *Writing the Memoir*, 65.
85 Parts of this section have been revised from Jillian A. Tullis Owen, Chris McRae, Tony E. Adams, and Alisha Vitale, "Truth Troubles," *Qualitative Inquiry* 15, no. 1 (2009), https://doi.org/10.1177/1077800408318316.
86 See Naima Brown-Smith, "Family Secrets," *Journal of Family Issues* 19, no. 1 (1998), 20–42, https://doi.org/10.1177/019251398019001003.
87 Dorothy Allison, *Two or Three Things I Know for Sure* (New York: Plume, 1996), 39.
88 Goodall, *Writing the New Ethnography*, 123.
89 Barrington, *Writing the Memoir*, 27.
90 Tullis Owen et al., "Truth Troubles," 188–189.
91 I included a revised version of this story in Bolen and Adams, "Narrative Ethics," 621. As Bochner writes, "our work is not about holding a mirror to the past through memory work, or about the authenticity of our memories," but instead about "how we use traces to make stories that give meaning to our lives now and change who we can be in the future." Arthur P. Bochner, "Notes toward an Ethics of Memory in Autoethnographic Inquiry," in *Ethical Futures in Qualitative Research: Decolonizing the Politics of Knowledge*, eds., Norman K. Denzin and Michael D. Giardina (Walnut Creek, CA: Left Coast Press, 2007), 206–207. Memory is fallible and our relationship to the past changes with time. This is a core premise of Carolyn Ellis's *Revision*, Mark Freeman's *Hindsight*, and Ragan Fox's "Diяty." Ellis, *Revision*; Mark Freeman, *Hindsight*; Ragan Fox, "Diяty."
92 Adapted from Herrmann, "The Future of Autoethnographic Criteria."
93 Norman Denzin, as quoted in Herrmann et al., "Pursuing, Practicing, and Portraying Qualitative Research."
94 Bochner, *Coming to Narrative*; Herrmann, "On Being a Homeless Work of Fiction."
95 Andrew F. Herrmann, "My Father's Ghost: Interrogating Family Photos," *Journal of Loss and Trauma* 10, no. 4 (2005), 337–346, https://doi.org/10.1080/15325020590956765. Herrmann, "The Ghostwriter"; Andrew F. Herrmann, "The Ghostwriter Writes No More: Narrative Logotherapy, and the Death of My Namesake," *Qualitative Inquiry* 22, no. 7 (2016), 1–12, https://doi.org/10.1177/1077800415622504.
96 Martin Heidegger, *Being and Time*, trans., John MacQuarrie and Edward Robinson (New York: Harper, 1962).
97 Herrmann, "The Future of Autoethnographic Criteria."
98 Shamla McLaurin, "Homophobia: An Autoethnographic Story," *The Qualitative Report* 8, no. 3 (2003), 481, https://doi.org/10.46743/2160-3715/2003.1882.
99 McLaurin, "Homophobia," 481.
100 McLaurin, "Homophobia," 482.
101 McLaurin, "Homophobia," 484.
102 McLaurin, "Homophobia," 484.
103 McLaurin, "Homophobia," 484.
104 McLaurin, "Homophobia," 484.
105 McLaurin, "Homophobia," 485.
106 See Purnell and Bowman, for a great discussion of happy endings and autoethnography. David Purnell and Jim Bowman, "'Happily Ever After': Are Traditional Scripts Just for Fairy Tales?," *Narrative Inquiry* 24, no. 1 (2014), 175–180, https://doi.org/10.1075/ni.24.1.09pur.

107 Bochner, "Criteria against Ourselves," 270.
108 McLaurin, "Homophobia," 481.
109 McLaurin, "Homophobia," 485.
110 McLaurin, "Homophobia," 485.
111 Tony E. Adams, "Supervising, Sharing, and Evaluating Autoethnography," 207–208.
112 Revised from Herrmann, "The Future of Autoethnographic Criteria," 127.

CHAPTER 4

The "Ethno" of Autoethnography

Assessing Culture and (Mis)uses of Others

Let us tell you what we don't do when we do autoethnography. We don't ever say, "Golly! I just had an experience. I want to share it with others!" We don't just sit with a notebook or at a screen and record all the happenings and ramblings from our day, and then turn these recordings into reports, and then try to publish these reports, and then hope others will read and understand our reports just because they are from and about us. We don't think every experience we have—at least those we select to record—is worthy of a research project, and we don't want our autoethnographies to resemble arrogant and narcissistic social media feeds.

When we do autoethnography, we often begin by thinking about experiences that made us pause, wonder, and reflect; to borrow the title of C & C Music Factory's classic song, "things that make you go hmmmm…," we focus on experiences that make us go hmmmm, those that tangle us, mark us, confuse us, generate curiosity—a conversation we overheard, someone's unusual reaction to us, a novel remark from an interviewee, being fascinated or frustrated by a particular text. We've detected something from these phenomena, and we're not sure what, or what will happen next, or how the experience will haunt us, change us, and alter our perceived life trajectory.

We begin to write these experiences, recognizing that, following Richardson, we will come to learn about them through the process of writing. We seek out relevant research, television shows, news stories, podcasts, and songs that may offer insights about the experience. We might decide to interview others, find a thread on Reddit, and conduct fieldwork in a certain location. We may think about the theories we know and, based on feedback from others, learn new theories to consider. We work to connect and compare our experiences with others and maybe even use their stories to feel and live better. For autoethnography, the auto isn't just about us; we must engage others, other texts, jarring and canonical discourses, all facets of the ethno.

*

DOI: 10.4324/9781003281771-5

Autobiographies and other forms of life writing foreground personal experience, yet they tend not to foreground "cultural analysis and interpretation," an important requirement for good autoethnography.[1] While the author's use of their personal experience is necessary for autoethnography, as we have noted before, the mere use of personal experience does not make a project autoethnographic. We must find ways to get out of ourselves, engage others, and assess how our experiences align with, or diverge from, extant research and representation.

In this chapter, we focus on assessing the ethno of autoethnography. "Ethno" refers to "culture," and "culture" refers to the (shared) principles, practices, and products of a social group, the people who, with their words and deeds and values and artifacts, comprise a community. In the broadest sense, ethnography thus refers to the process of studying and representing facets of and experiences with a culture/group/community. Karl Weick defines ethnographic research as "sustained, explicit, methodological observation and paraphrasing of social situations in relation to their naturally occurring contexts."[2] Van Maanen characterizes ethnography as "the peculiar practice of representing the social reality of others through the analysis of one's own experience in the world of these others."[3] The ethno aspect of autoethnography shifts the focus from us toward everything and everyone else.

The focus of the ethno is what Eric Eisenberg calls "the surround,"[4] those aspects of culture that bump up against the me/we. The primary goal of ethnographic research is to identify those points of intersection with the self, our tangles with cultural principles, practices, and products, and then, via concrete details and thick description, facilitate a nuanced understanding of these phenomena.[5] Consider this excerpt by Karen Lee Ashcraft:

> The three men glance my way, and I cringe as they pull up their masks begrudgingly, eyes rolling. I wince at the multiplying cues I don't belong, at the dawning: I just strolled into MAGA [Make America Great Again] town, I should've known; I should've avoided this place, stayed in a safer space. I'm in no mood for this today, and from the looks of it, neither are they.[6]

There is a lot of detail in this brief scene. Facial expressions. Small actions. Quick realizations. Cultural and political nuances. Multiple emotions. Ashcraft offers an example of the interplay of the graphy of the ethno and the graphy of the auto, coming together to create a tense and detailed scene of social life. This is thick description.

Authors use various techniques to accomplish the ethnographic goals of thick description, interpretation, and critique. Some ethnographers do fieldwork—sometimes referred to as "participant observation"[7] and "deep hanging out"[8]—by immersing themselves in "natural settings," spaces and situations that would exist regardless of the researcher's presence. They observe and take (field) notes of the patterns of discourse, interactions, and behavior in these spaces and situations and discern unique terms, norms, and experiences that comprise a group. William Whyte, for example, spent approximately a year in Chicago's Italian slums.[9] Karen Ho spent years participating and observing activities on Wall Street.[10]

Pete Simi and Robert Futrell went to back-yard parties and "Hate Music" concerts in their ethnographic research on White power groups in the United States.[11] Lauraine Leblanc spent more than a year in the field exploring how punk women resist gender norms.[12]

When I (Andrew) did fieldwork at a local comic bookstore, I observed customers and employees use the phrase "bag and board." Unless you are a member of the comic book community, you likely do not know what this term means. ("Bag and board" means to slide a comic book into a polyurethane bag with a cardboard back to protect it from damage.[13]) To offer a sense of the activities of the bookstore, Andrew had to observe, interpret, and explain the phrase for readers.

In this example, I *told* you information. But as we've mentioned before, showing through thick description is also a necessary part of writing good autoethnography. Consider Carolyn Ellis' description of her brother Rex's funeral:

> The people came. Three to four hundred of them. They occupied my parents and validated for me how important Rex had been. I became the greeter, letting them in, hugging, listening to them marvel at how I had changed, and then directing them to my parents, who sat side-by-side in their lazy boy chairs. Offering their sympathies, men looked sad and stoically held my father's hand and kissed my mother. Women were more likely to cry openly with my mother and often with my father, sometimes falling in sobs into my parents' arms. Older people comforted, while the younger ones stammered about not knowing what to say. That would come with experience. My mother cried continually and my father wiped tears constantly. I was the dry-eyed director, who craved and feared collapsing into my parents' embrace.[14]

Ellis includes a lot of important information in this ethnographic account. She provides more than mere information; she offers cultural details. She identifies rituals associated with some funerals. The guests coming and going and paying their respects. Ellis's parents mourn in their chairs and mourners come to them. And then there is Ellis herself, performing her part as the host, keeping grief at bay to get through the ritual. We can observe what Ellis observes and feel what she feels. Such descriptive care and talent are required for good autoethnography.

Some ethnographers conduct formal interviews with members of a community[15] or attend to the happenings of everyday comments and encounters that might indicate what it means and how it feels to be a member of a community,[16] experience a similar space or situation, or possess a particular trait or identity.[17] And some ethnographers analyze extant research, popular artifacts and texts,[18] as well as media portrayals of communities, experiences, traits, and identities.[19]

To be able to best assess an autoethnography, autoethnographers should show and/or tell which of these ethnographic practices they used and how. Leblanc, for example, noted:

> Formal interviews usually took place after I had spent time with punks in the city and thus had established some rapport. In conducting these semistructured interviews,

> I drew on an interview guide comprised of the main questions and follow-up probes. I began each interview with an explicit agreement to allow tape-recording. I assured confidentiality and explained that I would be using pseudonyms to identify speakers. I also agreed to full reciprocity and offered to answer any questions that they want to ask me.[20]

Leblanc does not simply tell us that she performed interviews. She provides details about the type of interview. She provides the context and the reasoning for the interviews. She informs readers how she will protect her interviewees and includes her interview guide. These details can allow readers to determine how to assess her process, character, and credibility as a researcher.

Although we do not expect autoethnographers to engage every ethnographic technique, a good autoethnographic project should use or emphasize at least one of them, or else the ethno component of autoethnography goes unfulfilled. When we assess autoethnographies, we expect a demonstrated awareness of and concerted effort to engage with others and/or prominent discourses about a topic; for us, an engagement with the ethno is a rigid and prescriptive requirement for doing good autoethnography.

Yet how one accomplishes this engagement, which ethnographic techniques an autoethnographer may pursue, is contingent upon a project. Assessing how well these techniques were actually used becomes increasingly subjective—no definitive mandates exist regarding how fieldwork should occur, who and how to interview, or what constitutes a sufficient review of the literature or analysis of a text. To assess autoethnography fairly means recognizing the myriad reasons for and fluid nature of actually doing the research, and what might be appropriate for one project may not be appropriate for another.

There are many good books on doing ethnographic research, and we have shared many of our favorites. Despite reading a lot of ethnographies and how-to books about ethnography, one thing is certain: no one does ethnography in the same way. "Research, particularly ethnographic research, is a messy process," Alexandra Plows writes. "Negotiating access, developing relationships with research participants, navigating the research dynamic, and what 'counts' as the research site, is inevitably a messy business."[21] Such mess makes ethnography and autoethnography fun and sometimes frustrating.

Given the myriad possibilities for the ethno, in this chapter we describe and assess how autoethnographers can move outside of themselves and how they consider what others think about or have written about a topic. We focus on assessing various types of fieldwork, formal interviews and informal conversations, and familiarity with existing research and popular texts. Although we offer various examples and questions to consider in each section, readers can determine which criteria to use to assess a specific project. Our only firm requirement is that an autoethnographer somehow engages the ethno. If you do not think about the ethno and if you do not consider how to get outside of your limited experiences and perspectives, then you will not do good autoethnography.

PARTICIPANT OBSERVATION IN NATURAL SETTINGS

As noted, some autoethnographers engage in participant observation. Although we embrace a broad definition of fieldwork for this book, historically the practice of participant observation has been referred to as "going into the field." A community may be bound by physical and/or virtual borders or by shared values, goals, and experiences. Autoethnographers engage in "deep hanging out" in relevant communal contexts[22]; to borrow a phrase from Goffman, they go "where the action is" and take (field) notes based on what they feel, see, hear, and experience.[23] If one wants to study the rural lives of Black women, or the happenings of a dialysis clinic, or experiences with online dating, then one must spend time with rural Black women, in a dialysis clinic, or on online dating sites.[24] The autoethnographer then uses their notes and observations to craft a thick description of the community. Although we do not describe techniques for doing participant observation—there are plenty of texts that explain the process[25]—we describe how to assess the practice as represented in autoethnographies.

Autoethnographers who use participant observation tend to spend a lot of time in key natural settings—at least a few months, possibly years, and sometimes even a lifetime. The purpose and premise of long-term immersion is to be present long enough to get a good sense of the principles, practices, and products of the community—to identify patterns of behavior and interaction as well as unique outliers. Wendy Leeds-Hurwitz suggests ethnographers typically spend one year doing fieldwork.[26] Leeds-Hurwitz's suggestion illustrates a possible criterion for assessment: we might assess an autoethnography based on the length of time the author spent in the field.

As with all research, there are ethical issues to consider when doing fieldwork. The longer we spend in a community's natural settings, the more we will learn about the actual happenings of the community; the shorter one stays, or the further one stays away, the less chance they may have to observe a community's day-to-day affairs. Further, as Goffman noted decades ago, the more time we spend with others, the more difficult it will be for them to maintain frontstage pretenses and performances.[27] With time, pretenses diminish, and participants may become more comfortable with us. The need to manage impressions becomes less important, and, with time, we get closer to what matters matter for community members, what they find to be meaningful. Participant observation allows us to get as close as possible to everyday life as it may occur absent a researcher's presence. With time, we will increasingly get glimpses of the coveted backstage, what community members may genuinely think and feel.

Is fieldwork deceptive? Possibly. Yet, doing fieldwork is really an exercise in impression management, something we all do, and we do fieldwork to go beyond, or learn more than, basic impressions. We don't share all information with strangers (e.g., finances, failures, sexual histories, etc.), yet the longer someone might hang with us, the more they will learn about us and the more we will learn about them. It takes great effort to maintain public performances for a long time, and with enough time, pretenses fade. As Carolyn Ellis wrote about her fieldwork in two fishing communities,

> Soon, however, at least to members of this extended family, I was just Carolyn coming to visit. Even those who knew my original purpose forgot I was doing research because 'writing a paper' had no relevance to their everyday lives. Who thought about research when there were funerals to go to, floods to escape, killings to be straightened out, sick babies to tend, welfare checks that didn't arrive on time, and doctors (always doctors) to visit?[28]

As Ellis astutely shows, the more time spent with others, the more these others might forget that we are doing research. They may become comfortable with us and share vital and vulnerable information about their/community life. It often takes time to establish relationships, yet we may need to establish relationships to learn about a community. This isn't only true when working with large communities and groups. When Jules Henry was doing ethnographic psychological research with families, after some time they may have forgotten that he was researching them.[29]

Here, accuracy also intertwines with pretense: ethnographers want to get as close as possible to an experience and/or community, to live and feel like a local, rather than a distanced and detached tourist/observer. Spending more time with others will influence the kind and quality of the information we will learn and gather; not spending enough time may result in thin descriptions and shallow findings. Although autoethnographers can determine the length appropriate for natural settings, they may have to account for why they didn't spend long enough immersed in the daily happenings of a community. We might also assess how the autoethnographer accessed the community, what they did when they were there, and what they did if and when they left.

*

Sometimes it may be difficult to do participant observation in a natural setting for a long time. Some ethnographers examine one-of-a-kind situations that Bob Krizek calls "non-routine public events."[30] An example of a non-routine public event was the closing and demolition of Comiskey Park, the beloved stadium where the Chicago White Sox played.[31] Nick Trujillo and Bob Krizek also did ethnographic research during the final baseball game at Texas Stadium in Arlington.[32] Katherine Miller explored the horrific Texas A&M University (TAMU) bonfire collapse that killed twelve people; TAMU then stopped the event.[33] Events such as the funeral of the Queen of England, an earthquake or airplane crash, the assassination of a celebrity or politician, or the disastrous FYRE festival can all be considered non-routine public events.

The point of studying a non-routine event is to locate the event within your experience and in tandem with the lives of others, "at the intersection of personal identities and not as the properties of distinct communities or cultures."[34] Rather than deep hanging out, these investigations foreground interpersonal connections. Unlike going to a field site for weeks, months, or even years, these types of events have a distinct end. The researcher doesn't spend a lot of time in the field because the event itself prohibits doing so; once the event ends, it's done.

Non-routine events can also include those that occur with irregular regularity. An ethnographer studying "Swifties" at a Taylor Swift concert during her Eras Tour could be considered studying a non-routine public event as "each performance becomes a special occasion."[35] However, what if that ethnographer decides to study successive tours? One of Andrew's favorite bands is The Cure. He's been to several concerts—one at Giants Stadium in 1989, when he was 23; one in 2016 at the PNC Music Pavilion in Charlotte, North Carolina, when he was 49; and one at Riot Fest in Chicago in 2023, when he was 57. Each could be considered a non-routine event and studied singularly through autoethnography. Or they could be studied in a way akin to longitudinal autoethnography, across a lifespan, like he has done with other projects.[36]

In his original conception of non-routine public events, Krizek suggested the researcher should "experience the event directly."[37] However, with the advent of live and recorded media, non-routine public events can now include the passing of the Olympic torch, acts of terrorism, the first post-pandemic Rolling Stones concert in St. Louis, and innumerable more.[38] The opportunities to do autoethnography on these types of events is boundless. Assessing autoethnographies of non-routine public events as inadequate solely because there wasn't any formal, in-person participant observation would be inappropriate. The events still happened, and they may have been important for many people, but there wasn't/isn't an easy way to find a distinct community for the events.

*

Not all autoethnographers can find a specific setting or community to do participant observation. Tony has written a lot about "coming out (of the closet)," the revealing of same-gender attraction to others, a shared experience for many people who identify with the LGBTQ+ community. But what natural settings exist for coming out? Where would he go to participate and observe a disclosure? Tony could (does) find venues that foreground coming out experiences, a coming-out support group or a YouTube campaign such as the *It Gets Better* project, but coming out can happen at any time. Further, for some, coming out is an intimate, private disclosure. Trying to participate and observe someone's actual coming out to someone else could be invasive and unethical.

We could apply a similar approach to topics such as microaggressions—those common, repeated, seemingly innocent slights that one might recognize as ageist, racist, ableist, or sexist, and which are a shared experience for folks who identify with a marginal, and possibly stigmatized, cultural identity. But what natural settings exist for microaggressions? Where would we go to participate and observe them? They can happen anywhere and at any time, and yet we need to figure out how to study them *in situ* to remedy them. These problematic patterns of behavior tied to an identity occur in everyday settings, and yet we often have no idea when they might happen. One engages in participant observation by living through them.

Finally, participant observation in natural settings may be difficult to accomplish for some groups. There may be ethical considerations to participating and observing members of Alcoholics Anonymous, actual therapeutic sessions, sex in public,[39] or places where fieldwork would put the researcher in physical danger.[40]

If a project could allow for participant observation in natural settings, then the autoethnographer should consider how to best do it. If not, they may need to justify why they didn't. Not all projects allow for participant observation, which is why we frame it as a possible practice for autoethnography, not a required technique.

*

There's one more place to hang out that we haven't discussed: online contexts.[41] Participating and observing in online contexts—an act sometimes called digital ethnography, cyber-ethnography, virtual ethnography, or netnography—presents a number of additional issues and challenges when conceiving of the field.[42] For virtual groups, the field is "an online world with fuzzy space and time boundaries."[43] In an interesting twist, going into the field might mean sitting at the desk in your office, relaxing on your sofa with your laptop, or using your phone at the local coffee shop.

Despite the opportunities and challenges online ethnography provides, understanding identity, community, and culture is still a prominent topic of investigation for qualitative researchers, including ethnographers and autoethnographers.[44] Online autoethnographers go online to hang out and do fieldwork, study interactions, and conduct interviews. Autoethnographers who do hybrid research combine these online activities with offline ones.[45] When assessing such works, we expect thick descriptions of the online sites and the (assumed) people, interviews, public comments, or guided conversations. We want to know about the place or space, as well as the metaphors and narratives and discourses that make the community a community. We also expect the author has read key texts about doing fieldwork online.[46]

ENGAGING AND REPRESENTING OTHERS

Historically, many ethnographers have been terribly invasive, colonialist, and abusive.[47] Bronislaw Malinowski, considered one of the "pioneers" (there's a colonizing term!) of ethnography, wrote, "The study of savage and coloured races possesses practical value, in the first sense, for purposes of colonial administration and the management of the relations between white and coloured people."[48] We assume this claim wasn't supposed to be a confession, but, in retrospect, it certainly reads that way.

These ethnographers would find a community in which they were not a member, hop into the community (often uninvited), observe how community members behave, leave the community, write about the community, and never again engage community members. Members were mined for data but weren't consulted after fieldwork, and sometimes the ethnographer's representation of the community would harm the community. As Reinharz remarked decades ago, traditional social scientific research, which includes ethnography,

> is frequently conducted on the rape model: The researchers take, hit, and run. They intrude into their subjects' privacy, disrupt their perceptions, utilize false pretenses,

> manipulate the relationship, and give little or nothing in return. When the needs of the researcher are satisfied, they break off contact with the subject.[49]

Conquergood expressed a similar concern about ethnography. He described "The Curator's Exhibitionism" approach to doing ethnography as one in which the researcher has a "fascination with the exotic, primitive, culturally remote."[50] Conquergood argued such an approach often results in disruptive fieldwork processes and sensationalized representations of ("exotic," "deviant") others.[51] (Note here how the ethno and the graphy intersect—the emphasis on studying *and* representing others.)

Many contemporary ethnographers—especially those who identify with critical, feminist, queer, postcolonial, and indigenous sensibilities—attempt to establish respectful and sincere ways of studying and representing others. These ethnographers conceptualize research as a relational, collaborative, and intersubjective endeavor.[52] They refuse to treat participants as research "subjects" only to be mined for data and they often try to meaningfully contribute to the people and communities they study.[53]

As such, ethnographers, and thus autoethnographers, who conduct interviews with, or intend to create representations of, communities must consider careful, strategic, and rapport-building recruitment of participants. These researchers must also consider how an account might implicate themselves, their participants, and maybe even their friends, family members, coworkers, and colleagues.[54] An autoethnographer who includes others in their work, and writes from the perspective of a community, might be held accountable to, and assessed by, these questions. How did they recruit interviewees? Did interviewees have a chance to review and approve the information they shared and how they may be represented? If not, why not? These questions do not solicit one right answer, yet an author must recognize that readers may assess their work and research ability based on how the author responds to these questions.

Given the use of personal experience, autoethnographers are often insiders to the community. Being an insider is helpful for several reasons. First, autoethnographers must carefully and respectfully represent the culture in which they work as they too will be affected by the representation. For instance, instead of a outside ethnographer writing about people with depression, an autoethnographer who writes about living with depression often has a personal investment in how depression is represented.[55] Likewise, an autoethnographer who defines herself as a Black, Southern, rural woman probably will care about how she represents a community of Black, Southern, rural women.[56]

An autoethnography might be assessed on the ways the researcher gained access to, and their interactions with, a community. Are they already an insider, a member of the community, or are they an outsider to a community they do not claim? How did they work with others, and what techniques did they use to capture others' stories? Answers to these questions are much more subjective—we do not have rigid criteria for assessing these decisions; our assessment would depend on if/how an author explains their processes and practices.[57]

*

In my (Tony) early training as a news reporter, I learned that, when interviewing people for a story, interviewees may be reserved and nervous at first, especially if the interview is being recorded. I also learned that after a few minutes, the interviewee may forget about the interview *as* an interview and about the recording, and subsequently may be less reserved and nervous, and subsequently may begin to share different, often more intimate and genuine insights. As a reporter, I would try to get people to talk about a topic longer than a few minutes because those few minutes would often contain basic or superficial commentary. (This strategy is a micro example of the need to spend a sufficient time with interviewees or in the field.) By interviewing others for more than a few minutes, I would likely learn something different from them, e.g., assuming the interviewee becomes comfortable with me, I might be privy to fewer frontstage pretenses and more backstage revelations.

In addition to this consideration of time, there are other ways to assess the interviews an autoethnographer might use in a project. These criteria aren't unique to autoethnography but rather to the design and doing of interview research. We can assess interviews based on the questions (not) asked, the duration of the interview, and maybe even the medium used for the interview. These decisions directly affect the kind of information we acquire, e.g., multiple interviews can allow for follow-up questions; in-person interviews allow for nonverbal cues that might be missed via phone or Zoom, yet they are not as convenient as phone or Zoom interviews, which might limit participation; and depending on the sensitivity of a topic, strangers and/or friends might be more reticent to share their experiences.

We can also assess who the interviewees were: Did they have the credentials or experience to discuss certain topics? How were they recruited? Were they compensated for their time? Did they have any input regarding how the researcher represented them? If one uses interviews for their autoethnographic project (and many do!), we encourage them to read about interview processes, including criteria for assessing interviews.[58] We also encourage autoethnographers to explain what they did and why they did what they did.

*

Sometimes we might learn information from others without ever asking for it. We might overhear a conversation or read a post on social media that relates to our project but, depending on the intimacy of the information, we may not be able to acquire approval to use it. For instance, microaggressions are difficult to study not only because we may not know who will commit them and when they will occur but also because the person committing the microaggression might not realize how the act is a microaggression and claim they acted with good intentions. They might also have an issue with us writing about them. Yet such informal and unsolicited information can be an important autoethnographic material: Even though the microaggression happened unsystematically and serendipitously, we might learn information that we could not acquire through organized and intentional efforts. These moments offer an "accidental," "surprising," and "unplanned" glimpse into a topic.[59] Yet such encounters require us to use great care: ethically, we should protect the privacy of these persons by masking or altering identifying details such as context, topics discussed, and a person's characteristics, especially if they are being used in ways they may never want or know.[60] Or we may experience consequences for violating one's privacy.

Not acquiring permission is another way to assess an autoethnographic project. For us, if an autoethnographer formally interviews someone for or uses the actual name of someone in a project, then permission is often necessary. (Yet we rarely, if ever, request permission to use and name/cite someone and their published/public work—you might cite us in your project, but not ask our permission to do so.) If an autoethnographer includes information about, or gleaned from unknown others, especially in public contexts, permission may be unnecessary, or not possible, or inappropriate to pursue. For example, Elizabeth Stephens describes how police officers killed her son.[61] Stephens does not mention officers by name, but to expect Stephens to seek permission from the officers who killed her son would be unnecessary and cruel. We imagine the officers might even refuse to grant her permission to tell her story, but they shouldn't be able to exert such control.

Although we may assess an author for not receiving approval from their Institutional Review Boards (IRBs), these boards only exist at some academic/research institutions.[62] Not all autoethnographers work at such institutions, e.g., therapists with private practices, independent scholars, and universities in certain countries. Journalists and news reporters also do not engage IRBs for permission to interview others; doing so would be antithetical to the notion of a "free press." Even though life writing is taught at many academic institutions, rarely do life writers pursue IRB permission for their work, and expecting creative writers, especially those working in fiction, to seek consent for those who have informed, or who may be implicated by, a work would be silly too. And what should one do if they write about someone who has died? Permission isn't possible, but that shouldn't prohibit the possibility of writing about the deceased. We do not want to suggest autoethnographers can write whatever they want; rather, we suggest the seemingly neutral expectation to acquire IRB permission is inappropriate. Such assessment says more about the assessor than the assessed. Not all autoethnographers formally include others, but some do, and when they do, not all autoethnographers receive permission to do so. Seeking permission might inhibit, even prohibit, an autoethnographer from sharing valuable insights about an important and understudied topic.

Further, just because we receive permission from the IRB to conduct a study doesn't mean that others will assess our work as ethical. Keith Berry and Tony conducted a virtual ethnography about a community of gay men interested in gaining weight. Although we included public comments from members, we did not interview or request any information from anyone for the project. Our IRB formally "exempted" our project. When we submitted the manuscript to a journal, the editor desk rejected it because they disagreed with our IRB's exemption. The editor assessed the project and the IRB's decision as inadequate—and there wasn't anything we could do. It would be inappropriate to tell members of our IRB that a journal editor determined they made a mistake. We submitted the project to another journal. The editor and the reviewers supported it, and it was published.[63]

*

If one has concerns about representing others, or if we, as assessors of these works, have concerns, we can help an author mask individuals and situations and maybe even encourage them to use composite characters, publish anonymously, use a pseudonym, or pursue techniques associated with fiction. But if one turns to fiction, they better demonstrate a good grasp of the fiction genre and fiction writing. We know several scholars who use fiction to represent their work—a good move ethically—but who are terrible (fiction) writers.

Several autoethnographers have espoused additional ethical criteria for autoethnography. We encourage you to read these texts.[64] We only stress that no universal ethical standards exist for doing autoethnography, so when we assess an autoethnographic manuscript in terms of ethics, we should recognize that our assumptions about ethics may not be shared by others, including the author. Conversely, we encourage authors to be aware of various ethical expectations as they can determine how to best respond when others use the expectations to assess their work. The autoethnographer who doesn't recognize the various ethical issues in representing a work may have a difficult time getting their work published and supported by others. They may also encounter several relational, professional, and legal consequences by not considering if and how their work implicates others.

ASSESSING THE USE OF TEXTS IN AUTOETHNOGRAPHY

I (Andrew) am on my couch binge-watching *The Walking Dead* when my phone pings. It's a notification from Google Scholar that someone cited something I wrote. It's exciting to get that ping—a good little dopamine hit.

I go to Google Scholar and notice someone cited an article Art Herbig and I wrote called "Polymediated Narrative: The Case of the *Supernatural* Episode 'Fan Fiction.'"[65] Our article is part of our work on polymediated narrative[66] and focuses on *Supernatural's* 200th episode, entitled "Fan Fiction." The meta, self-referential episode served as a love letter to audiences of the show. It included throwback quotes and inside jokes and made fun of its own unresolved issues, all wrapped-up in a murder mystery musical based on a prophetic book series, which narrated the main characters' lives.

I read the article citing our article and realize the author must not have read more than the title; they didn't know what our article actually said. The author must have read "Fan Fiction" in the title and determined the quotations were scare quotes, used to call attention to, even mock, the term/concept. The author referenced us as disparaging fan fiction, fiction written by fans based on the series. Yet, that claim was absolutely antithetical to what we wrote. Art and I discussed how fan fiction influenced the 200th episode and how the writers of the television series incorporated several themes and topics from *Supernatural* fan fiction into the episode itself.

I emailed the author who cited our article and mentioned that they seemed to not know what our article was about or how we felt about *Supernatural* fan fiction. The author was apologetic, which I appreciated. I also stressed that now people might read their article and what they said about our article and believe that Art and I ridiculed fan fiction. Hopefully, the citation lesson stuck.[67]

*

We can assess an autoethnography based on the sources used, how the author uses these sources, and what it contributes to existing research about a topic. Although we do not expect an author to find a definitive "gap" in existing research, we do expect authors to show how their work adds to existing conversations about a topic. As Tami Spry notes, "Good autoethnography is not simply a confessional tale of self-renewal; it is a provocative weave of story and theory."[68]

In *The Creative Qualitative Researcher*, Ron Pelias offers insights about good practices for citation—criteria we can use to assess if/how an author engages others in their work. Pelias offers the following suggestions:

- "Never cite someone you haven't read."
- "Cite only those you understand."
- "Always cite with accuracy."
- "Know what is historically relevant to your work."
- "Avoid the extended citation list."
- "Work to be as interesting as those you cite."
- "Cite yourself sparingly."
- "Always cite with generosity."

Pelias notes, "Citation carries consequences" as it marks an author's "academic positioning." "Your choice to include certain scholars in your work," he continues, "indicates to readers your values and allegiances. To cite is to engage in a relational and political act." In espousing these good practices, Pelias provides insights into how we can assess an author's citations.[69]

Some of Pelias' suggestions we cannot assess easily: we cannot know whether an author has read the work they cite, whether they understand the work they cite, if they are as interesting as the folks they cite, or if they are being generous when they cite others' work. However, we can assess the other practices, and we often do so when reviewing autoethnographic work.

If an author uses a "layered account" without engaging, or even citing, Carol Rambo's work, their manuscript becomes suspect. We expect the author to demonstrate an understanding of how Carol Rambo, the originator of this form, describes the form, how Rambo uses it, and why she uses it.[70] Although layered accounts are popular,[71] not understanding how and why Rambo developed the term is irresponsible, even unethical.

If an author uses autoethnography to study eating disorders, or "friendship as method," but doesn't engage the work of Lisa Tillmann, then we sense the author hasn't done sufficient reading about these topics.[72] If an author uses "relational ethics"[73] or "minor bodily stigma"[74] or "sociological introspection," then they should cite and engage Carolyn Ellis's conceptualization and application of these topics.[75] If an author does "exo-autoethnography," then they should consult with Anna Denejkina, the originator of this term, and analyze how she has used it in her work.[76] Take the originators' applications of these terms as models for your work. Not giving proper attribution risks being assessed as arrogant and lazy. You may even be charged with plagiarism. Know the origins and applications of key terms, and do not claim them as your own.

A similar consideration should be used when studying various sites and topics of autoethnography. If you are doing autoethnographic research on bars and/or bar culture, you would do well to read the works of Katherine Denker, Donna White, and Tony Adams.[77] If you delve into existential and phenomenological aspects of autoethnography, you would want to read work by Keith Berry, Jacquelyn Allen-Collinson, Amber Esping, Alec Grant, Helen Woodley, or Andrew's chapter on love in the second edition of the *Handbook of Autoethnography*.[78] If you are interested in writing an autoethnography about Dungeons & Dragons (D&D) or other role-playing games, you'll need to dive into nonacademic and academic literature about D&D. Read historical overviews about the game's development such as *The Elusive Shift: How Role-Playing Games Forged Their Identity*, *The Evolution of Fantasy Role-Playing Games*, and *Game Wizards: The Epic Battle for Dungeons & Dragons*.[79] Consulting with D&D relevant research that encapsulates everything from the Satanic panic, to D&D and deviance, to psychiatric problems among players is also useful.[80] (Yes, there were many studies like this.) Also consider how other autoethnographers have discussed gaming.[81] We recognize that we cannot know every work about a topic, but at the very least, start with a Google Scholar search for "autoethnography + [insert your topic here]."

While writing this book, we reviewed a manuscript about "workplace autoethnography" that, although it mentioned "organizational autoethnography," didn't engage the vast literature about organizational autoethnography—literature that, by its very nature, prioritizes places of work.[82] Consider this statement: "workplace autoethnography is still somewhat underused as a method of data inquiry, and oftentimes underutilized in the framework of academic institutions."[83] We disagree, particularly regarding the use of autoethnography in higher education by academics. A quick and basic Google search for "autoethnography and higher education" returned more than 50,000 results. The results include many classic autoethnographic texts.[84] Autoethnographies on higher education run the gamut of topics, including academic capitalism, encroaching neoliberalism, student-teacher relationships, being teaching assistants, tenure issues, spirituality, academic (un)employment, and more.[85] As such, the author's claim that autoethnography is underused, especially in academic institutions, makes us question how much the author has read about autoethnography.

The Case of Analytic Autoethnography

We encounter the most egregious transgressions of citation when people claim to do and use "analytic autoethnography." As reviewers, we have one simple request: If you use analytic autoethnography, then please read and engage what Leon Anderson, the person who coined the term, has written about the concept.[86] If you propose to do analytic autoethnography, in form and tone, it should resemble Anderson's analytic autoethnographies. We review an abundance of manuscripts espousing limited and twisted perspectives of analytic autoethnography. These authors argue analytic autoethnography allows them to remove personal bias from an autoethnographic manuscript, thus making their work reliable, valid, generalizable, and objective. These authors twist analytic autoethnography to fit their projects without demonstrating any understanding of how Anderson defined and applied it.

We have another more humorous and jarring example of how the term has been misunderstood. When Anderson submitted his manuscript, "Garfinkeling in Real Life," to the *Journal of Autoethnography*, we sent it out for review. In the manuscript, Anderson referred the work as analytic autoethnography, yet one reviewer, unaware that Anderson was the author (Anderson's name had been removed for review), remarked that the author wasn't using analytic autoethnography correctly. When we sent Anderson this feedback, we said he could address or dismiss the comment. Although we knew the author and the reviewer did not, we found it ironic that the very person who created the term was being told that he wasn't using the term correctly. This example also illustrates how once we publish something, we will lose much interpretive control of it; readers can use and interpret the work differently than intended.

From our perspective, Anderson conceptualized analytic autoethnography to push autoethnographers to bring all their methodological, theoretical, and interpretive skills to bear on their experiences and stories—do fieldwork, have guided conversations, consult with theory, solicit interviews, and examine texts. Although he conceptualized analytic autoethnography alongside evocative autoethnography, nowhere does he disparage the usefulness of evocative autoethnography; he never said do *this*, not *that*. Anderson even dismisses the false opposition between analytic and evocative autoethnography in his lead chapter in the first edition of the *Handbook of Autoethnography*, a collection coedited by (evocative) autoethnographer Carolyn Ellis.[87]

Consider the following excerpt about parachuting

> "Damnit!" I curse under my breath. I pull the right brake line down and dive in a 360-degree spiral to bleed off altitude and position myself for the downwind leg of my landing. I usually love this part, but my heart isn't in it now. Last time I was here I was so happy. Not now. I fucked up bad and I know it.
>
> I ought to sell my rig and take up bowling. But I'd probably suck at that, too.[88]

Analytic or evocative? Both. It's Leon Anderson. Writing now, in 2024, we feel the analytic-evocative debate has become tired and tiring. We have always understood Anderson's actual analytic autoethnographies as evocative reads, just as we have always found Ellis' actual evocative autoethnographies as astutely and artfully analytical.

We know authors will still use the term analytic autoethnography, and that's fine with us, as long as their manuscripts resemble the analytic autoethnographies written by the person who coined the phrase. If your analytical autoethnography doesn't engage what Anderson has written about analytic autoethnography or resemble Anderson's actual analytic autoethnographies, then you're not doing analytic autoethnography—you're doing something else.

*

Although citation is important, we also want to stress that not all autoethnographers will cite others' work or formally engage academic research on a topic. For this chapter, our goal is to push autoethnographers to get out of themselves, consider others, and engage the ethno. Citation is one way to do so but not the only way. Some autoethnographers may not cite any sources.

Consider Ron Pelias's "The Critical Life." Although Pelias does not include any formal citations, the craft of the text and the specificity of detail demonstrate Pelias's intimate knowledge of the nuances, complications, and potential distress that can stem from having to perpetually assess others. In "Maternal Connections," Carolyn Ellis does not formally cite or situate her account among existing daughter-mother stories, yet she offers a thick description of her experience that contributes to, even counters, dominant stories about illness, aging as a burden, and parental care and love.[89] Other examples include Devika Chawla's reflections on the significance of lost/found objects and David Kottenstette's vulnerable account of a gay man's life after the sudden death of his partner.[90] Although Chawla and Kottenstette do not cite academic literature, the cultural connections and complexities are teased out in deliberate writing and careful and compelling descriptions.[91] All of these accounts include others: the numerous others Pelias encounters in a day; Carolyn's mother, hospital staff, other parents, as well as larger discourses of caretaking and aging; how the assassination of Indira Gandhi affected Chawla's life, her family's life, and broader Hindu and Sikh communities; and Kottenstette's partner and others' cruel reactions to his partner's death. These articles are not just about one-self; they are about one's self-in-relation.

*

With this chapter, we have espoused ways to incorporate ethnographic techniques into our work. Go into the field, do participant observation, and take field notes—or not. Informally or formally engage others—or not. Analyze popular and academic texts related to your topic—or not. Although no easy or rigid formula exists for including the ethno in your autoethnographic work, we strongly suggest learning what ethnography is and how to do it; then incorporate ethnographic techniques into your work; and then, maybe, tell readers how you did so. Autoethnography isn't just about you; if you think it is, be prepared to be assessed accordingly.

NOTES

1 Heewon Chang, *Autoethnography as Method* (Walnut Creek, CA: Left Coast Press, 2008), 43.
2 Karl E. Weick, "Systemic Observational Methods," in *Handbook of Social Psychology: Theory and Method*, 3rd ed., eds., Gardner Lindzey and Elliot Aronson (New York: Random House, 1985), 567–634.
3 John Van Maanen, *Tales of the Field: On Writing Ethnography* (Chicago, IL: The University of Chicago Press, 1988), ix.
4 Eric M. Eisenberg, "Building a Mystery: Toward a New Theory of Communication and Identity," *Journal of Communication* 51, no. 3 (2009), 534–552, https://doi.org/10.1111/j.1460-2466.2001.tb02895.x. Eisenberg describes the surround as "the social world already in motion, complete with preexisting languages, relationships, social networks, and culturally

prescribed patterns of behavior." Eisenberg posits six aspects of the surround: cultural, societal, economic, interpersonal, spiritual, and biological.

5 Wolcott, *Ethnography Lessons.*

6 Karen Lee Ashcraft, *Wronged and Dangerous: Viral Masculinity and the Populist Pandemic* (Bristol: Bristol University Press, 2022), 1.

7 William Foote Whyte, "On Making the Most of Participant Observation," *The American Sociologist* 14, no. 1 (1979), 56–66, http://www.jstor.org/stable/27702360.

8 Clifford Geertz, "Deep Hanging Out," *New York Review of Books* (1998), https://www.nybooks.com/articles/1998/10/22/deep-hanging-out/.

9 William Foote Whyte, *Street Corner Society: The Social Structure of an Italian Slum* (Chicago, IL: University of Chicago Press, 2012).

10 Karen Ho, *Liquidated: An Ethnography of Wall Street* (Durham, NC: Duke University Press, 2009).

11 Pete Simi and Robert Futrell, *American Swastika: Inside the White Power Movement's Hidden Spaces of Hate*, 2nd ed. (Lanham, MD: Rowman & Littlefield, 2015).

12 Lauraine Leblanc, *Pretty in Punk: Girls' Gender Resistance in a Boys' Subculture* (New Brunswick, NJ: Rutgers University Press, 1999).

13 Andrew F. Herrmann, "Communication and Ritual at the Comic Book Shop: The Convergence of Organizational and Popular Cultures," *Journal of Organizational Ethnography* 7, no. 3 (2018), 285–301, https://doi.org/10.1108/JOE-06-2017-0027.

14 Ellis, "'There Are Survivors,'" 719.

15 Robin M. Boylorn, *Sweetwater: Black Women and Narratives of Resilience* (New York: Peter Lang, 2013); Goodall, *Casing a Promised Land*; Goodall, *A Need to Know*; Krizek, "From Cooperstown to Carmel: A Wingman's Stories of Nick Trujillo, or 'Playing Catch with Nick Trujillo.'" *Storytelling, Self, Society* 10, no. 1 (2014), 26–44, https://doi.org/10.1353/sss.2014.a813161. Jonathan Skinner, ed., *The Interview: An Ethnographic Approach* (London: Berg, 2012).

16 See Jacquelyn Allen-Collinson and John C. Hockey, "'Switch Off the Headwork!': Everyday Organisational Crossings in Identity Transformations from Academic to Distance Runner," in *The Routledge International Handbook of Organizational Autoethnography*, ed., Andrew F. Herrmann (New York: Routledge, 2020), 313–326; Luigi Gariglio, "On Fieldwork in the Hybrid Field: A 'Methodological Novel' on Ethnography, Photography, Fiction, and Creative Writing," *Qualitative Research* (2023), https://doi.org/10.1177/14687941221149584; Brinda India Jegatheesan, "I See the Stars: An Autoethnographer Speaks on Fieldwork and Flashbacks," *Qualitative Inquiry* 11, no. 5 (2005), 667–688, https://doi.org/10.1177/1077800405276810.

17 Karina Kuschnir, "Ethnographic Drawing: Eleven Benefits of Using a Sketchbook for Fieldwork," *Visual Ethnography* 5, no. 1 (2016), 103–134, https://doi.org/10.12835/ve2016.1-0060.

18 Marieke van Eijk, "Studying Health Care Institutions: Using Paperwork as Ethnographic Research Tools," *Ethnography* 23, no. 4 (2022), 539–558, https://doi.org/10.1177/1466138119871583.

19 Robin M. Boylorn, "As Seen on TV: An Autoethnographic Reflection on Race and Reality Television," *Critical Studies in Media Communication* 25, no. 4 (2008), 413–433, https://doi.org/10.1080/15295030802327758; Tasha R. Rennels, "Taking Out the Trash: Using Critical Autoethnography to Challenge Representations of White Working-Class People in Popular Culture," *The Popular Culture Studies Journal* 3, no. 1–2 (2015), 349–363; Colin

Whitworth, "Sissy That Performance Script! The Queer Pedagogy of *RuPaul's Drag Race*," in *RuPaul's Drag Race and the Shifting Visibility of Drag Culture*, eds., Neil Brennan and David Gudelunas (London: Palgrave Macmillan, 2017), 137–151, https://doi.org/10.1007/978-3-319-50618-0_10.

20 Leblanc, *Pretty in Punk*, 26–27.

21 Alexandra Plows, *Messy Ethnographies in Action* (Wilmington, DE: Vernon Press, 2018), xiii.

22 Geertz, "Deep Hanging Out."

23 Erving Goffman, *Where the Action Is* (Bristol: Lane, Penguin Press, 1969).

24 Boylorn, *Sweetwater*; Brommel, "Sensemaking in the Dialysis Clinic"; Wilkes, "Dialogic Autoethnography."

25 Robert M. Emerson, Rachel I. Fretz, and Linda L. Shaw, *Writing Ethnographic Fieldnotes*, 2nd ed. (Chicago, IL: University of Chicago Press, 2011); Lynne Hume and Jane Mulcock, *Anthropologists in the Field: Cases in Participant Observation* (New York: Columbia University Press, 2004); Danny L. Jorgensen, *Participant Observation: A Methodology for Human Studies* (Newbury Park: SAGE Publications, 1989); Judith Marti, *Starting Fieldwork: Methods and Experiences* (Long Grove, IL: Waveland Press, 2016); Van Maanen, *Tales of the Field.*

26 Wendy Leeds-Hurwitz, "Ethnography," in *Handbook of Language and Social Interaction*, eds., Kristine L. Fitch and Robert E. Sanders (New York: Psychology Press, 2004), 327–353.

27 Goffman, *Presentation of Self in Everyday Life.*

28 Ellis, "Emotional and Ethical Quagmires in Returning to the Field."

29 Jules Henry, *Pathways to Madness* (New York: Vintage Books, 1965).

30 Robert L. Krizek, "The Ethnography of Events: A Narrative Analysis of Non-Routine Public Events," PhD diss. (Arizona State University, 1995), https://www.proquest.com/dissertations-theses/ethnography-events-narrative-analysis-non-routine/docview/304164547/se-2.

31 Robert L. Krizek, "Goodbye Old Friend: A Son's Farewell to Comiskey Park," *OMEGA: Journal of Death and Dying* 25 (1992), 87–93. https://doi.org/10.2190/P5RF-G50T-MEYY-P8KU. Robert L. Krizek, "Remembrances and Expectations: The Investment of Identity in the Changing of Comiskey," *Elysian Fields Quarterly* 11, no. 2 (1992), 30–50.

32 Nick Trujillo and Bob Krizek, "Emotionality in the Stands and in the Field: Expressing Self through Baseball," *Journal of Sport and Social Issues* 18, no. 4 (1994), 303–325, https://doi.org/10.1177/019372394018004002.

33 Katherine Miller, "The Experience of Emotion in the Workplace: Professing in the Midst of Tragedy," *Management Communication Quarterly* 15, no. 4 (2002), 571–600, https://doi.org/10.1177/0893318902154003.

34 Robert L. Krizek, "Sport as Ethnography: An Embodied Practice Meets an Embodied Method," in *Defining Sport Communication*, ed., Andrew C. Billings (New York: Routledge, 2017), 69.

35 "Why Taylor Swift Tickets Are So Expensive." *Re-Edition Magazine*, https://www.reedition-magazine.com/to-the-minute/why-taylor-swift-tickets-are-so-expensive.

36 Herrmann, "Daniel Amos and Me."

37 Krizek, "The Ethnography of Events."

38 Robert L. Krizek, "Ethnography as the Excavation of Personal Narrative," in *Expressions of Ethnography: Novel Approaches to Qualitative Methods*, ed., Robin Clair (Albany: State University New York Press, 2003), 141–151.

39 Billy Huff, "On [Be]coming in Boystown," *Journal of Autoethnography* 3, no. 4 (2022), 427–444, https://doi.org/10.1525/joae.2022.3.4.427.

40 Deborah Jump, "They Didn't Know Whether to 'Fuck Me or Fight Me': An Ethnographic Account of North Town Boxing Gym," in *Mischief, Morality and Mobs*, ed., Dick Hobbs (New York: Routledge, 2016), 11–28.
41 Atay, "What Is Cyber or Digital Autoethnography?"; Michelle Calka, "Polymediation: The Relationship between Self and Media," in *Beyond New Media: Discourse and Critique in a Polymediated Age*, eds., Art Herbig, Andrew F. Herrmann and Adam W. Tyma (Lanham, MD: Lexington, 2015), 15–30.
42 Tabitha Hart, "Online Ethnography," in *The International Encyclopedia of Communication Research Methods*, ed., Jörg Matthes (New York: John Wiley & Sons, 2017), 1–8, https://doi.org/10.1002/9781118901731.iecrm0172.
43 Deniz Tunçalp and Patrick L. Lê, "(Re) Locating Boundaries: A Systematic Review of Online Ethnography," *Journal of Organizational Ethnography* 3, no. 1 (2014), 59, https://doi.org/10.1108/JOE-11-2012-0048.
44 Maha Bali, "Organizing Autoethnography on the Internet: Models and Challenges," in *The Routledge International Handbook of Organizational Autoethnography*, ed., Andrew F. Herrmann (New York: Routledge, 2020), 470–483; Herrmann, "People Get Emotional about Their Money"; Lori Kendall, *Hanging Out in the Virtual Pub: Masculinities and Relationships Online* (Berkeley: University of California Press, 2002); Annette N. Markham, *Life Online: Researching Real Experience in Virtual Space* (Thousand Oaks, CA: Altamira, 1998).
45 Liz Przybylski, *Hybrid Ethnography: Online, Offline, and In Between* (Thousand Oaks, CA: Sage Publications, 2020); Dunn and Myers, "Contemporary Autoethnography *Is* Digital Autoethnography."
46 Nancy K. Baym, *Personal Connections in the Digital Age* (New York: John Wiley & Sons, 2015); Zizi Papacharissi, *A Private Sphere: Democracy in a Digital Age* (New York: Polity, 2010); Howard Rheingold, *The Virtual Community, Revised Edition: Homesteading on the Electronic Frontier* (Cambridge: MIT Press, 2000); Sherry Turkle, *Life on the Screen* (New York: Simon and Schuster, 2011).
47 Herrmann, "The Historical and Hysterical Narratives"; Dvora Yanow, "Organizational Ethnography and Methodological Angst: Myths and Challenges in the Field," *Qualitative Research in Organizations and Management* 4, no. 2 (2009), 188, https://doi.org/10.1108/17465640910978427.
48 Bronislaw Malinowski, "Ethnology and the Study of Society," *Economica* 6, October (1922), 208, https://doi.org/10.2307/2548314.
49 Shulamit Reinharz, *On Becoming a Social Scientist: From Survey Research and Participant Observation to Experimental Analysis* (San Francisco, CA: Transaction Books, 1985), 95.
50 Dwight Conquergood, "Performing as a Moral Act: Ethical Dimensions of the Ethnography of Performance," *Text and Performance Quarterly* 5, no. 2 (1985), 6, https://doi.org/10.1080/10462938509391578.
51 The last two paragraphs have been adapted from Tony E. Adams, "Craving Bigger Bodies: Size, Sexuality, and Becoming Larger," in *Consuming Bodies: Body Commodification and Embodiment in Late Capitalist Societies*, eds., Jackie Hogan and Sarah Whetstone (New York: Routledge, forthcoming).
52 Ellis, "Telling Secrets, Revealing Lives"; Carolyn Ellis and Chris Patti. "With Heart: Compassionate Interviewing and Storytelling with Holocaust Survivors," *Storytelling, Self, Society* 10, no. 1 (2014), 93–118, https://doi.org/10.13110/storselfsoci.10.1.0093; Lisa M. Tillmann, *In Solidarity: Friendship, Family, and Activism Beyond Gay and Straight* (New York: Routledge, 2014).

53 Keyan G. Tomaselli, Lauren Dyll-Myklebust, and Sjoerd van Grootheest, “Personal/Political Interventions via Autoethnography: Dualisms, Knowledge, Power and Performativity in Research Relations,” in *The Handbook of Autoethnography*, eds., Stacy Holman Jones, Tony E. Adams, and Carolyn Ellis (Walnut Creek, CA: Left Coast Press, 2013), 576–598.
54 Ellis, “Telling Secrets.”
55 Barbara J. Jago, “Chronicling an Academic Depression,” *Journal of Contemporary Ethnography* 31, no. 6 (2002), 738, https://doi.org/10.1177/089124102237823. See also Barbara J. Jago, “Risk and Reward in Autoethnography: Revisiting ‘Chronicling an Academic Depression,’” in *Handbook of Autoethnography*, eds., Tony E. Adams, Stacy Holman Jones, and Carolyn Ellis (New York: Routledge, 2022), 383–390.
56 Robin M. Boylorn, “Bitter Sweet(water): Autoethnography, Relational Ethics, and the Possible Perpetuation of Stereotypes,” in *Doing Autoethnography*, eds., Sandra L. Pensoneau-Conway, Tony E. Adams, and Derek M. Bolen (Rotterdam: Sense, 2017), 7–17.
57 Keith Berry, *Bullied: Tales of Torment, Identity, and Youth* (New York: Routledge, 2016); Carolyn Ellis, “Telling Secrets.”
58 See Sarah J. Tracy, *Qualitative Research Methods: Collecting Evidence, Crafting Analysis, and Communicating Impact* (Hoboken, NJ: Wiley Blackwell, 2020).
59 Christopher N. Poulos, *Accidental Ethnography: An Inquiry into Family Secrecy*, 2nd ed. (New York: Routledge, 2018), 47.
60 Paragraph revised from Adams, *Narrating the Closet*, 161–162.
61 Stephens, “Homicide by Police.”
62 Zachary M. Schrag, *Ethical Imperialism: Institutional Review Boards and the Social Sciences, 1965–2009* (Baltimore, MD: Johns Hopkins University Press, 2010).
63 Tony E. Adams and Keith Berry, “Size Matters: Performing (Il)logical Male Bodies on FatClub.com,” *Text and Performance Quarterly* 33, no. 4 (2013), 308–325, https://doi.org/10.1080/10462937.2013.818704.
64 See Bochner, “Notes toward an Ethics of Memory”; Ellis, “Telling Secrets”; Ellis, “Emotional and Ethical Quagmires”; Tillmann-Healy, “Friendship as Method”; Stephen Andrew, *Searching for an Autoethnographic Ethic* (New York: Routledge, 2017); Jillian A. Tullis, “Self and Others: Ethics in Autoethnographic Research,” in *Handbook of Autoethnography*, 2nd ed., eds., Tony E. Adams, Stacy Holman Jones, and Carolyn Ellis (New York: Routledge, 2022), 101–113.
65 Art Herbig and Andrew F. Herrmann, “Polymediated Narrative: The Case of the Supernatural Episode ‘Fan Fiction,’” *International Journal of Communication* 10 (2016), 1–18, http://ijoc.org/index.php/ijoc/article/view/4397.
66 Herrmann, “Communicating, Sensemaking, and (Dis)Organizing”; Andrew F. Herrmann and Art Herbig, “Returning to Kolchak: Polymediated Narrative, Discourse, and Supernatural Drama,” *International Journal of Communication* 12 (2018), 222–240, https://ijoc.org/index.php/ijoc/article/view/7827/2224; Art Herbig, Andrew F. Herrmann, Alix R. Watson, A. W. Tyma, and J. Miller, “Critical Rhetoric and Collaboration: Missing Principle # 9 and ProfsDoPop.com,” *International Journal of Communication* 14 (2020), 885–898, https://ijoc.org/index.php/ijoc/article/view/8676/2967.
67 As an ethical consideration, I decided not to cite the author here. We all make mistakes and errors in judgment. Remember, citation is political.
68 Tami Spry, “Performing Autoethnography: An Embodied Methodological Praxis,” *Qualitative inquiry* 7, no. 6 (2001), 706–732, https://doi.org/10.1177/107780040100700605.
69 The original phrase is italicized. Ronald J. Pelias, *The Creative Qualitative Researcher: Writing that Makes Readers Want to Read* (New York: Routledge, 2019), 172. Adams and Herrmann,

"Expanding Our Autoethnographic Future"; Norman K. Denzin and Michael D. Giardina, "Introduction: The Elephant in the Room, OR Advancing the Conversation about the Politics of Evidence," in *Qualitative Inquiry and the Politics of Evidence*, eds., Norman K. Denzin and Michael D. Giardina (Walnut Creek, CA: Left Coast Press, 2008), 9–52.

70 Rambo Ronai, "Multiple Reflections of Child Sex Abuse."

71 Tony E. Adams, "Organizing Desire: The Queer Bar," in *The Routledge International Handbook of Organizational Autoethnography*, ed., Andrew F. Herrmann (New York: Routledge, 2020), 225–239. Sanne Frandsen and R. Duncan M. Pelly, "Organizational Resistance and Autoethnography," in *The Routledge International Handbook of Organizational Autoethnography*, ed., Andrew F. Herrmann (New York: Routledge, 2020), 252–268; Kari Lerum, "No One Cites Obituaries: Extricating from Sticky Grief," *Journal of Autoethnography* 4, no. 2 (2023), 255–274, https://doi.org/10.1525/joae.2023.4.2.255; Michaela D. E. Meyer, "The Cost of Winning the Pregnancy Lottery: An Autoethnographic Account of How My Life Was Consumed by Secondary Infertility," *Journal of Autoethnography* 3, no. 4, 544–560, https://doi.org/10.1525/joae.2022.3.4.544. Townsend, "A Groundhog Moment."

72 Tillmann-Healy, "A Secret Life in a Culture of Thinness"; Lisa M. Tillmann-Healy, "Friendship as Method," *Qualitative Inquiry* 9, no. 5 (2003), 729–749, https://doi.org/10.1177/1077800403254894.

73 Carolyn Ellis, "'I Just Want to Tell MY Story': Mentoring Students about Relational Ethics in Writing about Intimate Others," in *Ethical Futures in Qualitative Research: Decolonizing the Politics of Knowledge*, eds., Norman K. Denzin and Michael D Giardina (London: Routledge, 2016), 209–228.

74 Ellis, "'I Hate My Voice.'"

75 Ellis, "Sociological Introspection."

76 Anna Denejkina, "Exo-Autoethnography: An Introduction," *Forum Qualitative Sozialforschung/Forum: Qualitative Social Research* 18, no. 3 (2017), https://doi.org/10.17169/fqs-18.3.2754; Anna Denejkina, "Exo-Autoethnography as Method for Research on Intergenerational Trauma Transmission," in *Handbook of Autoethnography*, 2nd ed., eds., Tony E. Adams, Stacy Holman Jones, and Carolyn Ellis (New York: Routledge, 2022), 179–187.

77 Katherine J. Denker, "Power, Emotional Labor, and Intersectional Identity at Work: I Would Not Kiss My Boss But I Did Not Speak Up," in *Organizational Autoethnographies: Power and Identity in Our Working Lives*, ed., Andrew F. Herrmann (New York: Routledge, 2017), 32–52; Donna White, "Behind Bars: An Investigation of Bartenders in Missouri-St. Louis," *Lambda Alpha Journal* 30 (2000), 56–86, https://soar.wichita.edu/bitstream/handle/10057/1902/LAJv.30_.p56-86.pdf; Adams, "Organizing Desire."

78 Keith Berry, "The Ethnographic Choice: Why Ethnographers Do Ethnography," *Cultural Studies↔Critical Methodologies* 11, no. 2 (2011), 165–177; Jacquelyn Allen-Collinson, "Autoethnography as the Engagement of Self/Other, Self/Culture, Self/Politics, Selves/Futures," in *Handbook of Autoethnography*, eds., Stacy Holman Jones, Tony E. Adams, and Carolyn Ellis (Walnut Creek, CA: Left Coast Press, 2013), 281–299; Amber Esping, "Autoethnography and Existentialism: The Conceptual Contributions of Viktor Frankl," *Journal of Phenomenological Psychology* 41, no. 2 (2010), 201–215, https://doi.org/10.1163/156916210X532126; Alec Grant, ed., *Writing Philosophical Autoethnography* (New York: Routledge, 2024); Helen Woodley, "The Use of Kierkegaard as a Stimulus for Autoethnographical Journal Writing," *Journal of Autoethnography* 3, no. 4 (2022), 459–474, https://doi.org/10.1525/joae.2022.3.4.459. Andrew F. Herrmann, "Autoethnography as Acts of Love," in *Handbook of Autoethnography*,

2nd ed., eds., Tony E. Adams, Stacy Holman Jones, and Carolyn Ellis (New York: Routledge, 2022), 67–78.

79 Jon Peterson, *The Elusive Shift: How Role-Playing Games Forged Their Identity* (Cambridge: MIT Press, 2020); Michael J. Tresca, *The Evolution of Fantasy Role-Playing Games* (Jefferson, NC: McFarland, 2014); Jon Peterson, *Game Wizards: The Epic Battle for Dungeons & Dragons* (Cambridge: MIT Press, 2021).

80 Lisa A. DeRenard and Linda Mannik, "Alienation and the Game Dungeons and Dragons," *Psychological Reports* 66, no. 3_suppl (1990), 1219–1222, https://doi.org/10.2466/pr0.1990.66.3c.1219; Kurt Lancaster, "Do Role-Playing Games Promote Crime, Satanism and Suicide among Players as Critics Claim?," *Journal of Popular Culture* 28, no. 2 (1994), 67–79, https://doi.org/10.1111/j.0022-3840.1994.2802_67.x. James T. Richardson, Joel Best, and David G. Bromley, eds., *The Satanism Scare* (Piscataway, NJ: Transaction Publishers, 1991).

81 Aditya Deshbandhu, "Capturing the Holistic: The Need for Autoethnography in Game Studies," *Journal of Autoethnography* 4, no. 2 (2023), 277–282, https://doi.org/10.1525/joae.2023.4.2.277; Justin B. Hopkins, "Real? American? Hero? An Autoethnography about Playing Creatively and Cathartically with GI Joe," *American Journal of Play* 14, no. 3 (2022), 277–303, https://www.museumofplay.org/app/uploads/2022/12/14-3-Article-3-Real-American-Hero.pdf; Bonnie Nardi, *My Life as a Night Elf Priest: An Anthropological Account of World of Warcraft* (Ann Arbor: University of Michigan Press, 2010); Jason Pittman and Christopher Paul, "Seeking Fulfillment: Comparing Role-Play in Table-Top Gaming and World of Warcraft," *International Journal of Role-Playing* 1 (2008), 53–65, https://doi.org/10.33063/ijrp.vi1.187.

82 See Abby Arnold, "That Baby's Name: Birthing Autoethnographic Philanthropy, Healing and Organizational Change," in *The Routledge International Handbook of Organizational Autoethnography*, eds., Andrew F. Herrmann (New York: Routledge, 2020), 209–224; Catherine Lee, "Culture, Consent and Confidentiality in Workplace Autoethnography," *Journal of Organizational Ethnography* 7, no. 3 (2018), 302–319, https://doi.org/10.1108/JOE-06-2017-0032; Kurt Lindemann, "Working on It: Family Narratives of Masculinity, Disability, and Work-Life Balance," in *Organizational Autoethnographies: Power and Identity in Our Working Lives*, ed., Andrew F. Herrmann (New York: Routledge, 2017), 59–70; Sally Sambrook and Andrew F. Herrmann, "Organisational Autoethnography: Possibilities, Politics and Pitfalls," *Journal of Organizational Ethnography* 7, no. 3 (2018), 222–234, https://doi.org/10.1108/JOE-10-2018-075; Alix R. Watson, "Good ol' Boys and Their Analog Networks," in *Organizational Autoethnographies: Power and Identity in Our Working Lives*, ed., Andrew F. Herrmann (New York: Routledge, 2017), 125–143.

83 Marko Orel, "Workplace Autoethnography: Exploring the Place through Aspects of the Self," in Chiara Tagliaro, Marko Orel, and Ying Hua, eds., *Methodological Approaches for Workplace Research and Management* (New York: Routledge, 2023), 18–35.

84 Bryant Keith Alexander, "Performing Culture in the Classroom: An Instructional (Auto) ethnography," *Text and Performance Quarterly* 19, no. 4 (1999), 307–331, https://doi.org/10.1080/10462939909366272; Brenda J. Allen, Mark P. Orbe, and Margarita Refugia Olivas, "The Complexity of Our Tears: Dis/enchantment and (In)Difference in the Academy," *Communication Theory* 9, no. 4 (1999), 402–429, https://doi.org/10.1111/j.1468-2885.1999.tb00206.x; Bochner, "It's about Time"; Ellis, "A Meaningful Academic Life: Loving, Fulfilling, Challenging, and Flabbergasting," *Nauki o Wychowaniu. Studia Interdyscyplinarne* 8, no. 1 (2019), 243–249, http://doi.org/10.18778/2450-4491.08.16; Ellis, *Final Negotiations*;

Krizek, "Lessons: What the Hell Are We Teaching the Next Generation Anyway?," in *Fiction and Social Research: By Ice or Fire*, eds., Anna Banks and Stephen Banks (Walnut Creek, CA: AltaMira), 89–113; Miller, "The Experience of Emotion in the Workplace"; Daisy Pillay, Inbanathan Naicker, and Kathleen Pithouse-Morgan, eds., *Writing Academic Autoethnographies* (Rotterdam: Sense Publishers, 2016); Daisy Pillay, "Recreating a Graduate Supervisor through Art Making: An Autoethnographic Study," *Journal of Autoethnography* 1, no. 1 (2020), 99–104, https://doi.org/10.1525/joae.2020.1.1.99. Pelias, "The Critical Life"; Ronald J. Pelias, "The Academic Tourist: An Autoethnography," *Qualitative Inquiry* 9, no. 3 (2003), 369–373, https://doi.org/10.1177/1077800403009003003. Ronald J. Pelias, *A Methodology of the Heart: Evoking Academic and Daily Life* (Lanham, MD: AltaMira, 2004).

85 Art Herbig, "Understanding Privilege in a Pandemic: The Small Systems that Perpetuate the Large Structures," *Journal of Autoethnography* 2, no. 2 (2021), 242–247, https://doi.org/10.1525/joae.2021.2.2.242; Cortes Santiago, Ileana, Nastaran Karimi, and Zaira R. Arvelo Alicea, "Neoliberalism and Higher Education: A Collective Autoethnography of Brown Women Teaching Assistants," *Gender and Education* 29, no. 1 (2017), 48–65, https://doi.org/10.1080/09540253.2016.1197383; Herrmann, '"I Know I'm Unlovable'"; Daisy Pillay, "Recreating a Graduate Supervisor through Art Making"; Brian Johnston, "Framing Stories from the Academic Margins: Documentary as Qualitative Inquiry and Critical Community Engagement," in Andrew F. Herrmann, ed., *The Routledge International Handbook of Organizational Autoethnography* (New York: Routledge, 2020), 437–456; Christopher N. Poulos, "Transgressions," *International Review of Qualitative Research* 3, no. 1 (2010), 67–88, https://doi.org/10.1525/irqr.2010.3.1.67; Christopher N. Poulos, "Trouble in Paradise," *International Review of Qualitative Research* 12, no. 3 (2019), 268–277, https://doi.org/10.1525/irqr.2019.12.3.268; Sarah Stahlke, "Reflections on the Role of the Supervisor of an Autoethnographic Project," *Journal of Autoethnography* 1, no. 4 (2020), 388–394, https://doi.org/10.1525/joae.2020.1.4.388; Danielle M. Stern and Linda D. Manning, "Grieving Kathy: An Interactional Autoethnography of Cultivating Sustainable Organizations," in *The Routledge International Handbook of Organizational Autoethnography*, ed., Andrew F. Herrmann (New York: Routledge, 2020), 271–286;
Diana Wandix-White, "The Impact of Teacher Student (Dis)Connection on Black Student and Teacher Identity Development in U.S. Schools," *Journal of Autoethnography* 1, no. 3 (2020), 234–251, https://doi.org/10.1525/joae.2020.1.3.234.

86 Anderson, "Analytic Autoethnography": Anderson, "On Apples, Oranges, and Autopsies"; Anderson and Glass-Coffin, "I Learn by Going"; Anderson, "Time Is of the Essence"; Anderson, "Garfinkeling in Real Life."

87 Anderson and Glass-Coffin, "I Learn by Going."

88 Anderson, "Time Is of the Essence."

89 Carolyn Ellis, "Maternal Connections," in *Composing Ethnography: Alternative Forms of Qualitative Writing*, eds., Carolyn Ellis and Arthur P. Bochner (Walnut Creek, CA: AltaMira Press, 1996), 240–243.

90 Devika Chawla, "The Essay," *Journal of Autoethnography* 1, no. 4 (2020), 347–353, https://doi.org/10.1525/joae.2020.1.4.347; David Kottenstette, "Portrait at an Exhibition."

91 Paragraph revised from Adams et al., "Making Sense and Taking Action," 5.

Conclusion

Practical Advice and a Few Warnings

Autoethnography isn't easy. It isn't merely a way to add personal experience to a project or a license to write in first-person voice.

To do good autoethnography, one must understand the graphy, the auto, and the ethno. One must understand how autobiographers (and life writers) work, what ethnographers do, and how research and representation intertwine. "To us, ethnography is writing," Humphreys and Watson state. "The ethnography is the account."[1]

To do good autoethnography, one must identify important experiences, discern the meaning of these experiences, and make a case why others should care about these experiences. Events such as going to a grocery store, or riding a bus, or walking a dog, or working with a therapist, or teaching a course aren't necessarily special. Did a revelation occur while doing these tasks? Did you experience something news-worthy others need to know? Just because something happened doesn't mean we have to publish it, or that others will care about it. We may not care if others care, but if we do care about our work being read, understood, used, cited, purchased, and shared then we need to have a purpose for writing and make sure we write well.

To do good autoethnography, one must care about words, message design and distribution, the soundness of arguments, and how to balance impression management with vulnerable disclosures. One must know how to craft compelling descriptions, which terms to avoid, and what aesthetic flourishes might distract and detract from one's account. One must know how to story and storify experience and make sure our stories cohere and ring true.

To do good autoethnography, one should consider if and why they are frustrated or fascinated by certain texts, who else wrote about similar topics, whether they will do fieldwork, or interview or observe others, and how others might be implicated by their texts.

To do good autoethnography, one must embrace being homo assessors: we dwell in assessment across nearly every context—we make choices about what we pursue and what we want to avoid—and, in the case of impression management, we think about how others might assess us. Such recognition allows us to determine whose feedback matters and whose doesn't, as well as pushes us to assess ourselves, not only for the content of our autoethnographic projects—one's vulnerable assessment of self is how autoethnography often begins—but also to make the best projects possible.

DOI: 10.4324/9781003281771-6

To do good autoethnography, one must recognize that autoethnography isn't easy or easier than other methods for doing social research. If you think it is easy, then good luck.

*

When we launched the *Journal of Autoethnography*, we thought long and hard about the types of submissions we wanted. Obviously, we wanted people to submit autoethnographic projects. But we didn't want to unduly limit the types of autoethnographies people would submit—there are always new topics to explore, new theories to engage, and new ways to represent experience. After extensive deliberation, when we launched the journal, here's what we wrote on the "Author Guidelines" page:

> JoAE welcomes submissions that foreground autoethnography as a method of inquiry; highlight themes and issues of past and contemporary autoethnographic research; discuss theoretical, ethical, and/or pedagogical issues in autoethnography; and/or identify future directions for autoethnography.

The following criteria will be used to evaluate manuscripts:

- The use and application of autoethnography
- Original contribution to autoethnographic scholarship
- Engagement with relevant autoethnographic literature
- Quality of the writing[2]

We envisioned this book as an expanded treatise on these criteria, and for any kind of autoethnographic project, whether a journal article or a book-length manuscript. Submissions that don't meet any of these requirements are often desk rejected. Reviewers volunteer their time, and we do not want to waste their voluntary time reading a poorly constructed text. Further, we try not to be cruel with rejection—it can sting. We know—we too get our work rejected.

When we reject a manuscript, we try to offer constructive feedback. Here are a few sample statements we include in the decision letter:

> The manuscript resembles a life chronology—in content and form, there is too much "I did this and this and this" and "this happened, then this happened, then this happened." Sharing personal experience isn't necessarily autoethnography, and the use of first-person voice does not make a project autoethnographic.

> We need more concrete and focused experiences. Use dialogue. Take us into specific contexts. You write a lot about what you did, but we want to read about why you think you did what you did and how you feel about what you did. The manuscript should foreground formative and meaningful experiences, experiences from which you use to make valuable insights and arguments. We also encourage you to spend more time with the graphy aspect of the manuscript; focus on crafting a compelling story.

> The manuscript does not engage relevant autoethnographic research. Although engagement with autoethnographic research isn't always necessary, for this manuscript it is needed, given that many autoethnographers have also written about similar topics.
>
> The manuscript offers too much esoteric theorizing. It also introduces a breadth of topics without nuanced self-reflexive depth. Given the limited space, focus on fewer theories and topics.
>
> There are too many stylistic choices made in the text: Some words are italicized, some are underlined, and some are boldfaced. There's an array of indents and various spacings. The manuscript uses multiple fonts, font sizes, and font colors. We do not know what these choices mean, and the text is difficult to read and understand.
>
> This isn't what we would call autoethnography—your experiences, as the author, are not included in the manuscript. To us, the manuscript reads as a traditional ethnographic or interview project. For manuscripts to this journal, we expect to read a moderate amount about the subjectivity and stories of the author, not solely about the subjectivity and stories of others.
>
> There needs to be a more explicit "So what?" statement in the manuscript. Show and tell us why we/readers should care about your experiences.
>
> We encourage you to read our brief introductions to each volume of the journal. In these, you'll notice key aspects of our editorial vision and what we expect of manuscripts.

As we hope you can notice in this feedback, we use several criteria we outlined throughout the book to assess a manuscript. When we write a specific letter, we edit the letter appropriately. We often include more detailed suggestions and helpful examples. Sometimes we discuss storifying vignettes or adding dialogue to certain sections. Sometimes we suggest reading more autoethnographies about a topic and we provide the citations and links to these works. Sometimes we recommend streamlining the use of Buber, Bakhtin, Heidegger, Sartre, Kierkegaard, and Derrida to two of these philosophers to help with focus and cohesion. If a manuscript isn't necessarily autoethnography but rather good qualitative research, we suggest sending the manuscript to a broader qualitative journal such as *Departures in Critical Qualitative Research*, *Qualitative Inquiry*, or *The Qualitative Report* or to a journal related to the topic of the manuscript such as *Journal of Loss and Trauma*, *Qualitative Research in Organizations and Management*, or the *International Journal of Qualitative Studies in Education*. We want to help authors make the submission the best it can be regardless of whether they publish in the journal. We are also mindful of submissions we receive from students. We don't want to discourage folks who are getting their heads and hearts wrapped around doing autoethnography.

Further, we try to be mindful of Sparkes' warning about creating lists of criteria, especially if these lists become "rigid and inflexible."[3] We have some rigid and inflexible criteria—an autoethnographic manuscript must prioritize the auto, ethno, and graphy: it must foreground the author's personal experience, it must consider/engage others, and it must be a compelling read. But how an author chooses to accomplish these tasks is much less firm, more flexible, and increasingly subjective.

As we conclude, we want to offer a few final observations to synthesize the advice we offer throughout this book.

CONCERNS ABOUT "COLLABORATIVE AUTOETHNOGRAPHY"

In the past few years, we have developed concerns about what some authors call "collaborative autoethnography." These texts typically consist of two or more authors doing and writing autoethnography together. At the journal, we, and reviewers, assess these submissions using the same criteria we do for all autoethnographies. Yet the mere concept of collaborative autoethnography introduces several dilemmas, and many of these manuscripts are rejected.[4]

Could we do "collaborative autobiography" (or collaborative life writing)? Like oxymoronic phrases such as "jumbo shrimp," "act natural," and "unbiased opinion," "collaborative autobiography" feels like an oxymoron. Autobiography privileges the self; to add another self, maybe even a third self can dilute the depth and focus of a project.

Let's shift to ethnography. Can we do "collaborative ethnography?" Can we conduct interviews or do fieldwork together? Sure, but doing so can be difficult for another person and especially difficult with three+ collaborators.

Good collaborative autobiographies are rare. Good collaborative ethnographies are rare. Good collaborative autoethnographies are very rare. When the researcher is the focus and the instrument, it takes great effort to collaborate with someone. You can't observe what they observe, feel what they feel, or explain their experiences. As Parry reminds us, we can have the same experience, but our interpretations and narratives of the experience might be vastly different.[5] We see and feel things differently, we communicate about these things differently, and we story things differently. The auto—the self, one's experience—is a core component of autoethnography and it takes great work to include two (or more!) people as the focus.

For example, we have reviewed several collaborative autoethnographies, sometimes even with five to six authors, in which each person shares a paragraph or two about their experiences. A paragraph or two—it's hard to offer thick description using such little experience *and* be able to convey the nuances and meanings of this experience. These texts feel like they began with one person saying they have one experience with [insert topic] and then they find a few others who have opinions about the topic. They each share an experience or two, assemble the experiences together, and claim the project is finished. In form and content, they read like this:

A Collaborate Autoethnography of Grocery Stores

AUTHOR 1: "I went to a grocery store. It did not sell my favorite coffee."
AUTHOR 2: "I too have been to a grocery store. The prices were fair."
AUTHOR 3: "I worked in a grocery store."
AUTHOR 4: "I was named after a grocery store."
AUTHOR 5: "I haven't been a grocery store, but I would like to go one day!"
AUTHOR 1: "Author 4, I like your name."
AUTHOR 4: "Thank you, Author 1. It was my grandmother's favorite store, and I am my grandmother's favorite. I'm sorry the store you visited did not sell your coffee."
AUTHOR 1: "I found the coffee at another store."
AUTHOR 4: "I am happy for you."
AUTHOR 2: "Author 3, was it difficult working at a grocery store?"
AUTHOR 3: "Author 2, only on weekends, when it was busy."
AUTHOR 5: "Author 3, I would like to visit the store where you worked!"
AUTHOR 3: "We should all visit the store where I worked. The employees are nice and the prices are fair."
AUTHOR 1: "Author 2, did you have to collect the grocery buggies?"
AUTHOR 2: "Sometimes. What coffee do you like?"
AUTHOR 1: "Folger's coffee."
AUTHOR 4: "I like Folger's coffee!"
AUTHOR 3: "As a child, I used to ride in the grocery carts."
AUTHOR 5: "Me too!"

Do you want to read more? Many of the so-called collaborative autoethnographies read like this. They fail to tell a compelling story, nor do they offer much depth or connection between the experiences; each author reports bits of information, and these bits are placed together without much explanation for readers. The more authors, the more so-called "collaborators," the more chance to make an unorganized mess of thin description.

Additionally, we have noticed that several collaborative autoethnographies follow the sterile introduction-literature review-methods-findings-analysis-conclusion formula. This formula further impedes the ability to write good autoethnography. Few good autoethnographies use this formula; a collaborative autoethnography really shouldn't use the formula.

Folks, do the math (didn't think we'd include more math in this book, eh?): You have about 30 pages to use for a journal article. If you use three pages for the introduction and conclusion and five pages for the literature review, method, findings, and analysis sections, you have 26 pages (3 + 5 + 5 + 5 + 5 + 3 = 26) not including references. Personal experience must be used and interrogated for good autoethnography, and yet, with collaborative texts, personal experience is often relegated to a five-page "findings" section. Not only is there limited space for each author's personal experience (a concern about the auto), but the experience that is storied and shared will likely be very thin, especially with multiple authors (a concern about the graphy). Finally, the very structure will likely make a boring read (graphy, again). We're not sure what to call these projects—we understand them more as co-authored *narratives-under-analysis* where each author uses their experiences as data. Fine, but that's not autoethnography.

If you want to do collaborative autoethnography, we suggest reviewing good collaborative autoethnographies that maintain an appropriate focus and where the authors work to create seamless, thick, and compelling accounts of their experiences.[6] For example, "Coming Unhinged: A Twice-Told Multivoiced Autoethnography" works as a collaborative article because it is strictly limited to *one* incident.[7] Similarly, "The IRB's Stone Wall: Rollercoaster of Doom" works because it's about *one* dilemma.[8] We also recommend Carolyn Ellis, Christine Kiesinger, and Lisa Tillmann's work with interactive interviewing,[9] Carolyn Ellis and Jerry Rawicki's work with collaborative witnessing,[10] Carolyn and Art's collaborative writing in *Evocative Autoethnography*,[11] and even the work done by Nick Trujillo as he was teaching his graduate students to write and publish collaborative ethnographies.[12]

Once you have your project, maintain a narrow focus, and make sure the experiences shared are only related to that focus. The larger the scope and grander the topic, the more difficult collaboration will be. Also attend to graphy—make it a compelling read, break out of the introduction-literature review-method-findings-analysis-conclusion formula, and write it as a story so that it falls under the auspices of *narrative analysis* and not *narratives-under-analysis*.[13]

PUBLICATION AND REPUTATION

When the lead special issue editor and I (Andrew) were writing the introduction to a journal's special issue on organizational autoethnography, the primary journal editor asked us to cite an article from the previous issue of the journal. The article wasn't published yet. We hadn't read it. I was hesitant.

Why did the editor ask us to cite an article that wasn't yet published and that we hadn't read? Pressure. While there are many problems with the idea and its implementation, an academic journal's reputation is generally based on one number—its impact factor.[14] The impact factor was conceived on the idea that "a citation indicates an article has influenced someone and therefore, the more often an article is cited, the greater its influence on the scientific community."[15]

The impact factor is a simple mathematical formula (more math!). You take the number of articles in a journal that are cited over a two-year period and divide that number by the number of articles that were published in the journal over that same period. If your journal published 300 articles and those articles were cited 250 times, your impact factor is 0.83.

In the academic market, the higher the impact factor, the more presumed prestige for your journal. The more prestigious your journal, the more valuable your journal is. The more valuable your journal is, the more subscriptions you may sell and the more can you charge for it. Capitalism.

My co-editor and I succumbed. We added the citation. We shouldn't have.

Within a few weeks, a complaint was filed regarding the article we cited. The individuals written about in that article were livid. While they were given pseudonyms, they were still easily recognizable. They were also all women, mostly people of color, and in precarious academic positions and didn't have the protections of tenure. Lawyers got involved and the women demanded that the journal retract the article.

The journal editor didn't know about the submitted article's ethical issue. There's not necessarily fault there. The questionable issue was asking us to cite the article. This activity is called coercive self-citation and is used to bolster a journal's impact factor and therefore its value.[16] While there is nothing wrong with an editor or a reviewer suggesting an author read an article related to the author's topic—doing so can help the author demonstrate they're familiar with existing research (though, as Pelias warns, "Never cite someone you haven't read"[17])—coercing someone to add a reference is ethically problematic.

As soon as I realized what was happening, I emailed the lead editor of the special issue. Our introduction was going to press. We needed to delay its publication. We needed to remove all mentions of that article. We tried to stop the press to make those changes. It was too late. The citation is there.

It still irks me that I have a publication with a citation for an article that was retracted because "there was a lack of sufficient anonymization of the participants in the article."[18] I won't cite like this again, even if I am being pressured by an editor.

*

Given the use of personal experience and revelation of intimate details, if you pursue publication for your autoethnographic work, consider how readers could use your work against you. "Do not underestimate the afterlife of a published narrative," Jillian Tullis writes.[19] "Assume everyone in your story will read it," advises Carolyn Ellis.[20] Once you publicly reveal aspects of yourself, confess your vulnerabilities and failures, you cannot retract the revelations. You can become so identified with one work that the work becomes your identity for readers.

Take Ted and Alice for example. They wrote about the difficult choice they had to make about an unplanned pregnancy.

> As university professors, Alice and Ted had formulated abstract theories and strong convictions about "rights to choose." Now they were faced not with a hypothetical "What if?" but with a real "What now?" For Alice and Ted, the events of the following week were intense and emotionally charged. Each of them knew that this could be their last chance to experience parenthood and each realized the responsibility associated with the birth of a child as well. After an agonizing appraisal of their options, they decided that Alice should have an abortion. The abortion occurred 10 days after the pregnancy was confirmed.[21]

The issue isn't the writing itself, but rather what the authors share about their lives. At the time, "Ted" and "Alice" were barely veiled pseudonyms for "Art Bochner" and

"Carolyn Ellis." For some readers, they became known as the abortion-couple. "You become the story you write and publish," Ellis writes. "Nowhere for me is this more true than in this account of our decision to terminate our pregnancy. We became the couple who had an abortion and wrote about it."[22]

Andrew's first published autoethnography described how his engagement failed a month before the wedding.[23] Students have since referred to him as "Professor Break Up." And in Chapter 3, Tony assessed Shamla McLaurin's character based on her comments about homophobia, how he considers her unsafe based on the words she used, and how he would never recommend her as a social worker or therapist.

Harry Wolcott received negative responses to his writing about Sneaky Kid because he committed several research violations (e.g., misrepresenting data) and because he had a sexual affair with a kid, his only research participant.[24]

Barbara Jago shared concerns about making her struggles with depression public. She feared "risking personal and professional humiliation" and wondered how readers might assess her. She asked: "Am I undermining my credibility (as an author, teacher, human being) by the very act of testimony?"[25]

And Karl Andersson's article about "masturbation as an ethnographic method" was published in *Qualitative Research* and then retracted because Andersson described masturbating to (illegal) Japanese comics portraying children and teenage boys.[26]

Do you want to admit to being arrested or engaging in illegal activities? Do you want to share how you perpetrated sexual assault? Do you want to describe your dislike of students, or your incessant suicide ideations, or the peer who commits rampant microaggressions? Although we cannot predict how readers will react to the personal experiences we share, how they may assess our character and credibility, these examples illustrate the need for autoethnographers to be "judicious and self-protective to some degree in published work."[27] We do not have easy or definitive advice on what it means to actually be judicious and self-protective, just recognize that while you can write whatever and however you want in private, the moment you make your work public, you open your work and life to assessment. As Jago observes,

> You can't do "good" autoethnographic work without constantly questioning the ethics of your pursuit. As soon as you put that "I" on the page, you can't avoid asking if your revelations might be harmful to you or anyone else.[28]

We do not want to scare you or suggest you shouldn't share your work. Instead, recognize that when we do autoethnography, when we share personal experience, others can assess our work and life based on what we share. "The self that does the writing is a pimp who'd slit my throat for a good line," Sophie Tamas notes, "but I am crazy in love with her."[29] (Now that's a good line!) If you fear publishing certain information but feel as though you must, consider writing anonymously, or use a pseudonym, or turn to fiction.[30] Just be mindful of how you describe yourself and others; consider impression management and recognize descriptions have consequences. If you are worried about how you represent others, seek feedback from these others or from others you trust. Maybe even pursue legal counsel. Be cautious about writing about where you work and when referencing anyone by their actual name. Once you publish content, even a seemingly innocent post on social media, it may be saved and shared for days, years, and decades.

READING AND WRITING TO DISCOVER YOUR AUTHORIAL VOICE

Have you ever recorded your voice and played it back and realized your voice doesn't sound like you? That somehow your voice is different outside your head than inside your head? You're not wrong. Most of what we hear when we talk is through bone conduction; our voice makes literal vibrations inside our skulls.[31] A recording of your voice doesn't include these internal vibrations, which is why you sound different to yourself. Voice is an instrument, and we may not realize how we play it. This is one reason why, as communication professors, we ask students to practice and record multiple oral presentations—and then ask them to listen to themselves. We want students to improve their oral presentation skills, as well as have a sense of how their voice/instrument sounds.

Similarly, one way to find and develop your authorial voice is to write, and write, and write. Consider the following excerpts from three.

> There is no lying in the kitchen. And no god there either. He [sic] couldn't help you anyway. You either can–or can't–make an omelet. You either can or can't chop an onion, shake a pan, keep up with the other cooks, replicate again and again, perfectly, the dishes that need to be done. No credential, no amount of bullshit, no well-formed sentences or pleas for mercy will change the basic facts.[32]
>
> He's my husband. I'm supposed to respect him, accept him on a deeper level than accept someone I was just dating. He's the father of my kids. His demeanor is different now, but if it changed, it could change back. People say he's going to break up with me while I have tiny children, like he did with the mother of his first two children when they were infants, but no way! How he was with his other family won't be the way he is with me.[33]
>
> I have thrown in with Sting and Stewart, but now having to face the hard-core (punk) scene, the moment of truth is upon us. With the music we have in hand and the way we play, I feel as if I am smiling into a severe hailstorm with my aggression in place but my musical values at the bottom of a deep black ocean. The songs that make up our set are terrible. [...] In a nutshell, we suck.[34]

The first voice sounds experienced, no stranger to the demands of cooking. The writing is gruff, the sentences—sharp; turns of a phrase, pointed, probably like the knives in the kitchen. The second voice conveys hope and horror, someone struggling to make sense of a failing relationship; the sentences hint at tension and trepidation. The third voice is filled with desperate determination. And while all three are memoirs, Anthony Bourdain, Brittney Spears, and Andy Summers have different authorial voices.

We encourage you to learn and develop your writing voice, to consider who and what you sound like as an author. According to Mhilli,

> authorial voice is the identity of the author reflected in written discourse, where written discourse should be understood as an ever evolving and dynamic source of language features available to the writer to choose from to express their voice.[35]

Although authors influence each other, no one author sounds exactly like the other. We are both autoethnographers, but we have different authorial voices. Andrew thinks Tony's authorial voice is compassionate, while Tony thinks Andrew's authorial voice is macabre and sarcastic.

Discovering and developing your voice is extremely important if you want to write good autoethnography. There's only one way to find it—and that's by writing. A lot. Remember, this too: no one is going to give you time to write, you must make the time. Write when you are in the mood to write and learn how to write when you are not in the mood.

Further, remember what Stephen King said about becoming a writer. You need to read too. And to help you find your voice, you need to read a lot. Read books about writing—some of our favorites include Ray Bradbury,[36] Mary Karr,[37] Stephen King,[38] Anne Lamott,[39] bell hooks,[40] John Van Maanen,[41] Carolyn Ellis,[42] Kurt Vonnegut,[43] Harold L. (Bud) Goodall,[44] Ursula K. Le Guin,[45] as well as Loren Niemi and Nancy Donoval.[46] Read science fiction. Read theoretical physics. Read classic literature. Read poetry. Read romance novels. Read horror. Read erotica. Read mysteries. Read memoirs. Pick your favorite books and then analyze these books in terms of their content (what they did [not] include) and form (how they organized and represented the content). And then try to apply that analysis to your work.

Although I spend much of my life writing, most of the memoirs I (Andrew) read are not by writers about writing. Most are by musicians. As Tony shared in his opening life history, there's a connection between music and writing. Both are forms of art and take craft seriously. I find musicians' memoirs especially interesting because musicians not only hone their craft, but they also often do so in public.[47] That's nerve-wracking if you ask me. Take *One Train Later: A Memoir* by Andy Summers, the guitarist for The Police, who we quoted earlier.[48] Throughout, Summers describes themes such as his love of the guitar, how the guitar called to him, and how he plays the instrument. Sure, he mentions Sting, Jimi Hendrix, John Belushi, world tours, his interest in photography, and his family. But his memoir isn't about those things. He mentions those only as they connect to his love of the guitar. In the excerpt above, about Summers' "musical values at the bottom of a deep black ocean," describes how his new band tried fooling audiences that they were punks. (Hint: They didn't.)

I (Tony) have two favorite books: John Durham Peters' *Speaking into the Air: A History of the Idea of Communication* and Ocean Vuong's (autofiction) novel *On Earth We're Briefly Gorgeous.*[49] Peters' book offers a dense, well-researched, and brilliant discussion about various, often competing views of communication, and how many contemporary technologies emerged from a cultural desire to connect with others—not only friends and lovers but also extraterrestrials and the dead. Vuong's writing captivates me, not only in how he describes his family but also his experiences of feeling like an outsider regarding his ethnicity, nationality, and sexuality. Like Peters and Vuong, I try to merge dense theory and research with vivid and vulnerable prose, and I do so with form: I work to make my primary text accessible, closer to a fifth-grade reading level I used when writing news, and I use endnotes for citations and esoteric discussions. (I learned this technique from Stacy Holman Jones.[50])

*

You can go back in time and search out lost writing. Find works written by underrepresented groups that have been generally overlooked and silenced. For example, when working on *The Routledge International Handbook of Organizational Autoethnography*, Andrew learned he had serious gaps in his knowledge about ethnography in organizations around the turn of the 20th century. There was an entire literature written by anthropologists mostly from the first-person point of view, and quite a few called for social action. To wit:

> I was within six feet of the door when registration began. In half an hour I was fully twenty feet away, with a great wall of human beings in front of me. This plainly was no place for politeness; the fight for first place there would put a Grand Street bargain-counter crush to shame and make a football hero look to his laurels. The race was not to the strong but to the canny. Gay girls soon began to pay toll in kisses or promises and were shoved up ahead. I was beaten about for over two hours and I saw women grow dizzy and faint and drop out.[51]

Despite his background in organizational communication, ethnography, and autoethnography, he wasn't familiar with these authors. There was an entire organizational literature from the Gilded Age and the Progressive Era in the United States, some written in the first person—some with calls for action, some written by women and persons of color he never knew about.[52] What could those authors tell us? What commonalities and concerns did they have that might resonate with (organizational) autoethnographers today? In the words of Rocky Balboa, "I have gaps." We all do. We read to find them.

*

How to begin an autoethnographic project? Maybe start with those experiences that give you pause, make you go hmmm. You have questions about these experiences (why do they make you pause?) and these questions may become a reason for writing, or maybe even formal research questions. Why do you feel that way because of something that happened, what did you learn, how did you change?

Have you encountered frustrating patterns of experience—incessant questions, remarks, stares, silences, latent or blatant disregard? If so, when? Why are these experiences frustrating? And have others written about them? Show and tell us.

Have you seen a film, or listened to a podcast, or watch a YouTube clip that frustrated you, excited you? Do you have a favorite novel or work of nonfiction? What makes these texts your favorite? Analyze the form and content of these texts, determine what you like and what you don't, and then try to approach your work accordingly.

Have you completed a project in which you couldn't share your personal experiences, but wish you could have, as you had more insights to offer? If you have done research before, are there lessons from the research experience that you could share to help others with their work?

These prompts and questions might generate the start of an autoethnographic project. Take this start and spend a few minutes tomorrow writing about/around it and a few more minutes the following day. Ask yourself—what do others need to know and why might they need to know this? We're certain that several of your experiences would have a lot to teach us—the difficult part is identifying these experiences, explaining why they are meaningful, and crafting them into an enticing text. You can do it, just take care in the craft of your work.

SCENES FROM THE EDITORS (REDUX)

ANDREW: This submission connects autoethnography and Harold Garfinkel's work with ethnomethodology. It's an engaging account of an author purposefully challenging taken-for-granted social rules and expectations.

TONY: Let's send it out for review.[53]

TONY: We have received a manuscript using autoethnographic poetry. I'm not good at assessing poetry.

ANDREW: Me neither.

TONY: But I *feel* the aggravation and sadness the author conveys.

ANDREW: Let's send it to reviewers who do autoethnographic poetry.[54]

ANDREW: This author explores how their research into far-right online spaces has negatively affected their mental and physical health.

TONY: I read that one last night. It's compelling.

ANDREW: Let's send it out for review.

TONY: Cool. I know two reviewers we could ask.[55]

TONY: Have you read this manuscript? It's a gem. The reviewers loved it too.

ANDREW: Yes! The author is a brilliant writer and storyteller. I didn't want the manuscript to end.

TONY: Me neither. We get to read some beautiful work for the journal.

ANDREW: Agreed. Accept.[56]

NOTES

1 Michael Humphreys and Tony Watson, "Ethnographic Practices: From 'Writing-Up Ethnographic Research' to 'Writing Ethnography,'" in *Organizational Ethnography: Studying the Complexities of Everyday Life*, eds., Sierk Ybema, Dvaora Yanow and Frank Kamsteeg (Thousand Oaks, CA: SAGE, 2009), 40.

2 https://docs.google.com/document/d/131WfN_f7GoTu_6Mo-Uu00rPIAiA3vVr7GlmPFMsWn_w/edit.
3 Sparkes, "Autoethnography: Accept, Revise, Reject? Sparkes," 295.
4 A co-authored autoethnography is not necessarily a collaborative autoethnography; for us, co-authors can have disparate tasks with a project whereas collaboration implies doing a process together.
5 As Parry writes, "while each of us is the central character in our own stories, we are also characters in the stories of all those others with whom we are connected whether by marriage, family, friendship, or simply by being an inhabitant of the earth." Alan Parry, "A Universe of Stories," *Family Process* 30, no. 1 (1991), 6, https://doi.org/10.1111/j.1545-5300.1991.00037.x.
6 See David Carless and Kitrina Douglas, "Collaborative Autoethnography: From Rhythm and Harmony to Shared Stories and Truths," in *Handbook of Autoethnography*, 2nd ed., eds., Tony E. Adams, Stacy Holman Jones, and Carolyn Ellis (New York: Routledge, 2022), 155–165; Dunn and Myers, "Contemporary Autoethnography *Is* Digital Autoethnography"; Klevan and Grant, *An Autoethnography of Becoming a Qualitative Researcher*; David Purnell and Daniel Wade Clarke, "Finding Our Fathers," *Qualitative Inquiry* 25, no. 9–10 (2019), 907–914, https://doi.org/10.1177/1077800418810978; Leah Vande Berg and Nick Trujillo, *Cancer and Death: A Love Story in Two Voice* (New York: Hampton Press, 2008). Although not labeled as an "autoethnography," we also suggest Irvin D. Yalom and Marilyn Yalom, *A Matter of Death and Life* (Stanford, CA: Redwood Press, 2021).
7 Carolyn Ellis, Arthur P. Bochner, Carol Rambo, Keith Berry, Hannah Shakespeare, Craig Gingrich-Philbrook, Tony E. Adams, Robert E. Rinehart, and Derek M. Bolen, "Coming Unhinged: A Twice-Told Multivoiced Autoethnography," *Qualitative Inquiry* 24, no. 2 (2018), 119–133, https://doi.org/10.1177/1077800416684874.
8 Townsend et al., "The IRB's Stone Wall."
9 Carolyn Ellis, Christine Kiesinger, and Lisa M. Tillmann-Healy, "Interactive Interviewing: Talking about Emotional Experience," in *Reflexivity & Voice*, ed., Rosanna Hertz (Thousand Oaks, CA: Sage), 119–149.
10 Carolyn Ellis and Jerry Rawicki, "More Than Mazel? Luck and Agency in Surviving the Holocaust," *Journal of Loss and Trauma* 19, no. 2 (2014); 99–120, https://doi.org/10.1080/15325024.2012.738574; Carolyn Ellis and Jerry Rawicki, "Collaborative Witnessing of Survival during the Holocaust: An Exemplar of Relational Autoethnography," *Qualitative Inquiry* 19, no. 5 (2013), 366–380, https://doi.org/10.1177/1077800413479562; Jerry Rawicki and Carolyn Ellis, "Lechem Hara (Bad Bread) Lechem Tov (Good Bread): Survival and Sacrifice during the Holocaust," *Qualitative Inquiry* 17, no. 2 (2011), 155–157, https://doi.org/10.1177/1077800410392337.
11 Bochner and Ellis, *Evocative Autoethnography*.
12 Communication Studies 298, California State University, Sacramento, "Fragments of Self at the Postmodern Bar," *Journal of Contemporary Ethnography* 26 no. 3 (1997), 251–292, https://doi.org/10.1177/089124197026003001; Communication Studies 298, California State University, Sacramento, "Shopping for Family," *Qualitative Inquiry* 5 no. 2 (1999), 147–180, https://doi.org/10.1177/107780049900500201; Nick Trujillo, "Teaching Ethnography in the Twenty-First Century Using Collaborative Learning," *Journal of Contemporary Ethnography* 28, no. 6 (1999), 705–719.
13 Bochner and Herrmann, "Practicing Narrating Inquiry II."
14 Eugene Garfield, "The History and Meaning of the Journal Impact Factor," *JAMA* 295, no. 1(2006), 90–93, https://doi.org/10.1001/jama.295.1.90.
15 Peng Dong, Marie Loh, and Adrian Mondry, "The 'Impact Factor' Revisited," *Biomedical Digital Libraries* 2, no. 1 (2005), 1–8, https://doi.org/10.1186/1742-5581-2-7.

16 Allen Wilhite, Eric A. Fong, and Seth Wilhite, "The Influence of Editorial Decisions and the Academic Network on Self-Citations and Journal Impact Factors," *Research Policy* 48, no. 6 (2019), 1513–1522, https://doi.org/10.1016/j.respol.2019.03.003.
17 The original phrase is italicized. Pelias, *The Creative Qualitative Researcher*, 172.
18 https://www.emerald.com/insight/content/doi/10.1108/JOE-07-2018-074/full/html.
19 Tullis, "Self and Others," 110, original in italics. See also Joy Castro, ed., *Family Trouble: Memoirists on the Hazards and Rewards of Revealing Family* (Lincoln: University of Nebraska Press, 2013); Caroline Brettell, *When They Read What We Write: The Politics of Ethnography* (Westport, CT: Bergin & Garvey, 1993).
20 Ellis, "Telling Secrets," 25.
21 Arthur P. Bochner and Carolyn Ellis, "Personal Narrative as a Social Approach to Interpersonal Communication," *Communication Theory* 2, no. 2 (1992), 168, https://doi.org/10.1111/j.1468-2885.1992.tb00036.x. See also Carolyn Ellis and Arthur P. Bochner, "Telling and Performing Personal Stories: The Constraints of Choice in Abortion," in *Investigating Subjectivity: Research on Lived Experience*, eds., Carolyn Ellis and Michael G. Flaherty (Newbury Park, CA: Sage, 1992), 79–101.
22 Ellis, *Revision*, 194.
23 Andrew F. Herrmann, "How Did We Get This Far Apart? Disengagement, Relational Dialectics, and Narrative Control," *Qualitative Inquiry* 13, no. 7 (2007), 989–1007, https://doi.org/10.1177/1077800407304468.
24 See Wolff-Michael Roth, "Autobiography as Scientific Text: A Dialectical Approach to the Role of Experience. Review Essay: Harry F. Wolcott (2002). Sneaky Kid and Its Aftermath," *Forum Qualitative Sozialforschung / Forum: Qualitative Social Research* 5, no. 1 (2003), Art. 9, http://nbn-resolving.de/urn:nbn:de:0114-fqs040199.
25 Jago, "Chronicling an Academic Depression," 738; Jago, "Risk and Reward in Autoethnography."
26 Andersson, "I Am Not Alone."
27 Leon Anderson and Bonnie Glass-Coffin, "I Learn by Going," 76.
28 Jago, "Chronicling an Academic Depression," 753.
29 Sophie Tamas, "The Shadow Manifesto," *International Review of Qualitative Research* 10, no. 1 (2017), 111, https://doi.org/10.1525/irqr.2017.10.1.110.
30 Anonymous, "A Letter to the Male 'Good Apples' about How You May Be Viewed by Your Female Colleagues," *Journal of Management Inquiry* 30, no. 1 (2021), 98–101, https://doi.org/10.1177/1056492620965039; Anonymous, "Cleaning a Tarnished Bloodstained Anchor?," *International Review of Qualitative Research* 12, no. 3 (2019), 215–218, https://www.jstor.org/stable/26855537; Anonymous, "Highlighting Numbers: Students Stalking Faculty and the Lasting Impacts of a Flawed System," *Journal of Autoethnography* 2, no. 2 (2021), 143–160, https://doi.org/10.1525/joae.2021.2.2.143; Sergeant Sofie, Peels Hanna, Sandvoort Henriëtte, Beau Pseudonym, Schelfhout Patrick, and De Schauwer Elisabeth, "A Collective Biography on Working Relationships in Inclusive Research Teams," *Disability & Society* (2022), 1–18, https://doi.org/10.1080/09687599.2022.2071228.
31 Dieter Maurer and Theodor Landis, "Role of Bone Conduction in the Self-Perception of Speech," *Folia Phoniatrica et Logopaedia* 42, no. 5 (1990), 226–229, https://doi.org/10.1159/000266070.
32 Anthony Bourdain, *Medium Raw* (New York: HarperCollins, 2010), 209.
33 Britney Spears, *The Woman in Me* (New York: Gallery Books, 2023), 122.
34 Andy Summers, *One Train Later* (New York: St. Martin's Press, 2006), 177.
35 Olga Mhilli, "Authorial Voice in Writing: A Literature Review," *Social Sciences & Humanities Open* 8, no. 1 (2023), 10, https://doi.org/10.1016/j.ssaho.2023.100550.

36 Ray Bradbury, *Zen in the Art of Writing* (New York: Rosetta Books, 2017).
37 Mary Kerr, *The Art of Memoir* (New York: HarperCollins, 2015).
38 King, *On Writing*.
39 Lamott, *Bird by Bird*.
40 bell hooks, *Remembered Rapture* (New York: Henry Holt and Company, 1999).
41 Van Maanen, *Tales of the Field*.
42 Ellis, *The Ethnographic I*.
43 Kurt Vonnegut and Suzanne McConnell, *Pity the Reader: On Writing with Style* (New York: Rosetta Books, 2019).
44 Goodall, Jr., *Writing Qualitative Inquiry*.
45 Ursula K. Le Guin and David Naimon, *Conversations on Writing* (Brooklyn, NY: Tin House Books, 2018).
46 Lauren Niemi and Nancy Donoval, *Point of View and the Emotional Arc of Stories: A Handbook for Writers and Storytellers* (Marion, MI: Parkhurst Brothers, 2020).
47 Stewart Copeland, *Strange Things Happen: A Life with The Police, Polo, and Pygmies* (New York: It Books, 2009); Miles Davis and Quincy Troupe, *Miles* (New York: Simon and Schuster, 1990); Ice-T, *Ice: A Memoir of Gangster Life and Redemption-from South Central to Hollywood* (London: One World, 2012); Liz Phair, *Horror Stories: A Memoir* (New York: Random House, 2019); Frank Zappa and Peter Occhiogrosso, *The Real Frank Zappa Book* (New York: Simon and Schuster, 1989).
48 Summers, *One Train Later*.
49 John Durham Peters, *Speaking Into the Air: A History of the Idea of Communication* (Chicago, IL: University of Chicago Press, 1999); Ocean Vuong, *On Earth We're Briefly Gorgeous* (New York, Penguin, 2019).
50 Stacy Holman Jones, "(M)othering Loss: Telling Adoption Stories, Telling Performativity," *Text and Performance Quarterly* 25, no. 2 (2005), 113–135, https://doi.org/10.1080/10462930500122716.
51 Annie Marion MacLean, "With Oregon Hop Pickers," *American Journal of Sociology* 15, no. 1 (1909), 83–95.
52 Frances R. Donovan, *The Woman Who Waits* (Boston, MA: RG Badger, 1920). Annie Marion MacLean, "Two Weeks in Department Stores," *American Journal of Sociology* IV, no. 6 (1899), 721–741. Annie Marion MacLean, "Life in the Pennsylvania Coal Fields with Particular Reference to Women," *American Journal of Sociology* 14, no. 3 (1908), 329–351. Annie Marion MacLean, "Four Months in a Model Factory," *Century* 106 (1923), 436–444. Anonymous, *Four Years in the Underbrush: Adventures as a Working Woman in New York* (New York: Scribners, 1921); Jane A. Stewart, "The Model Public Bath at Brookline," *American Journal of Sociology* 5, no. 4 (1900), 470–474; Amey E. Tanner, "Glimpses at the Mind of a Waitress," *American Journal of Sociology* 13, no. 1 (1907), 48–55.
53 Anderson, "Garfinkeling in Real Life."
54 Anandam Kavoori, "Re-making the World: Autoethnographic Interventions," *Journal of Autoethnography* 2, no. 3 (2023), 290–292, https://doi.org/10.1525/joae.2021.2.3.290.
55 Riley Clare Valentine, "Blankets, Rosaries, and Cajun French: The Impacts of Researching Far-Right Online Discourse on the Researcher," *Journal of Autoethnography* 4, no. 3 (2023), 315–329, https://doi.org/10.1525/joae.2023.4.3.315.
56 Kottenstette, "Portrait at an Exhibition"; Chawla, "The Essay"; Jennifer L. Adams, "Writing Others' Stories: Autoethnographic Reflections on Historical Research, Representation, and Bakhtin," *Journal of Autoethnography* 3, no. 1 (2021), 4–18, https://doi.org/10.1525/joae.2022.3.1.4; Singh et al., "Walking the Doors"; Joe Cleary, "A Suburban Funeral," *Journal of Autoethnography* 3, no. 3 (2022), https://doi.org/10.1525/joae.2022.3.3.283.

Bibliography

Abbott, Andrew. "From Causes to Events: Notes on Narrative Positivism." *Sociological Methods & Research* 20, no. 4 (1992), 428–455, https://doi.org/10.1177/0049124192020004002.

Adams, Jennifer L. "Writing Others' Stories: Autoethnographic Reflections on Historical Research, Representation, and Bakhtin." *Journal of Autoethnography* 3, no. 1 (2021), 4–18, https://doi.org/10.1525/joae.2022.3.1.4.

Adams, Tony E. "Seeking Father: Relationally Reframing a Troubled Love Story." *Qualitative Inquiry* 12, no. 4 (2006), 704–723, https://doi.org/10.1177/1077800406288607.

———. "A Review of Narrative Ethics." *Qualitative Inquiry* 14, no. 2 (2008), 175–194, https://doi.org/10.1177/1077800407304417.

———. *Narrating the Closet: An Autoethnography of Same-Sex Attraction*. Walnut Creek, CA: Left Coast Press, 2011.

———. "Frames of Homosexuality: Comparing *Los Angeles Times'* Coverage of California's Proposition 6 (1978) and Proposition 8 (2008)." *Sexuality & Culture* 17 (2013), 213–228, https://doi.org/10.1007/s12119-012-9145-2.

———. "Review: Jane Speedy (2015). Staring at the Park: A Poetic Autoethnographic Inquiry." *Forum Qualitative Sozialforschung Forum: Qualitative Social Research* 16, no. 3 (2015), https://doi.org/10.17169/fqs-16.3.2416.

———. "Foreword." In *Critical Autoethnography and Spiritual Discovery*, edited by Gresilda A. Tilley-Lubbs, xv–xvii. Oxford: Peter Lang, 2017.

———. "Autoethnographic Responsibilities." *International Review of Qualitative Research* 10, no. 1 (2017), 62–66, https://doi.org/10.1525/irqr.2017.10.1.62.

———. "Supervising, Sharing, and Evaluating Autoethnography." In *International Perspectives on Autoethnographic Research and Practice*, edited by Lydia Turner, Nigel P. Short, Alec Grant, and Tony E. Adams, 201–210. New York: Routledge, 2018.

———. "Organizing Desire: The Queer Bar." In *The Routledge International Handbook of Organizational Autoethnography*, edited by Andrew F. Herrmann, 225–239. New York: Routledge, 2020.

———. "Craving Bigger Bodies: Size, Sexuality, and Becoming Larger." In *Consuming Bodies: Body Commodification and Embodiment in Late Capitalist Societies*, edited by Jackie Hogan and Sarah Whetstone. New York: Routledge, forthcoming.

Adams, Tony E. and Keith Berry. "Size Matters: Performing (Il)logical Male Bodies on FatClub.com." *Text and Performance Quarterly* 33, no. 4 (2013), 308–325, https://doi.org/10.1080/10462937.2013.818704.

Adams, Tony E. and Derek M. Bolen, eds., "Queer Autoethnography" [Forum]. *QED: Journal in GLBTQ Worldmaking* 4 (2017), 110–197.

Adams, Tony E., Robin M. Boylorn, and Lisa M. Tillmann, eds., *Advances in Autoethnography and Narrative Inquiry: Reflections on the Legacy of Carolyn Ellis and Arthur Bochner*. New York: Routledge, 2021.

Adams, Tony E. and Andrew F. Herrmann, "Expanding Our Autoethnographic Future." *Journal of Autoethnography* 1, no. 1 (2020), 1–8, https//doi.org/10.1525/joae.2020.1.1.1.

———. "Good Autoethnography." *Journal of Autoethnography* 4, no. 1 (2023), 1–9, https://doi.org/10.1525/joae.2023.4.1.1.

Adams, Tony E. and Stacy Holman Jones, eds., "On Studying Ourselves and Others." *Liminalities: A Journal of Performance Studies* 9 (2013), http://liminalities.net/9-2/.

Adams, Tony E. and Stacy Holman Jones. "The Art of Autoethnography." In *Handbook of Arts-Based Research*, edited by Patricia Leavy, 141–164. New York: The Guilford Press, 2018.

Adams, Tony E., Stacy Holman Jones, and Carolyn Ellis. *Autoethnography.* New York: Oxford University Press, 2015.

———, eds., *Handbook of Autoethnography*, 2nd ed. New York: Routledge, 2022.

———. "Making Sense and Taking Action: Creating a Caring Community of Autoethnographers." In *Handbook of Autoethnography*, 2nd ed., edited by Tony E. Adams, Stacy Holman Jones, and Carolyn Ellis, 1–20. New York: Routledge, 2022.

Adams, Tony E. and Jimmie Manning. "Autoethnography and Family Research." *Journal of Family Theory and Review* 7 (2015), 350–366, https://doi.org/10.1111/jftr.12116.

Adams, Tony E. and Jonathan Wyatt, eds., "On (Writing) Fathers." *Qualitative Inquiry* 18 (2012), 119–209.

Alexander, Bryant Keith. "Performing Culture in the Classroom: An Instructional (Auto)ethnography." *Text and Performance Quarterly* 19, no. 4 (1999), 307–331, https://doi.org/10.1080/10462939909366272.

Allen, Brenda. *Difference Matters*, 3rd ed. Long Grove, IL: Waveland Press, 2023.

Allen, Brenda J., Mark P. Orbe, and Margarita Refugia Olivas. "The Complexity of Our Tears: Dis/enchantment and (In)Difference in the Academy." *Communication Theory* 9, no. 4 (1999), 402–429, https://doi.org/10.1111/j.1468-2885.1999.tb00206.x.

Allen-Collinson, Jacquelyn. "Autoethnography as the Engagement of Self/Other, Self/Culture, Self/Politics, Selves/Futures." In *Handbook of Autoethnography*, edited by Stacy Holman Jones, Tony E. Adams, and Carolyn Ellis, 281–299. Walnut Creek, CA: Left Coast Press, 2013.

Allen-Collinson, Jacquelyn and John C. Hockey. "'Switch Off the Headwork!': Everyday Organisational Crossings in Identity Transformations from Academic to Distance Runner." In *The Routledge International Handbook of Organizational Autoethnography*, edited by Andrew F. Herrmann, 313–326. New York: Routledge, 2020.

Allison, Dorothy. *Two or Three Things I Know for Sure.* New York: Plume, 1996.

Alshammari, Shahd. "Narrative Reflections on Losing a Companion Animal: In Memory of Flake." *Journal of Autoethnography* 1, no. 4 (2020), 378–387, https://doi.org/10.1525/joae.2020.1.4.378.

American Psychological Association. "Bias-Free Language Guidelines." *Publication Manual of the American Psychological Association*, 131–149. Washington, DC: American Psychological Association, 2020.

Anderson, Leon. "Analytic Autoethnography." *Journal of Contemporary Ethnography* 35, no. 4 (2006), 373–395, https://doi.org/10.1177/0891241605280449.

———. "On Apples, Oranges, and Autopsies: A Response to Commentators." *Journal of Contemporary Ethnography* 35, no. 4 (2006), 450–465, https://doi.org/10.1177/0891241606287395.

———. "Time is of the Essence: An Analytic Autoethnography of Family, Work, and Serious Leisure." *Symbolic Interaction* 34, no. 2 (2011), 133–157, https://doi.org/10.1525/si.2011.34.2.133.

———. "Garfinkeling in Real Life: The Candid Sociology of "Neon Leon." *Journal of Autoethnography* 2, no. 4 (2021), 369–379, https://doi.org/10.1525/joae.2021.2.4.369.

Anderson, Leon and Bonnie Glass-Coffin. "I Learn by Going: Autoethnographic Modes of Inquiry." In *Handbook of Autoethnography*, edited by Stacy Holman Jones, Tony E. Adams, and Carolyn Ellis, 57–83. Walnut Creek, CA: Left Coast Press, 2013.

Anderson, Patrick. *Autobiography of a Disease*. New York: Routledge, 2017.

Andersson, Karl. "I Am Not Alone—We Are All Alone: Using Masturbation as an Ethnographic Method in Research on *Shota* Subculture in Japan." *Qualitative Research* 22 (2022), https://doi.org/10.1177/14687941221096600.

Andrew, Stephen. *Searching for an Autoethnographic Ethic*. New York: Routledge, 2017.

Anonymous. *Four Years in the Underbrush: Adventures as a Working Woman in New York*. New York: Scribners, 1921.

Anonymous. "Cleaning a Tarnished Bloodstained Anchor?" *International Review of Qualitative Research* 12, no. 3 (2019), 215–218, https://www.jstor.org/stable/26855537.

Anonymous. "A Letter to the Male 'Good Apples' about How You May Be Viewed by Your Female Colleagues." *Journal of Management Inquiry* 30, no. 1 (2021), 98–101, https://doi.org/10.1177/1056492620965039.

Anonymous. "Highlighting Numbers: Students Stalking Faculty and the Lasting Impacts of a Flawed System." *Journal of Autoethnography* 2, no. 2 (2021), 143–160, https://doi.org/10.1525/joac.2021.2.2.143.

Anonymous. "Why Taylor Swift Tickets Are So Expensive." *Re-Edition Magazine*, https://www.reeditionmagazine.com/to-the-minute/why-taylor-swift-tickets-are-so-expensive.

Arnold, Abby. "That Baby's Name: Birthing Autoethnographic Philanthropy, Healing and Organizational Change." In *The Routledge International Handbook of Organizational Autoethnography*, edited by Andrew F. Herrmann, 209–224. New York: Routledge, 2020.

Ashcraft, Karen Lee. *Wronged and Dangerous: Viral Masculinity and the Populist Pandemic*. Bristol: Bristol University Press, 2022.

Atay, Ahmet. "Digital Life Writing: The Failure of a Diasporic, Queer, Blue Tinker Bell." *Interactions: Studies in Communication & Culture* 2, no. 1 (2018), 183–193, https://doi.org/10.1386/iscc.9.2.183_1.

———. "What Is Cyber or Digital Autoethnography?" *International Review of Qualitative Research* 13, no. 3 (2020), 267–279, https://doi.org/10.1177/1940844720934373.

Bal, P. Matthijs and Martijn Veltkamp. "How does Fiction Reading Influence Empathy? An Experimental Investigation on the Role of Emotional Transportation." *PloS One* 8, no. 1 (2013), e55341, https://journals.plos.org/plosone/article?id=10.1371/journal.pone.0055341.

Bali, Maha. "Organizing Autoethnography on the Internet: Models and Challenges." In *The Routledge International Handbook of Organizational Autoethnography*, edited by Andrew F. Herrmann, 470–483. New York: Routledge, 2020.

Banks, Anna and Stephen P. Banks, eds., *Fiction and Social Research: By Ice or Fire*. Walnut Creek, CA: Sage, 1998.

Barley, Karen D. "Life Is Like a Box of Derwents-An Autoethnography Colouring in the Life of Child Sexual Abuse." *The Qualitative Report* 25, no. 2 (2020), 504–524, https://doi.org/10.46743/2160-3715/2020.4155.

Barrington, Judith. *Writing the Memoir: From Truth to Art*. Portland, OR: The Eighth Mountain Press.

Batchelor, Bob. "Creating Public Intellectuals: Popular Culture's Move from the Niche to the Mainstream in the Twenty-first Century." In *Popular Culture in the Twenty-First Century*, edited by Myc Wiatrowski and Cory Barker, 2–15. Newcastle upon Tyne: Cambridge Scholars Publishing, 2013.

Baym, Nancy K. *Personal Connections in the Digital Age*. New York: John Wiley & Sons, 2015.

Behar, Ruth. "Ethnography in a Time of Blurred Genres." *Anthropology and Humanism* 32, no. 2 (2007), 153, https://doi.org/10.1525/ahu.2007.32.2.145.

Bernstein, Jacob. "The Many People Behind 'The Woman in Me.'" *New York Times*, October 31, 2023, https://www.nytimes.com/2023/10/31/style/britney-spears-ghostwriters.html.

Berry, Keith. "Implicated Audience Member Seeks Understanding: Reexamining the 'Gift' of Autoethnography." *International Journal of Qualitative Methods* 5, no. 3 (2006), 94–108, https://doi.org/10.1177/160940690600500309.

———. "The Ethnographic Choice: Why Ethnographers do Ethnography." *Cultural Studies ↔ Critical Methodologies* 11, no. 2 (2011), 165–177, https://doi.org/10.1177/1532708611401336.

———. *Bullied: Tales of Torment, Identity, and Youth.* New York: Routledge, 2016.

———. "The Consumed Self: Understanding the Stories I Cannot Have." In *Doing Autoethnography*, edited by Sandra L. Pensoneau-Conway, Tony E. Adams, and Derek M. Bolen, 19–27. Rotterdam: Sense, 2017.

———. "Things I Don't Have to Do." In *Living Sexuality: Storying LGBTQ Relationships, Identities, and Desires*, edited by Keith Berry, Cathy M. Gillotti, and Tony E. Adams, 43–50. Rotterdam: Brill | Sense, 2020.

———. "Things I Must Still Do." In *Living Sexuality: Storying LGBTQ Relationships, Identities, and Desires*, edited by Keith Berry, Cathy M. Gillotti, and Tony E. Adams, 143–153. Rotterdam: Brill | Sense, 2020.

———. "Autoethnography." In *The Cambridge Handbook of Identity*, edited by Michael Bamberg, Carolin Demuth, and Meike Watzlawik, 324–344. Cambridge: Cambridge University Press, 2022.

———. "Meditations on the Story I Cannot Write: Reflexivity, Autoethnography, and the Possibilities of Maybe." In *Handbook of Autoethnography*, 2nd ed., edited by Tony E. Adams, Stacy Holman Jones, and Carolyn Ellis, 29–40. New York: Routledge, 2022.

Berry, Keith, Catherine M. Gillotti, and Tony E. Adams. *Living Sexuality: Stories of LGBTQ Relationships, Identities, and Desires.* Leiden: Brill | Sense, 2020.

Billig, Michael. *Learn to Write Badly: How to Succeed in the Social Sciences.* Cambridge: Cambridge University Press, 2013.

Black, Jessica E. and Jennifer L. Barnes. "Fiction and Morality: Investigating the Associations between Reading Exposure, Empathy, Morality, and Moral Judgment." *Psychology of Popular Media* 10, no. 2 (2021), 149–164.

Blee, Kathleen M. "Studying the Enemy." In *Our Studies, Ourselves: Sociologists' Lives and Work*, edited by Barry Glassner and Rosanna Hertz, 13–23. New York: Oxford University Press, 2003.

Bloch, Charlotte. *Passion and Paranoia: Emotions and the Culture of Emotion in Academia.* London: Routledge, 2016.

Bloom, Lynn Z. "That Way Be Monsters: Myths and Bugaboos about Teaching Personal Writing." Paper presented at the Conference on College Composition and Communication, Minneapolis, MN, April 2000.

Bloomfield, Arthur Edward. *How to Recognize the Antichrist.* Bloomington, MN: Bethany House Publishers, 1975.

Bochner, Arthur P. "Perspectives on Inquiry II: Theories and Stories." In *Handbook of Interpersonal Communication*, edited by Mark L. Knapp and Gerald R. Miller, 21–41. Thousand Oaks, CA: Sage, 1994.

———. "It's about Time: Narrative and the Divided Self." *Qualitative Inquiry* 3, no. 4 (1997), 418–438.

———. "Criteria against Ourselves." *Qualitative Inquiry* 6, no. 2 (2000), 266–272, https://doi.org/10.1177/107780040000600209.

———. "Narrative's Virtues." *Qualitative Inquiry* 7, no. 2 (2001), 131–157, https://doi.org/10.1177/107780040100700201.

———. "Perspectives on Inquiry III: The Moral of Stories." In *Handbook of Interpersonal* Communication, 3rd ed., edited by Mark L. Knapp and John A. Daly, 73–101. Thousand Oaks, CA: Sage, 2002.

———. "Response to 'Ethnography in Interpersonal Communication." Paper presented at the National Communication Association, Chicago, IL, November 12, 2004.

———. "Notes toward an Ethics of Memory in Autoethnographic Inquiry." In *Ethical Futures in Qualitative Research: Decolonizing the Politics of Knowledge*, edited by Norman K. Denzin and Michael D. Giardina, 197–208. Walnut Creek, CA: Left Coast Press, 2007.

———. *Coming to Narrative: A Personal History of Paradigm Change in the Human Sciences.* Walnut Creek, CA: Left Coast Press, 2014.

Bochner, Arthur P. "Autoethnography as a Way of Life: Listening to Tinnitus Teach." *Journal of Autoethnography* 1, no. 1 (2020), 81–92, https://doi.org/10.1525/joae.2020.1.1.81.

Bochner, Arthur P. and Carolyn Ellis. "Personal Narrative as a Social Approach to Interpersonal Communication." *Communication Theory* 2, no. 2 (1992), 168, https://doi.org/10.1111/j.1468-2885.1992.tb00036.x.

Bochner, Arthur P. and Carolyn Ellis, eds., *Ethnographically Speaking: Autoethnography, Literature, and Aesthetics.* Lanham, MD: Altamira Press, 2002.

———. *Evocative Autoethnography: Writing Lives and Telling Stories.* New York: Routledge, 2016.

Bochner, Arthur P. and Andrew F. Herrmann. "Practicing Narrative Inquiry II: Making Meanings Move." In *The Oxford Handbook of Qualitative Inquiry*, 2nd ed., edited by Patricia Leavy, 285–328. Oxford: Oxford University Press, 2020.

Bolen, Derek M. and Tony E. Adams. "Narrative Ethics." In *The Routledge International Handbook on Narrative and Life History*, edited by Ivor Goodson, Ari Antikainen, Pat Sikes, and Molly Andrews, 618–629. New York: Routledge, 2017.

Booth, Wayne C. *The Rhetoric of Fiction.* Chicago: University of Chicago Press, 1961.

Bordwell, David. *The Way Hollywood Tells It: Story and Style in Modern Movies.* Berkeley: University of California Press, 2006.

Bourdain, Anthony. *Medium Raw.* New York: HarperCollins, 2010.

Boylorn, Robin M. "As Seen on TV: An Autoethnographic Reflection on Race and Reality Television." *Critical Studies in Media Communication* 25, no. 4 (2008), 413–433, https://doi.org/10.1080/15295030802327758.

———. "Gray or for Colored Girls Who Are Tired of Chasing Rainbows: Race and Reflexivity." *Cultural Studies ↔ Critical Methodologies* 11, no. 2 (2011), 178–186, https://doi.org/10.1177/1532708611401336.

———. *Sweetwater: Black Women and Narratives of Resilience.* New York: Peter Lang, 2013.

———. "Bitter Sweet(water): Autoethnography, Relational Ethics, and the Possible Perpetuation of Stereotypes." In *Doing Autoethnography*, edited by Sandra L. Pensoneau-Conway, Tony E. Adams, and Derek M. Bolen, 7–17. Rotterdam: Sense, 2017.

———. "'Keep Remembering': Racialized Memory at The Lynching Memorial." *Journal of Autoethnography* 2, no. 1 (2021), 83–87, https://doi.org/10.1525/joae.2021.2.1.83.

Boylorn, Robin M. and Mark P. Orbe. *Critical Autoethnography: Intersecting Cultural Identities in Everyday Life.* New York: Routledge, 2021.

Bradbury, Ray. *Zen in the Art of Writing.* New York: Rosetta Books, 2017.

Braithwaite, Andrea. "From Brand to Genre: The Hallmark Movie." *Television & New Media* 24, no. 5 (2023), 488–498, https://doi.org/10.1177/15274764231171070.

Brettell, Caroline. *When They Read What We Write: The Politics of Ethnography.* Westport, CT: Bergin & Garvey, 1993.

Brody, Howard. *Stories of Sickness*, 2nd ed. Oxford: Oxford University Press, 2002.

Brommel, Bernard J. "Sensemaking in the Dialysis Clinic." In *Organizational Autoethnographies: Power and Identity in Our Working Lives*, edited by Andrew F. Herrmann, 87–106. New York: Routledge, 2017.

Brown-Smith, Naima. "Family Secrets." *Journal of Family Issues* 19, no. 1 (1998), 20–42, https://doi.org/10.1177/019251398019001003.

Bruner, Jerome. "Life as Narrative." *Social Research* 54, no. 11 (1986), 11–32, https://www.jstor.org/stable/40970444.

Burke, Kenneth. *The Philosophy of Literary Form: Studies in Symbolic Action*, 3rd ed. Berkeley: University of California Press, 1974.

Burton, Tim. *Big Fish.* Film. Columbia Pictures, 2003.

Calafell, Bernadette Marie. "Captain Sisko and Me: Reflections of a Fatherless Daughter." *Journal of Autoethnography* 5, no. 2 (2024): 181–195, doi: https://doi.org/10.1525/joae.2024.5.2.181

Calka, Michelle. "Polymediation: The Relationship between Self and Media." In *Beyond New Media: Discourse and Critique in a Polymediated Age*, edited by Art Herbig, Andrew F. Herrmann, and Adam W. Tyma, 15–30. Lanham, MD: Lexington, 2015.

Calvino, Italo. *Italian Folktales.* Boston, MA: Houghton Mifflin Harcourt, 2013.

Carbado, Devon W. "Privilege." In *Black Queer Studies: A Critical Anthology*, edited by E. Patrick Johnson and Mae G. Henderson, 190–212. Durham, NC: Duke University Press.

Carless, David and Kitrina Douglas. "Collaborative Autoethnography: From Rhythm and Harmony to Shared Stories and Truths." In *Handbook of Autoethnography*, 2nd ed., edited by Tony E. Adams, Stacy Holman Jones, and Carolyn Ellis, 155–165. New York: Routledge, 2022).

Carter, Shelly. "How Much Subjectivity Is Needed to Understand Our Lives Objectively?" *Qualitative Health Research* 12, no. 9 (2002), 1184–1201, https://doi.org/10.1177/1049732302238244.

Castro, Joy, ed., *Family Trouble: Memoirists on the Hazards and Rewards of Revealing Family.* Lincoln: University of Nebraska Press, 2013.

Chandler, Raymond. *The Long Goodbye.* New York: Knopf Doubleday, 1988.

Chang, Heewon. *Autoethnography as Method.* Walnut Creek, CA: Left Coast Press, 2008.

Chawla, Devika. "The Essay." *Journal of Autoethnography* 1, no. 4 (2020), 347–353, https://doi.org/10.1525/joae.2020.1.4.347.

Cleary, Joe. "A Suburban Funeral." *Journal of Autoethnography* 3, no. 3 (2022), https://doi.org/10.1525/joae.2022.3.3.283.

Coles, Robert. *The Call of Stories: Teaching and the Moral Imagination.* Boston, MA: Houghton Mifflin, 1989.

Communication Studies 298. "Fragments of Self at the Postmodern Bar." *Journal of Contemporary Ethnography* 26, no. 3 (1997), 251–292, https://doi.org/10.1177/089124197026003001.

———. "Shopping for Family." *Qualitative Inquiry* 5, no. 2 (1999), 147–180, https://doi.org/10.1177/107780049900500201.

Conquergood, Dwight. "Performing as a Moral Act: Ethical Dimensions of the Ethnography of Performance." *Text and Performance Quarterly* 5, no. 2 (1985), 6, https://doi.org/10.1080/10462938509391578.

Copeland, Stewart. *Strange Things Happen: A Life with The Police, Polo, and Pygmies.* New York: It Books, 2009.

Couser, G. Thomas. *Recovering Bodies: Illness, Disability, and Life Writing.* Madison: University of Wisconsin Press, 1997.

Crawford, Lyall. "Personal Ethnography." *Communication Monographs* 63, no. 2, 158–170, https://doi.org/10.1080/03637759609376384.

Crites, Stephen. "The Narrative Quality of Experience." *Journal of the American Academy of Religion* 39, no. 3 (1971), 291–311, http://www.jstor.org/stable/1461066.

Cruz, Joelle, James McDonald, Kirsten Broadfoot, Andy Kai-chun Chuang, and Shiv Ganesh. "'Aliens' in the United States: A Collaborative Autoethnography of Foreign-Born Faculty." *Journal of Management Inquiry* 29, no. 3 (2020), 272–285, https://doi.org/10.1177/1056492618796561.

Cuellar, M. "The Makings of a Boyfriend: Doing Sexuality through Parasocial Relationships." *The Popular Culture Studies Journal* 3, no. 2 (2015), 270–298.

Cvetkovich, Ann. *Depression: A Public Feeling.* Durham, NC: Duke University Press, 2012.

Davis, Miles and Quincy Troupe. *Miles.* New York: Simon and Schuster, 1990.

Defenbaugh, Nicole. *Dirty Tale: A Narrative Journey of the IBD Body.* Creskill, NJ: Hampton Press, 2011.

Denejkina, Anna. "Exo-Autoethnography: An Introduction." *Forum Qualitative Sozialforschung/Forum: Qualitative Social Research* 18, no. 3 (2017), https://doi.org/10.17169/fqs-18.3.2754.

———. "Exo-Autoethnography as Method for Research on Intergenerational Trauma Transmission." In *Handbook of Autoethnography*, 2nd ed., edited by Tony E. Adams, Stacy Holman Jones, and Carolyn Ellis, 179–187. New York: Routledge, 2022.

Denker, Katherine J. "Power, Emotional Labor, and Intersectional Identity at Work: I Would Not Kiss My Boss But I Did Not Speak Up." In *Organizational Autoethnographies: Power and Identity in Our Working Lives*, edited by Andrew F. Herrmann, 32–52. New York: Routledge, 2017.

Denzin, Norman K. *Interpretive Biography*. Newbury Park, CA: Sage, 1989.

———. *Interpretive Ethnography: Ethnographic Practices for the 21st Century*. Thousand Oaks, CA: Sage Publications, 1997.

Denzin, Norman K. and Michael D. Giardina. "Introduction: The Elephant in the Room, OR Advancing the Conversation about the Politics of Evidence." In *Qualitative Inquiry and the Politics of Evidence*, edited by Norman K. Denzin and Michael D. Giardina, 9–52. Walnut Creek, CA: Left Coast Press, 2008.

DeRenard, Lisa A. and Linda Mannik. "Alienation and the Game Dungeons and Dragons." *Psychological Reports* 66, no. 3_suppl (1990), 1219–1222, https://doi.org/10.2466/pr0.1990.66.3c.1219.

Deshbandhu, Aditya. "Capturing the Holistic: The Need for Autoethnography in Game Studies." *Journal of Autoethnography* 4, no. 2 (2023), 277–282, https://doi.org/10.1525/joae.2023.4.2.277.

Díaz, Estefanía and Silvia Bénard. "Composing a Sense of Belonging: Our Journey through the Maze and Its Ports of Arrival." *Journal of Autoethnography* 4, no. 4 (2023), 474–488, https://doi.org/10.1525/joae.2023.4.4.474.

Di Leo, Jeffrey R. "The Paranoid Imperative: Affect, Emotion, and Neoliberal Academe." *symploke* 29, no. 1 (2021), 163–178, https://doi.org/10.1353/sym.2021.0009.

Dodell-Feder, David and Diana I. Tamir. "Fiction Reading has a Small Positive Impact on Social Cognition: A Meta-analysis." *Journal of Experimental Psychology: General* 147, no. 11 (2018), 1713–1727, https://doi.org/10.1037/xge0000395.

Dong, Peng, Marie Loh, and Adrian Mondry. "The 'Impact Factor' Revisited." *Biomedical Digital Libraries* 2, no. 1 (2005), 1–8, https://doi.org/10.1186/1742-5581-2-7.

Donovan, Frances R. *The Woman Who Waits*. Boston, MA: RG Badger, 1920.

Dunn, Tasha R. *Talking White Trash: Mediated Representations and Lived Experiences of White Working-Class People*. New York: Routledge, 2019.

Dunn, Tasha R. and W. Benjamin Myers. "Contemporary Autoethnography *Is* Digital Autoethnography: A Proposal for Maintaining Methodological Relevance in Changing Times." *Journal of Autoethnography* 1, no. 1 (2020), 43–59, https://doi.org/10.1525/joae.2020.1.1.43.

Durham, Aisha. "Textual Experience: A Relational Reading of Culture." In *Handbook of Autoethnography*, 2nd ed., edited by Tony E. Adams, Stacy Holman Jones, and Carolyn Ellis, 321–328. New York: Routledge, 2022.

Eadie, William F. *When Communication Became a Discipline*. Lanham, MD: Rowman & Littlefield, 2021.

Eisenberg, Eric M. "Building a Mystery: Toward a New Theory of Communication and Identity." *Journal of Communication* 51, no. 3 (2009), 534–552, https://doi.org/10.1111/j.1460-2466.2001.tb02895.x.

Eisenberg, Eric M., H. Lloyd Goodall, Angela Trethewey, and Marianne LeGreco, *Organizational Communication: Balancing Creativity and Constraint*. Boston, MA: Bedford/St. Martin's, 2016.

Ellis, Carolyn. "Sociological Introspection and Emotional Experience." *Symbolic Interaction* 14, no. 1 (1991), 23–50, https://doi.org/10.1525/si.1991.14.1.23.

———. "'There Are Survivors': Telling a Story of Sudden Death." *The Sociological Quarterly* 34, no. 4 (1993), 711–730.

———. "Emotional and Ethical Quagmires in Returning to the Field." *Journal of Contemporary Ethnography* 24, no. 1 (1995), 68–98, https://doi.org/10.1177/089124195024001003.

———. "Maternal Connections." In *Composing Ethnography: Alternative Forms of Qualitative Writing*, eds., Carolyn Ellis and Arthur P. Bochner, 240–243. Walnut Creek, CA: AltaMira Press, 1996.

———. "Evocative Autoethnography: Writing Emotionally about Our Lives." In *Representation and the Text: Re-framing the Narrative Voice*, edited by William G. Tierney and Yvonna S. Lincoln, 115–139. Albany: SUNY Press, 1997.

———. "'I Hate My Voice': Coming to Terms with Minor Bodily Stigmas." *The Sociological Quarterly* 39, no. 4 (1998), 517–537, https://doi.org/10.1111/j.1533-8525.1998.tb00516.x.

———. "Creating Criteria: An Ethnographic Short Story." *Qualitative Inquiry* 6, no. 2 (2000), 273–277, https://doi.org/10.1177/107780040000600210.

———. *The Ethnographic I: A Methodological Novel about Autoethnography.* Walnut Creek, CA: AltaMira, 2004.

———. "The Emotional Life: Honoring Ronald J. Pelias." *Studies in Symbolic Interaction* 29 (2006), 9–15, https://doi.org/10.1016/S0163-2396(06)29002-1.

———. "Telling Secrets, Revealing Lives: Relational Ethics in Research with Intimate Others." *Qualitative Inquiry* 13, no. 1 (2007), 3–29, https://doi.org/10.1177/1077800406294947.

———. "'I Just Want to Tell MY Story': Mentoring Students about Relational Ethics in Writing about Intimate Others." In *Ethical Futures in Qualitative Research: Decolonizing the Politics of Knowledge*, edited by Norman K. Denzin and Michael D. Giardina, 209–228. London: Routledge, 2007.

———. "Fighting Back or Moving On: An Autoethnographic Response to Critics." *International Review of Qualitative Research* 2, no. 3 (2009), 371–378, https://doi.org/10.1525/irqr.2009.2.3.371.

———. *Final Negotiations: A Story of Love, Loss, and Chronic Illness, Revised and Expanded Edition.* Philadelphia, PA: Temple University Press, 2018.

———. "A Meaningful Academic Life: Loving, Fulfilling, Challenging, and Flabbergasting." *Nauki o Wychowaniu. Studia Interdyscyplinarne* 8, no. 1 (2019), 243–249, http://doi.org/10.18778/2450-4491.08.16.

Ellis, Carolyn and Tony E. Adams. "Practicing Autoethnography and Living the Autoethnographic Life." In *The Oxford Handbook of Qualitative Research*, 2nd ed., edited by Patricia Leavy, 359–396. New York: Oxford University Press, 2020.

Ellis, Carolyn and Arthur P. Bochner. "Telling and Performing Personal Stories: The Constraints of Choice in Abortion." In *Investigating Subjectivity: Research on Lived Experience*, edited by Carolyn Ellis and Michael G. Flaherty, 79–101. Newbury Park, CA: Sage, 1992.

———. "Autoethnography, Personal Narrative, Reflexivity: Researcher as Subject." In *Handbook of Qualitative Research*, 2nd ed., edited by Norman K. Denzin and Yvonna S. Lincoln, 733–768. Thousand Oaks, CA: Sage, 2000.

Ellis, Carolyn and Arthur P. Bochner, eds., *Composing Ethnography: Alternative Forms of Qualitative Writing.* Walnut Creek, CA: AltaMira Press, 1996.

Ellis, Carolyn, Arthur P. Bochner, Carol Rambo, Keith Berry, Hannah Shakespeare, Craig Gingrich-Philbrook, Tony E. Adams, Robert E. Rinehart, and Derek M. Bolen. "Coming Unhinged: A Twice-Told Multivoiced Autoethnography." *Qualitative Inquiry* 24, no. 2 (2018), 119–133, https://doi.org/10.1177/1077800416684874.

Ellis, Carolyn, Christine Kiesinger, and Lisa M. Tillmann-Healy. "Interactive Interviewing: Talking about Emotional Experience." In *Reflexivity & Voice*, edited by Rosanna Hertz, 119–149. Thousand Oaks, CA: Sage, 1997.

Ellis, Carolyn and Patti, Chris. "With Heart: Compassionate Interviewing and Storytelling with Holocaust Survivors." *Storytelling, Self, Society* 10, no. 1 (2014), 93–118, https://doi.org/10.13110/storselfsoci.10.1.0093.

Ellis, Carolyn and Jerry Rawicki. "Collaborative Witnessing of Survival during the Holocaust: An Exemplar of Relational Autoethnography." *Qualitative Inquiry* 19, no. 5 (2013), 366–380, https://doi.org/10.1177/1077800413479562.

———. "More Than Mazel? Luck and Agency in Surviving the Holocaust." *Journal of Loss and Trauma* 19, no. 2 (2014), 99–120, https://doi.org/10.1080/15325024.2012.738574.

Ellis, Cassidy D. "Introduction: Bodies on the Line—Living Reproductive (In)Justice." *Journal of Autoethnography* 4, no. 4 (2023), 538–544, https://doi.org/10.1525/joae.2023.4.4.538.

Emerson, Robert M., Rachel I. Fretz, and Linda L. Shaw. *Writing Ethnographic Fieldnotes*, 2nd ed. Chicago, IL: University of Chicago Press, 2011.

Entman, Robert M. "Framing: Toward Clarification of a Fractured Paradigm." *Journal of Communication* 43 (1993), 51–58, https://doi.org/10.1111/j.1460-2466.1993.tb01304.x.

Entman, Robert M. "Media Framing Biases and Political Power: Explaining Slant in News of Campaign 2008." *Journalism* 11, no. 4 (2010), 389–408, https://doi.org/10.1177/1464884910367587.

Esping, Amber. "Autoethnography and Existentialism: The Conceptual Contributions of Viktor Frankl." *Journal of Phenomenological Psychology* 41, no. 2 (2010), 201–215, https://doi.org/10.1163/156916210X532126.

Faulkner, Sandra L. "That Baby Will Cost You (REDUX): The Story of an Intended Ambivalent Pregnancy (and Motherhood)." In *Handbook of Autoethnography*, 2nd ed., edited by Tony E. Adams, Stacy Holman Jones, and Carolyn Ellis, 443–450. New York: Routledge, 2022.

Faulkner, Sandra L. and Sheila Squillante. *Writing the Personal: Getting your Stories onto the Page.* Rotterdam: Sense Publishers, 2016.

Ferdinand, Renata. "Skin Tone and Popular Culture: My Story as a Dark Skinned Black Woman." *The Popular Culture Studies Journal* 3, no. 2 (2015), 324–348.

———. *An Autoethnography of African American Motherhood: Things I Tell My Daughter*, 49–68. New York: Routledge, 2022, https://doi.org/10.4324/9780367822897.

Fisher, Walter. "Narration as a Human Communication Paradigm: The Case of Public Moral Argument." *Communications Monographs* 51, no. 1 (1984), 1–22, https://doi.org/10.1080/03637758409390180.

Fledderus, France. "Insights and Outlooks: Why Highfalutin Language has to Go." *Discourses in Music*, 4, no. 2 (2003), http://library.music.utoronto.ca/discourses-in-music/v4n2io.html.

Fox, Ragan. "You Are Not Allowed to Talk about Production: Narratization On (and Off) the Set of CBS's *Big Brother*." *Critical Studies in Media Communication* 30, no. 3 (2013), 189–208, https://doi.org/10.1080/15295036.2012.755051.

———. "Diяty." *Text and Performance Quarterly* 39, no. 3 (2019), 250, https://doi.org/10.1080/10462937.2019.1643906.

———. "Recalling Emotional Recall: Reflecting on the Methodological Significance of Affective Memory in Autoethnography." *Text and Performance Quarterly* 41, no. 1–2 (2021), 61–80, https://doi.org/10.1080/10462937.2021.1915497.

Frandsen, Sanne and R. Duncan M. Pelly. "Organizational Resistance and Autoethnography." In *The Routledge International Handbook of Organizational Autoethnography*, edited by Andrew F. Herrmann, 252–268. New York: Routledge, 2020.

Frank, Arthur W. *The Wounded Storyteller.* Chicago, IL: University of Chicago Press, 1995.

Frankfurt, Harry G. *On Truth.* New York: Random House, 2010.

Freeman, Mark. *Hindsight: The Promise and Peril of Looking Back.* New York: Oxford University Press, 2010.

Freeman, Melissa. "The Hermeneutical Aesthetics of Thick Description." *Qualitative Inquiry* 20, no. 6 (2014), 827.

Fruchtenbaum, Arnold G. *The Footsteps of the Messiah: A Study of the Sequence of Prophetic Events.* San Antonio, TX: Ariel Press, 1982.

Gadamer, Hans-Georg. *Truth and Method*, 2nd ed., translated by Joel Weinsheimer and Donald G. Marshall. New York: Continuum, 2000.

García-Iglesias, Jaime. "The Maroon Boxer Briefs: Exploring Erotic Reflexivity in Interview Research." *Qualitative Research* 21, no. 5 (2021), 703–718, https://doi.org/10.1177/1468794120927676.

Garfield, Eugene. "The History and Meaning of the Journal Impact Factor." *JAMA* 295, no. 1 (2006), 90–93, https://doi.org/10.1001/jama.295.1.90.

Gariglio, Luigi. "On Fieldwork in the Hybrid Field: A 'Methodological Novel' on Ethnography, Photography, Fiction, and Creative Writing." *Qualitative Research* (2023), https://doi.org/10.1177/14687941221149584.

Geertz, Clifford. *The Interpretation of Cultures.* New York: Basic Books, 1973.

———. *Works and Lives: The Anthropologist as Author*. Stanford, CA: Stanford University Press, 1988.
———. "Deep Hanging Out." *New York Review of Books* (1998), https://www.nybooks.com/articles/1998/10/22/deep-hanging-out/.
Gerber, David A. "The 'Careers' of People Exhibited in Freak Shows: The Problem of Volition and Valorization." In *Freakery: Cultural Spectacles of the Extraordinary*, edited by Rosemarie Garland Thomson, 38–54. New York: New York University Press, 1996.
Gergen, Kenneth J. "Pursuing Excellence in Qualitative Inquiry." *Qualitative Psychology* 1, no. 1 (2014), 49, https://doi.org/10.1037/qup0000002.
Gerrard, Eve and David McNaughton. "Conditional Unconditional Forgiveness." In *The Ethics of Forgiveness: A Collection of Essays*, edited by Christel Fricke, 97–196. New York: Routledge, 2011.
Gingrich-Philbrook, Craig. "Autoethnography's Family Values: Easy Access to Compulsory Experiences." *Text and Performance Quarterly* 25, no. 4 (2005), 297–314, https://doi.org/10.1080/10462930500362445.
———. "Evaluating (Evaluations of) Autoethnography." In *Handbook of Autoethnography*, edited by Stacy Holman Jones, Tony E. Adams, and Carolyn Ellis, 609–626. Walnut Creek, CA: Left Coast Press, 2013.
Goffman, Erving. *The Presentation of Self in Everyday Life* (New York: Doubleday, 1956).
———. *Where the Action Is*. London: Allen Lane The Penguin Press, 1969.
Goldschmidt, Walter. "Anthropology and the Coming Crisis: An Autoethnographic Appraisal." *American Anthropologist* 79, no. 2 (1977), 294, https://www.jstor.org/stable/673841.
Goodall, Jr., H. L. *Casing a Promised Land: The Autobiography of an Organizational Detective as Cultural Ethnographer*. Carbondale: Southern Illinois University Press, 1994.
———. *Divine Signs: Connecting Spirit to Community*. Carbondale: Southern Illinois University Press, 1996.
———. *Writing the New Ethnography*. Thousand Oaks, CA: AltaMira Press, 2000.
———. "Commentary: Narrative Ethnography as Applied Communication Research." *Journal of Applied Communication Research* 32, no. 3 (2004), 185–194, https://doi.org/10.1080/0090988042000240130.
———. *A Need to Know: The Clandestine History of a CIA Family*. Walnut Creek, CA: Left Coast Press, 2006.
———. *Writing Qualitative Inquiry: Self, Stories, and Academic Life*. Thousand Oaks, CA: Left Coast Press, 2008.
Grant, Alec. "Autoethnography." In *Critical Qualitative Health Research: Exploring Philosophies, Politics and Practices*, edited by Kay Aranda, 159–176. New York: Routledge, 2020.
———. *Writing Philosophical Autoethnography*. New York: Routledge, 2024.
Grant, Alec and Susan Young. "Troubling Tolichism in Several Voices: Resisting Epistemic Violence in Creative Analytical and Critical Autoethnographic Practice." *Journal of Autoethnography* 3, no. 1 (2022), 103–117, https://doi.org/10.1525/joae.2022.3.1.103.
Greenberg, Julie A. "When Is a Man a Man, and When Is a Woman a Woman?" *Florida Law Review* 52, no. 4 (2000), 745–768.
———. *Intersexuality and the Law*. New York: New York University Press, 2012.
Guignon, Charles B, ed., *The Cambridge Companion to Heidegger*. Cambridge: Cambridge University Press, 1993.
———. *On Being Authentic*. London: Routledge, 2004.
———. *The Existentialists: Critical Essays on Kierkegaard, Nietzsche, Heidegger, and Sartre*. Lanham, MD: Rowman & Littlefield, 2004.
———. "The History of Being." In *A Companion to Heidegger*, edited by Hubert L. Dreyfus and Mark A. Wrathall, 392–406. Oxford: Blackwell, 2005.
———. "Identity, History, Tradition." In *The Blackwell Companion to Hermeneutics*, edited by Niall Keane and Chris Lawn, 130–142. New York: John Wiley & Sons, 2016.

Guignon, Charles, and Kevin Aho. "Authenticity and Social Critique." In *The Cambridge History of Philosophy, 1945–2015*, edited by Kelly Becker and Iain D. Thomas, 389–398. Cambridge: Cambridge University Press, 2019.

Gullion, Jessica Smartt. *Writing Ethnography*, 2nd ed. Lieden: Brill, 2022.

Gutkind, Lee. *Keep It Real.* New York: W.W. Norton & Company.

Hall, Delbert A. *Rigging Math Made Simple.* Johnson City, TN: Spring Knoll Press, 2013.

Hamlet, Janice D. "Still Standing, Still Here: Lessons Learned from Mediated Mentors in My Academic Journey." *The Popular Culture Studies Journal* 3, no. 2 (2015), 299–323.

Hart, Tabitha. "Online Ethnography." In *The International Encyclopedia of Communication Research Methods*, edited by Jörg Matthes, 1–8. New York: John Wiley & Sons, 2017.

Hayano, David M. "Auto-Ethnography: Paradigms, Problems, and Prospects." *Human Organization* 38, no. 1 (1979), 99–104, https://www.jstor.org/stable/44125560.

Heidegger, Martin. *Being and Time*, translated by John MacQuarrie and Edward Robinson. New York: Harper, 1962.

Heider, Karl G. "What Do People Do? Dani Auto-Ethnography." *Journal of Anthropological Research* 31, no. 1 (1975), 3–17, https://www.jstor.org/stable/3629504.

Henry, Jules. *Pathways to Madness.* New York: Vintage Books, 1965.

Herbig, Art. "Understanding Privilege in a Pandemic: The Small Systems That Perpetuate the Large Structures." *Journal of Autoethnography* 2, no. 2 (2021), 242–247, https://doi.org/10.1525/joae.2021.2.2.242.

Herbig, Art and Andrew F. Herrmann. "Polymediated Narrative: The Case of the Supernatural Episode 'Fan Fiction.'" *International Journal of Communication* 10 (2016), 1–18, http://ijoc.org/index.php/ijoc/article/view/4397.

Herbig, Art, Andrew F. Herrmann, Alix R. Watson, A. W. Tyma, and J. Miller. "Critical Rhetoric and Collaboration: Missing Principle # 9 and ProfsDoPop.com." *International Journal of Communication* 14 (2020), 885–898, https://ijoc.org/index.php/ijoc/article/view/8676/2967.

Herrmann, Andrew F. "My Father's Ghost: Interrogating Family Photos." *Journal of Loss and Trauma* 10, no. 4 (2005), 337–346, https://doi.org/10.1080/15325020590956765.

———. "Reflexivity, Narrative and Ethical Undecidability: On Not Presenting 'Home Is Where the Heart Was." Paper presented at the Second Annual International Congress of Qualitative Inquiry, Urbana, IL, 2006.

———. "Stockholders and Mediated Intertextuality." *Florida Communication Journal* 34, no. 2 (2006), 105–114.

———. "Stockholders in Cyberspace: Weick's Sensemaking Online." *Journal of Business Communication* 44, no. 1 (2007), 13–35, https://doi.org/10.1177/0021943606295778.

———. "How Did We Get This Far Apart? Disengagement, Relational Dialectics, and Narrative Control." *Qualitative Inquiry* 13, no. 7 (2007), 989–1007, https://doi.org/10.1177/1077800407304468.

———. "'People Get Emotional about Their Money': Performing Masculinity in a Financial Discussion Board." *Journal of Computer-Mediated Communication* 12, no. 2 (2007), 499–522, https://doi.org/10.1111/j.1083-6101.2007.00335.x.

———. "Kierkegaard and Dialogue: The Communication of Capability." *Communication Theory* 18, no. 1 (2008), 71–92, https://doi.org/10.1111/j.1468-2885.2007.00314.x.

———. "Narratives and Sensemaking in the New Corporate University: The Socialization of First Year Communication Faculty." PhD dissertation, University of South Florida, 2008, http://scholarcommons.usf.edu/etd/291.

———. "'Losing Things Was Nothing New': A Family's Story of Foreclosure." *Journal of Loss & Trauma* 16, no. 6 (2011), 497–510, https://doi.org/10.1080/15325024.2011.576982.

———. "Criteria against Ourselves? Embracing the Opportunities of Qualitative Inquiry." *International Review of Qualitative Research* 5, no. 2 (2012), 135–152, https://doi.org/10.1525/irqr.2012.5.2.135.

———. "'I Know I'm Unlovable'" Desperation, Dislocation, Despair, and Discourse on the Academic Job Hunt." *Qualitative Inquiry* 18, no. 3 (2012), 247–255, https://doi.org/10.1177/1077800411431561.

———. "Never Mind the Scholar, Here's the Old Punk: Identity, Community, and the Aging Music Fan." *Studies in Symbolic Interaction* 39 (2012), 153–170, https://doi.org/10.1108/S0163-2396(2012)0000039007.

———. "Narrative as an Organizing Process: Identity and Story in a New Nonprofit." *Qualitative Research in Organizations and Management: An International Journal* 6, no. 33, (2012), 246–264, https://doi.org/10.1108/17465641111188411.

———. "Daniel Amos and Me: The Power of Pop Culture and Autoethnography." *The Popular Culture Studies Journal* 1, no. 2 (2013), 6–17.

———. "Ghosts, Vampires, Zombies, and Us: The Undead as Autoethnographic Bridges." *International Review of Qualitative Research* 7, no. 3 (2014), 327–341, https://doi.org/10.1525/irqr.2014.7.3.327.

———. "The Ghostwriter: Living a Father's Unfinished Narrative." In *On (Writing) Families: Autoethnographies of Presence and Absence, Love and Loss*, edited by Jonathan Wyatt and Tony E. Adams, 95–101. Rotterdam: Brill, 2014.

———. "Communicating, Sensemaking, and (Dis)Organizing: Theorizing the Complexity of Polymediation." In *Beyond New Media: Discourse and Critique in a Polymediated Age*, edited by Art Herbig, Andrew F. Herrmann, and Adam Tyma, 61–82. Lanham, MD: Lexington, 2015.

———. "Walking in Kierkegaard's Instant and Walking Out of American Christendom." *Departures in Critical Qualitative Research* 4, no. 2 (2015), 91–119.

———. "On Being a Homeless Work of Fiction: Narrative Quests and Questions." *International Review of Qualitative Research* 9, no. 1 (2016), 29–43, https://doi.org/10.1525/irqr.2016.9.1.29.

———. "The Ghostwriter Writes No More: Narrative Logotherapy, and the Death of My Namesake." *Qualitative Inquiry* 22, no. 7 (2016), 1–12, https://doi.org/10.1177/1077800415622504.

———. *Organizational Autoethnographies: Power and Identity in Our Working Lives.* New York: Routledge, 2017.

———. "Broken Promises: Psychological Contract Breach, Organizational Exit, and Occupational Change." In *Organizational Autoethnographies: Power and Identity in Our Working Lives*, edited by Andrew F. Herrmann, 144–162. New York: Routledge, 2017.

———. "Communication and Ritual at the Comic Book Shop: The Convergence of Organizational and Popular Cultures." *Journal of Organizational Ethnography* 7, no. 3 (2018), 285–301, https://doi.org/10.1108/JOE-06-2017-0027.

———. "Purity, Nationalism, and Whiteness: The Fracturing of Fundamentalist Evangelicalism." *International Review of Qualitative Research* 13, no. 4 (2020), 414–432, https://doi.org/10.1177/1940844720937813.

———, ed., *The Routledge International Handbook of Organizational Autoethnography.* New York: Routledge, 2020.

———. "The Historical and Hysterical Narratives of Organization and Autoethnography." In *The Routledge International Handbook of Organizational Autoethnography*, edited by Andrew F. Herrmann, 13–41. New York: Routledge, 2020.

———. "Autoethnography as Acts of Love." In *Handbook of Autoethnography*, 2nd ed., edited by Tony E. Adams, Stacy Holman Jones and Carolyn Ellis, 67–78. New York: Routledge, 2022.

———. "The Future of Autoethnographic Criteria." *International Review of Qualitative Research* 15, no. 1 (2022), 125–135, https://doi.org/10.1177/19408447211049513.

Herrmann, Andrew F. and Tony E. Adams. "Learning to be Editors." *Journal of Autoethnography* 2, no. 1 (2021), 1–4, https://doi.org/10.1525/joae.2021.2.1.1.

———. "Autoethnography and the 'So What?' Question." *Journal of Autoethnography* 3, no. 1 (2022), 1–3, https://doi.org/10.1525/joae.2022.3.1.1.

Herrmann, Andrew F., Tony E. Adams, and Sara B. Dykins Callahan. "Pursuing, Practicing, and Portraying Qualitative Research: An Interview with Norman K. Denzin." *Qualitative Inquiry* (2023), https://doi.org/10.1177/10778004231202939.

Herrmann, Andrew F. and Kristen DiFate. "The New Ethnography." *Storytelling, Self, Society* 10, no. 1 (2014), 3–118.

———. "Introduction to the Special Issue: The New Ethnography: Goodall, Trujillo, and the Necessity of Storytelling." *Storytelling, Self, Society* 10, no. 1 (2014), 3–10.

Herrmann, Andrew F. and Art Herbig. "Not Another Pop Culture Series! Studying the World(s) We Occupy." In *Communication Perspectives on Popular Culture*, edited by Andrew F. Herrmann and Art Herbig, iii–xiv. Lanham, MD: Rowman & Littlefield, 2016.

———. "Returning to Kolchak: Polymediated Narrative, Discourse, and Supernatural Drama." *International Journal of Communication* 12 (2018), 222–240, https://ijoc.org/index.php/ijoc/article/view/7827/2224.

———. "An Autoethnography of Working, Failing, and Reworking Public Scholarship." In *Popularizing Scholarly Research: Research Methods and Practices*, edited by Patricia Leavy, 104–131. New York: Oxford University Press, 2021.

Ho, Karen. *Liquidated: An Ethnography of Wall Street.* Durham, NC: Duke University Press, 2009.

Holman Jones, Stacy. "(M)othering Loss: Telling Adoption Stories, Telling Performativity." *Text and Performance Quarterly* 25, no. 2 (2005), 113–135, https://doi.org/10.1080/10462930500122716.

Holman Jones, Stacy, Tony E. Adams, and Carolyn Ellis, eds., *Handbook of Autoethnography.* Walnut Creek, CA: Left Coast Press, 2013.

Holt, Nicholas L. "Representation, Legitimation, and Autoethnography: An Autoethnographic Writing Story." *International Journal of Qualitative Methods* 2, no. 1 (2003), 18–28, https://doi.org/10.1177/160940690300200102.

hooks, bell. *Remembered Rapture.* New York: Henry Holt and Company, 1999.

Hopkins, Justin B. "Real? American? Hero? An Autoethnography about Playing Creatively and Cathartically with GI Joe." *American Journal of Play* 14, no. 3 (2022), 277–303, https://www.museumofplay.org/app/uploads/2022/12/14-3-Article-3-Real-American-Hero.pdf.

Huff, Billy. "On [Be]coming in Boystown." *Journal of Autoethnography* 3, no. 4 (2022), 427–444, https://doi.org/10.1525/joae.2022.3.4.427.

Hughes, Sherick, Julie L. Pennington, and Sara Makris. "Translating Autoethnography across the AERA Standards: Toward Understanding Autoethnographic Scholarship as Empirical Research." *Educational Researcher* 41, no. 6 (2012), 209–219, https://doi.org/10.3102/0013189X12442983.

Hume, Lynne and Jane Mulcock. *Anthropologists in the Field: Cases in Participant Observation.* New York: Columbia University Press, 2004.

Humphrey, Vernon F. "I Can't Be Blind, I Can See." *Journal of Autoethnography* 1, no. 4 (2020), 370–377, https://doi.org/10.1525/joae.2020.1.4.370.

Humphreys, Michael and Tony Watson. "Ethnographic Practices: From 'Writing-Up Ethnographic Research' to 'Writing Ethnography.'" In *Organizational Ethnography: Studying the Complexities of Everyday Life*, edited by Sierk Ybema, Dvaora Yanow, and Frank Kamsteeg, 40–55. Thousand Oaks, CA: Sage, 2009.

Hunniecutt, Jeni R. "Veteran Identity (Perceptions) in Higher Education: A Veteran/Scholar/Advocate's Story." *Journal of Veterans Studies* 8, no. 2 (2022), 36–50.

———. *Rethinking Reintegration and Veteran Identity: A New Consciousness.* London: Palgrave Macmillan, 2022.

Ice-T, *Ice: A Memoir of Gangster Life and Redemption-from South Central to Hollywood.* London: One World, 2012.

Irwin, Katherine. "Into the Dark Heart of Ethnography: The Lived Ethics and Inequality of Intimate Field Relationships." *Qualitative Sociology* 29 (2006), 155–175.

Jacke, Janina. "Unreliability and Narrator Types. On the Application Area of ›Unreliable Narration‹." *Journal of Literary Theory* 12, no. 1 (2018), 3–28, https://doi.org/10.1515/jlt-2018-0002.

Jago, Barbara J. "Chronicling an Academic Depression." *Journal of Contemporary Ethnography* 31, no. 6 (2002), 738, https://doi.org/10.1177/089124102237823.

———. "Risk and Reward in Autoethnography: Revisiting 'Chronicling an Academic Depression." In *Handbook of Autoethnography*, edited by Tony E. Adams, Stacy Holman Jones, and Carolyn Ellis, 383–390. New York: Routledge, 2022.

Jegatheesan, Brinda India. "I See the Stars: An Autoethnographer Speaks on Fieldwork and Flashbacks." *Qualitative Inquiry* 11, no. 5 (2005), 667–688, https://doi.org/10.1177/1077800405276810.

Johnson, Alexis Zoe Waters. "Living in Silence: An Autoethnography of Relating, Coping, and Navigating Daily Challenges with Hearing Impairment." *Journal of Autoethnography* 2, no. 11 (2021), 39–54, https://doi.org/10.1525/joae.2021.2.1.39.

Johnson, Amber. "Confessions of a Video Vixen: My Autocritography of Sexuality, Desire, and Memory." *Text and Performance Quarterly* 34, no. 2 (2014), 182–200, https://doi.org/10.1080/10462937.2013.879991.

Johnson, Amber and Lore/tta LeMaster, *Gender Futurity, Intersectional Autoethnography: Embodied Theorizing from the Margins.* New York: Routledge, 2020.

Johnston, Brian. "Framing Stories from the Academic Margins: Documentary as Qualitative Inquiry and Critical Community Engagement." In *The Routledge International Handbook of Organizational Autoethnography*, edited by Andrew F. Herrmann, 437–456. New York: Routledge, 2020.

Johnson, Kevin. "At Stake in the Rules of Communication Is Democratic Life Itself: Does 'the Marketplace of Ideas' Matter Anymore?" *Communication and Democracy* 56, no. 2 (2022), 205–209, https://doi.org/10.1080/27671127.2022.2141740.

Johnston, Matthew S. "Through Madness and Back Again: An Autoethnography of Psychosis." *Journal of Autoethnography* 1, no. 2 (2020), 137–155, https://doi.org/10.1525/joae.2020.1.2.137.

Joo, Thomas W. "The Worst Test of Truth: The Marketplace of Ideas as Faulty Metaphor." *Tulane Law Review* 89, no. 2 (2014), 383–433.

Jorgensen, Danny L. *Participant Observation: A Methodology for Human Studies.* Newbury Park: SAGE Publications, 1989.

Jump, Deborah. "They Didn't Know Whether to 'Fuck Me or Fight Me': An Ethnographic Account of North Town Boxing Gym." In *Mischief, Morality and Mobs*, edited by Dick Hobbs, 11–28. New York: Routledge, 2016.

Karr, Mary. *The Art of Memoir.* New York: Harper Perennial, 2015.

Kavoori, Anandam. "Re-making the World: Autoethnographic Interventions." *Journal of Autoethnography* 2, no. 3 (2023), 290–292, https://doi.org/10.1525/joae.2021.2.3.290.

Kendall, Lori. *Hanging Out in the Virtual Pub: Masculinities and Relationships Online.* Berkeley: University of California Press, 2002.

Kerr, Mary. *The Art of Memoir.* New York: HarperCollins, 2015.

Keskin, Burhanettin. "When 'Even' Is Uneven: 'Inclusion' as Exclusion." *Journal of Autoethnography* 2, no. 4 (2021), 396–404, https://doi.org/10.1525/joae.2021.2.4.396.

Key, Adam. "The Silent A: A Critical Soundtrack of Asexuality." *Journal of Autoethnography* 2, no. 4 (2021), 446–465, https://doi.org/10.1525/joae.2021.2.4.446.

Kierkegaard, Søren A. *Journals and Papers*, 7 Vol. Bloomington: Indiana University Press, 1967–1978.

Kiesinger, Christine E. "My Father's Shoes: The Therapeutic Value of Narrative Reframing." In *Ethnographically Speaking: Autoethnography, Literature, and Aesthetics*, edited by Arthur P. Bochner and Carolyn Ellis, 95–114. Walnut Creek, CA: Altamira. 2002.

King, Stephen. *The Stand: The Complete and Uncut Edition.* New York: Doubleday, 1990.

———. *On Writing: A Memoir of the Craft*. New York: Pocket Books, 2000.

———. *Danse Macabre*. New York: Gallery Books, 2010.

Klevan, Trude and Alec Grant. *An Autoethnography of Becoming a Qualitative Researcher*. New York: Routledge, 2022.

Kottenstette, David T. "Portrait at an Exhibition: An Unlikely Affair with Grief." *Journal of Autoethnography* 1, no. 1 (2020), 29–42, https://doi.org/10.1525/joae.2020.1.1.29.

Krizek, Robert L. "Goodbye Old Friend: A Son's Farewell to Comiskey Park." *OMEGA: Journal of Death and Dying* 25 (1992), 87–93, https://doi.org/10.2190/P5RF-G50T-MEYY-P8KU.

———. "Remembrances and Expectations: The Investment of Identity in the Changing of Comiskey." *Elysian Fields Quarterly* 11, no. 2 (1992), 30–50.

———. "The Ethnography of Events: A Narrative Analysis of Non-Routine Public Events." PhD dissertation. Arizona State University, 1995, https://www.proquest.com/dissertations-theses/ethnography-events-narrative-analysis-non-routine/docview/304164547/se-2.

———. "Lessons: What the Hell Are We Teaching the Next Generation Anyway?" In *Fiction and Social Research: By Ice or Fire*, edited by Anna Banks and Stephen Banks, 89–113. Walnut Creek, CA: AltaMira, 1998.

———. "Ethnography as the Excavation of Personal Narrative." In *Expressions of Ethnography: Novel Approaches to Qualitative Methods*, edited by Robin Clair, 141–151. Albany: State University New York Press, 2003.

———. "From Cooperstown to Carmel: A Wingman's Stories of Nick Trujillo, or 'Playing Catch with Nick Trujillo.'" *Storytelling, Self, Society* 10, no. 1 (2014), 26–44, 10.1353/sss.2014.a813161.

———. "Sport as Ethnography: An Embodied Practice Meets an Embodied Method." In *Defining Sport Communication*, edited by Andrew C. Billings, 59–78. New York: Routledge, 2017.

Kuschnir, Karina. "Ethnographic Drawing: Eleven Benefits of Using a Sketchbook for Fieldwork." *Visual Ethnography* 5, no. 1 (2016), 103–134, https://doi.org/10.12835/ve2016.1-0060.

Lambert, Ashlee A. "'What Are You?' An Autocritography of Language, Stereotypes, and Microaggressions." *Journal of Autoethnography* 2, no. 1 (2021), 13–25, https://doi.org/10.1525/joae.2021.2.1.13.

Lamott, Anne. *Bird by Bird: Some Instructions on Writing and Life*. New York: Anchor Books, 1994.

Lancaster, Kurt. "Do Role-Playing Games Promote Crime, Satanism and Suicide among Players as Critics Claim?" *Journal of Popular Culture* 28, no. 2 (1994), 67–79, https://doi.org/10.1111/j.0022-3840.1994.2802_67.x.

Le Guin, Ursula K., and David Naimon. *Conversations on Writing*. Brooklyn, NY: Tin House Books, 2018.

Leary, Mark R. *Impression Management and Interpersonal Behaviors*. Madison: Brown & Benchmark, 1995.

Leavy, Patricia. "Fiction and the Feminist Academic Novel." *Qualitative Inquiry* 18, no. 6 (2012), 517.

———. *Fiction as Research Practice: Short Stories, Novellas, and Novels*. Walnut Creek, CA: Left Coast Press, 2013.

———. *Re/Invention: Methods of Social Fiction*. New York: Guilford, 2023.

Leblanc, Lauraine. *Pretty in Punk: Girls' Gender Resistance in a Boys' Subculture*. New Brunswick, NJ: Rutgers University Press, 1999.

Lee, Catherine. "Culture, Consent and Confidentiality in Workplace Autoethnography." *Journal of Organizational Ethnography* 7, no. 3 (2018), 302–319, https://doi.org/10.1108/JOE-06-2017-0032.

Leeds-Hurwitz, Wendy. "Ethnography." In *Handbook of Language and Social Interaction*, edited by Kristine L. Fitch and Robert E. Sanders, 327–353. New York: Psychology Press, 2004.

Leilani, Raven. *Luster: A Novel*. New York: Farrar, Straus and Giroux, 2020.

Lengelle, Reinekke. *Writing the Self in Bereavement: A Story of Love, Spousal Loss, and Resilience.* New York: Routledge, 2021.

Lerum, Kari. "No One Cites Obituaries: Extricating from Sticky Grief." *Journal of Autoethnography* 4, no. 2 (2023), 255–274, https://doi.org/10.1525/joae.2023.4.2.255.

Lindemann, Kurt. "Working On It: Family Narratives of Masculinity, Disability, and Work-Life Balance." In *Organizational Autoethnographies: Power and Identity in Our Working Lives*, edited by Andrew F. Herrmann, 59–70. New York: Routledge, 2017.

Lindsey, Hal. *There's a New World Coming.* Santa Ana, CA: Vision House, 1973.

Lindsey, Hal and Carole C. Carlson. *The Late Great Planet Earth.* Grand Rapids, MI: Zondervan, 1970.

Longley, Kyle, Jeremy Mayer, Michael Schaller, and John W. Sloan. *Deconstructing Reagan: Conservative Mythology and America's Fortieth President.* New York: Routledge, 2015.

Lorde, Audre. "The Uses of Anger." *Women's Studies Quarterly* 9, no. 3 (1981), 7–10.

———. *Sister Outsider.* Berkeley: The Crossing Press, 1984.

Luri de Almeida, Moana. "The Evil Woodcutter and the Amazon Jungle: What Comics Have Taught Me about the Environment." *The Popular Culture Studies Journal* 3, no. 2 (2015), 386–414.

MacLean, Annie Marion. "Two Weeks in Department Stores." *American Journal of Sociology* IV, no. 6 (1899), 721–741.

———. "Life in the Pennsylvania Coal Fields with Particular Reference to Women." *American Journal of Sociology* 14, no. 3 (1908), 329–351.

———. "With Oregon Hop Pickers." *American Journal of Sociology* 15, no. 1 (1909), 83–95.

———. "Four Months in a Model Factory." *Century* 106 (1923), 436–444.

Malinowski, Bronislaw. "Ethnology and the Study of Society." *Economica* 6 (October 1922), 208, https://doi.org/10.2307/2548314.

Mandel, Barrett John. "The Autobiographer's Art." *Journal of Aesthetics and Art Criticism* 27, no. 2 (1968), 218, https://doi.org/10.2307/428849.

Manning, Jimmie. "Ipsedixitism, Ipseity, and Ipsilateral Identity: The Fear of Finding Ourselves in the Fissures between Phishing and Catfish." In *Beyond New Media: Discourse and Critique in a Polymediated Age*, edited by Art Herbig, Andrew F. Herrmann, and Adam Tyma, 83–107. Lanham, MD: Lexington Books, 2015.

Manning, Jimmie and Tony E. Adams, eds., "Connecting the Personal and the Popular: Autoethnography and Popular Culture." *The Popular Culture Studies Journal* 3 (2015), 187–519.

Mar, Raymond A., Keith Oatley, Jacob Hirsh, Jennifer Dela Paz, and Jordan B. Peterson. "Bookworms versus Nerds: Exposure to Fiction versus Non-fiction, Divergent Associations with Social Ability, and the Simulation of Fictional Social Worlds." *Journal of Research in Personality* 40, no. 5 (2006), 694–712, https://doi.org/10.1016/j.jrp.2005.08.002.

Markham, Annette N. *Life Online: Researching Real Experience in Virtual Space.* Thousand Oaks, CA: Altamira, 1998.

Marti, Judith. *Starting Fieldwork: Methods and Experiences.* Long Grove, IL: Waveland Press, 2016).

Maurer, Dieter and Theodor Landis. "Role of Bone Conduction in the Self-Perception of Speech." *Folia Phoniatrica et Logopaedia* 42, no. 5 (1990), 226–229, https://doi.org/10.1159/000266070.

McCloy, James F. and Ray Miller, Jr., *The Jersey Devil.* Wilmington, DE: Middle Atlantic Press, 1976.

McCombs, Maxwell E., and Donald L. Shaw. "The Agenda-Setting Function of Mass Media." *The Public Opinion Quarterly* 36, no. 2 (1972), 176–187, https://doi.org/10.1086/267990.

McCombs, Maxwell and Salma I. Ghanem. "The Convergence of Agenda Setting and Framing." In *Framing Public Life*, edited by Stephen D. Reese, Oscar H. Gandy, Jr., and August E. Grant, 67–81. Mahwah, NJ: Lawrence Erlbaum, 2001.

McDonald, Matthew G. "Epiphanies: An Existential Inquiry." *Existential Analysis* 18, no. 1 (2007), 17–30.

McIntosh, Peggy. "White Privilege and Male Privilege: A Personal Account of Coming to See Correspondences through Work in Women's Studies." In *Understanding Diversity: Readings, Cases, and Exercises*, edited by Carol P. Harvey and June Allard, 130–139. New York: Harper-Collins, 1995.

McKerrow, Raymie E. "Coloring Outside the Tines: The Limits of Civility." *Vital Speeches of the Day* 67 (2001), 279–280.

McLaurin, Shamla. "Homophobia: An Autoethnographic Story." *The Qualitative Report* 8, no. 3 (2003), 481, https://doi.org/10.46743/2160-3715/2003.1882.

McLuhan, Marshall. *Understanding Media: The Extensions of Man*. Cambridge: MIT Press, 1994.

Meyer, Michaela D. E. "The Cost of Winning the Pregnancy Lottery: An Autoethnographic Account of How My Life Was Consumed by Secondary Infertility." *Journal of Autoethnography* 3, no. 4, 544–560, https://doi.org/10.1525/joae.2022.3.4.544.

Meyerowitz, Joanne. *How Sex Changed: A History of Transsexuality in the United States*. Cambridge, MA: Harvard University Press, 2002.

Meyrowitz, Joshua. "Multiple Media Literacies." *Journal of Communication* 48, no. 1 (1998), 100–102, https://doi.org/10.1111/j.1460-2466.1998.tb02740.x.

Mhilli, Olga. "Authorial Voice in Writing: A Literature Review." *Social Sciences & Humanities Open* 8, no. 1 (2023), 10, https://doi.org/10.1016/j.ssaho.2023.100550.

Miller, Katherine. "The Experience of Emotion in the Workplace: Professing in the Midst of Tragedy." *Management Communication Quarterly* 15, no. 4 (2002), 571–600, https://doi.org/10.1177/0893318902154003.

Minai, Naveen. "Desi Butch (Where the 'Twain Shall Meet): Queer Autoethnography." *Journal of Autoethnography* 3, no. 2 (2022), 160–168, https://doi.org/10.1525/joae.2022.3.2.160.

Mnouer, Mounia. "A Woman's Journey of Decolonization and Indigenous Amazigh Identity." *Journal of Autoethnography* 4, no. 3 (2023), 348–358, https://doi.org/10.1525/joae.2023.4.3.348.

Mockler, Nicole. "Being Me: In Search of Authenticity." In *Creative Spaces for Qualitative Researching: Living Researchi*, edited by Joy Higgs, Angie Titchen, Debbie Horsfall, and Donna Bridges, 159–168. Rotterdam: Sense, 2011.

Mykhalovskiy, Eric. "Reconsidering Table Talk: Critical Thoughts on the Relationship between Sociology, Autobiography and Self-indulgence." *Qualitative Sociology*, 19 (1996), 131–151, https://doi.org/10.1007/BF02393251.

Nardi, Bonnie. *My Life as a Night Elf Priest: An Anthropological Account of World of Warcraft*. Ann Arbor: University of Michigan Press, 2010.

Niemi, Lauren and Nancy Donoval. *Point of View and the Emotional Arc of Stories: A Handbook for Writers and Storytellers*. Marion, MI: Parkhurst Brothers, 2020.

Nititham, Diane Sabenacio. "Positionalities of Precarity: An Autoethnography of 'Making It' in the Neoliberal Academy." *Journal of Autoethnography* 3, no. 1 (2022), 38–56, https://doi.org/10.1525/joae.2022.3.1.38.

Okely, Judith and Helen Callaway, eds., *Anthropology & Autobiography*. New York: Routledge, 1992.

Ong, Walter J., *The Technologizing of the Word*. New York, Methuen, 1982.

Orel, Marko. "Workplace Autoethnography: Exploring the Place through Aspects of the Self." In *Methodological Approaches for Workplace Research and Management*, edited by Chiara Tagliaro, Marko Orel, and Ying Hua, 18–35. New York: Routledge, 2023.

Papacharissi, Zizi. *A Private Sphere: Democracy in a Digital Age*. New York: Polity, 2010.

Parks, Elizabeth S. "The Hybrid I/Eye: A Critical Autoethnography of Intersecting Race and Disability Identities." *Journal of Autoethnography* 2, no. 1 (2021), 26–38, https://doi.org/10.1525/joae.2021.2.1.26.

Parry, Alan. “A Universe of Stories.” *Family Process* 30, no. 1 (1991), 6, https://doi.org/10.1111/j.1545-5300.1991.00037.x.

Patton, Michael Quinn. *Qualitative Research and Evaluation Methods*, 3rd ed. Thousand Oaks, CA: Sage, 2002.

Patrick, Stephanie. “Lights, Camera, Silence: How Casting Processes Foster Compliance in Film and Television Performers.” *The Popular Culture Studies Journal* 3, no. 2 (2015), 223–244.

Paxton, Blake. *At Home with Grief: Continued Bonds with the Deceased*. New York: Routledge, 2018.

Pelias, Ronald J. “An Autobiographic Ethnography of Performance in Everyday Discourse.” *Journal of Dramatic Theory and Criticism* 8, no. 2 (1994), 163–172.

———. “The Critical Life.” *Communication Education* 49, no. 3 (2000), 220–228, https://doi.org/10.1080/03634520009379210.

———. “The Academic Tourist: An Autoethnography.” *Qualitative Inquiry* 9, no. 3 (2003), 369–373, https://doi.org/10.1177/1077800403009003003.

———. *A Methodology of the Heart: Evoking Academic and Daily Life*. Lanham, MD: Rowman Altamira, 2004.

———. “Writing into Position: Strategies for Composition and Evaluation.” In *The SAGE Handbook of Qualitative Research*, 4th ed., edited by Norman K. Denzin and Yvonna S. Lincoln, 659–668. Thousand Oaks: Sage, 2011.

———. *Performance: An Alphabet of Performative Writing*. Walnut Creek, CA: Left Coast Press, 2014.

———. *The Creative Qualitative Researcher: Writing that Makes Readers Want to Read*. New York: Routledge, 2019.

Pensoneau-Conway, Sandra L., Tony E. Adams, and Derek M. Bolen, eds., *Doing Autoethnography*. Rotterdam: Brill, 2017.

Peters, John Durham. *Speaking Into the Air: A History of the Idea of Communication*. Chicago, IL: University of Chicago Press, 1999.

Peterson, Jon. *The Elusive Shift: How Role-Playing Games Forged Their Identity*. Cambridge: MIT Press, 2020.

———. *Game Wizards: The Epic Battle for Dungeons & Dragons*. Cambridge: MIT Press, 2021.

Phair, Liz. *Horror Stories: A Memoir*. New York: Random House, 2019.

Pillay, Daisy. “Recreating a Graduate Supervisor through Art Making: An Autoethnographic Study.” *Journal of Autoethnography* 1, no. 1 (2020), 99–104, https://doi.org/10.1525/joae.2020.1.1.99.

Pillay, Daisy, Inbanathan Naicker, and Kathleen Pithouse-Morgan, eds., *Writing Academic Autoethnographies*. Rotterdam: Sense Publishers, 2016.

Pittman, Jason and Christopher Paul. “Seeking Fulfillment: Comparing Role-Play in Table-Top Gaming and World of Warcraft.” *International Journal of Role-Playing* 1 (2008), 53–65, https://doi.org/10.33063/ijrp.vi1.187.

Plows, Alexandra. *Messy Ethnographies in Action*. Wilmington, DE: Vernon Press, 2018.

Polkinghorne, Donald E. *Narrative Knowing and the Human Sciences*. Albany: State University of New York Press, 1988.

Poulos, Christopher N. “Transgressions.” *International Review of Qualitative Research* 3, no. 1 (2010), 67–88, https://doi.org/10.1525/irqr.2010.3.1.67.

———. *Accidental Ethnography: An Inquiry into Family Secrecy*, 2nd ed. New York: Routledge, 2018.

———. “Trouble in Paradise.” *International Review of Qualitative Research* 12, no. 3 (2019), 268–277, https://doi.org/10.1525/irqr.2019.12.3.268.

———. *Essentials of Autoethnography*. Washington, DC: American Psychological Association, 2021.

Przybylski, Liz. *Hybrid Ethnography: Online, Offline, and In Between*. Thousand Oaks, CA: Sage Publications, 2020.

Purnell, David and Jim Bowman. "'Happily ever after': Are Traditional Scripts Just for Fairy Tales?" *Narrative Inquiry* 24, no. 1 (2014), 175–180, https://doi.org/10.1075/ni.24.1.09pur.

Purnell, David and Daniel Wade Clarke. "Finding Our Fathers." *Qualitative Inquiry* 25, no. 9–10, (2019), 907–914, https://doi.org/10.1177/1077800418810978.

Quiller-Coach, Arthur. *On the Art of Writing*. New York: G. P. Putnam's Sons, 1916.

Rabinowitz, Peter J. "Truth in Fiction: A Reexamination of Audiences." *Critical inquiry* 4, no. 1 (1977), 121–141, https://doi.org/10.1086/447927.

Rambo Ronai, Carol. "The Reflexive Self through Narrative." In *Investigating Subjectivity: Research on Lived Experience*, edited by Carolyn Ellis and Michael G. Flaherty, 102–124. Thousand Oaks, CA: Sage, 1992.

———. "Multiple Reflections of Child Sex Abuse: An Argument for a Layered Account." *Journal of Contemporary Ethnography* 23, no. 4 (1995), 395–426, https://doi.org/10.1177/089124195023004001.

———. "My Mother Is Mentally Retarded." In *Composing Ethnography: Alternative Forms of Qualitative Writing*, edited by Carolyn Ellis and Arthur P. Bochner, 109–131. Walnut Creek, CA: AltaMira, 1996.

Rambo, Carol. "Remixing/Reliving/Revisioning 'My Mother Is Mentally Retarded.'" In *Handbook of Autoethnography*, 2nd ed., edited by Tony E. Adams, Stacy Holman Jones, and Carolyn Ellis, 401–410. New York: Routledge, 2022.

Rawicki, Jerry and Carolyn Ellis, "Lechem Hara (Bad Bread) Lechem Tov (Good Bread): Survival and Sacrifice during the Holocaust." *Qualitative Inquiry* 17, no. 2 (2011), 155–157, https://doi.org/10.1177/1077800410392337.

Reinharz, Shulamit. *On Becoming a Social Scientist: From Survey Research and Participant Observation to Experimental Analysis*. San Francisco, CA: Transaction Books, 1985.

———. *Feminist Methods in Social Research*. Oxford: Oxford University Press, 1992.

Rennels, Tasha R. "Taking Out the Trash: Using Critical Autoethnography to Challenge Representations of White Working-Class People in Popular Culture." *The Popular Culture Studies Journal* 3, no. 1–2 (2015), 349–363.

Rheingold, Howard. *The Virtual Community, Revised Edition: Homesteading on the Electronic Frontier*, Cambridge: MIT Press, 2000.

Richardson, James T., Joel Best, and David G. Bromley, eds., *The Satanism Scare*. Piscataway, NJ: Transaction Publishers, 1991.

Richardson, Laurel. "Narrative and Sociology." *Journal of Contemporary Ethnography* 19, no. 1 (1990), 129, https://doi.org/10.1177/089124190019001006.

———. *Fields of Play: Constructing an Academic Life*. New Brunswick, NJ: Rutgers University Press, 1997.

———. "Evaluating Ethnography." *Qualitative Inquiry* 6, no. 2 (June 2000), 253–255, https://doi.org/10.1177/107780040000600207.

———. *A Story of a Marriage through Dementia and Beyond: Love in a Whirlwind*. New York: Routledge, 2022.

Ricoeur, Paul. *History and Truth*, translated by Charles A. Kelbley. Evanston, IL: Northwestern University Press, 1965.

Ritchie, Donald A. *Doing Oral History*. Oxford: Oxford University Press, 2014.

Rossing, Barbara R. *The Rapture Exposed: The Message of Hope in the Book of Revelation*. New York: Basic Books, 2004.

Roth, Wolff-Michael. "Autobiography as Scientific Text: A Dialectical Approach to the Role of Experience. Review Essay: Harry F. Wolcott (2002). Sneaky Kid and Its Aftermath." *Forum Qualitative Sozialforschung / Forum: Qualitative Social Research* 5, no. 1 (2003), Art. 9, http://nbn-resolving.de/urn:nbn:de:0114-fqs040199.

Ryle, Gilbert. "The Thinking of Thoughts: What Is 'Le Penseur' Doing?" In *Collected Essays 1929-1968*, Vol. 2, edited by Julia Tanney, 494–510. London: Hutchinson, 1971.

Salvo, James M. *Reading Autoethnography: Reflections on Justice and Love*. New York: Routledge, 2020.

Sambrook, Sally and Andrew F. Herrmann. "Organizational Autoethnography." *Journal of Organizational Ethnography* 7, no. 3 (2012), 222–387.

———. "Organisational Autoethnography: Possibilities, Politics and Pitfalls." *Journal of Organizational Ethnography* 7, no. 3 (2018), 222–234, https://doi.org/10.1108/JOE-10-2018-075.

Santiago, Cortes, Ileana, Nastaran Karimi, and Zaira R. Arvelo Alicea. "Neoliberalism and Higher Education: A Collective Autoethnography of Brown Women Teaching Assistants." *Gender and Education* 29, no. 1 (2017), 48–65, https://doi.org/10.1080/09540253.2016.1197383.

Schrag, Zachary M. *Ethical Imperialism: Institutional Review Boards and the Social Sciences, 1965–2009.* Baltimore, MD: Johns Hopkins University Press, 2010.

Schroeder, Robert. "Evaluative Criteria for Autoethnographic Research: Who's to Judge?" In *The Self as Subject: Autoethnographic Research into Identity, Culture, and Academic Librarianship*, edited by Anne-Marie Deitering and Robert Schroeder, 315–346. Chicago, IL: ACRL Publications, 2017.

Short, Nigel P. and Alec Grant. "Burnard (2007): Autoethnography or a Realist Account?" *Journal of Psychiatric and Mental Health Nursing* 16, no. 2 (2009), 196–198, https://doi.org/10.1111/j.1365-2850.2008.01348.x.

Sikes, Pat. *Autoethnography.* Thousand Oaks, CA: Sage, 2011.

Simi, Pete and Robert Futrell. *American Swastika: Inside the White Power Movement's Hidden Spaces of Hate*, 2nd ed. Lanham, MD: Rowman & Littlefield, 2015.

Singh, Kanwarjeet, Jane Southcott, and Damien Lyons. "Walking the Doors—To Be to Become: An Autoethnography of Diasporic Beings and Multiple Becomings." *Journal of Autoethnography* 3, no. 1 (2021), 19–37, https://doi.org/10.1525/joae.2022.3.1.19.

Skinner, Jonathan, ed., *The Interview: An Ethnographic Approach.* London: Berg, 2012.

Smith, Brett. "Narrative Analysis." In *Analysing Qualitative Data in Psychology*, 3rd ed., edited by Evanthia Lyons and Adrian Coyle, 235–252. Walnut Creek, CA: Sage, 2021.

Smith, Brett and Javier Monforte. "Stories, New Materialism and Pluralism: Understanding, Practising and Pushing the Boundaries of Narrative Analysis." *Methods in Psychology* 2 (2020), https://doi.org/10.1016/j.metip.2020.100016.

Sofie, Sergeant, Peels Hanna, Sandvoort Henriëtte, Beau Pseudonym, Schelfhout Patrick, and De Schauwer Elisabeth. "A Collective Biography on Working Relationships in Inclusive Research Teams." *Disability & Society* (2022), 1–18, https://doi.org/10.1080/09687599.2022.2071228.

Sparkes, Andrew C. "Autoethnography and Narratives of Self: Reflections on Criteria in Action." *Sociology of Sport Journal* 17, no. 1 (2000), 21–43, https://doi.org/10.1123/ssj.17.1.21.

———. "Creating Criteria for Evaluating Autoethnography: Pedagogical Possibilities and Problems with Lists." In *International Perspectives on Autoethnographic Research and Practice*, edited by Lydia Turner, Nigel P. Short, Alec Grant, and Tony E. Adams, 256–267. New York: Routledge, 2018.

———. "Autoethnography: Accept, Revise, Reject? An Evaluative Self Reflects." *Qualitative Research in Sport, Exercise and Health* 12, no. 2 (2020), 289–302, https://doi.org/10.1080/2159676X.2020.1732453.

———. "When Judgment Calls: Making Sense of Criteria for Evaluating Different Forms of Autoethnography." In *Handbook of Autoethnography*, 2nd ed., edited by Tony E. Adams, Stacy Holman Jones, and Carolyn Ellis, 263–276. New York: Routledge, 2022.

Spears, Britney. *The Woman in Me.* New York: Gallery Books, 2023.

Speedy, Jane. *Staring at the Park: A Poetic Autoethnography.* Walnut Creek, CA: Routledge, 2015.

Spry, Tami. "Performing Autoethnography: An Embodied Methodological Praxis." *Qualitative Inquiry* 7, no. 6 (2001), 706–732, https://doi.org/10.1177/107780040100700605.

———. *Body, Paper, Stage: Writing and Performing Autoethnography.* New York: Routledge, 2011.

Stahlke, Sarah. "Reflections on the Role of the Supervisor of an Autoethnographic Project." *Journal of Autoethnography* 1, no. 4 (2020), 388–394, https://doi.org/10.1525/joae.2020.1.4.388.

Standaert, Michael. *Skipping towards Armageddon: The Politics and Propaganda of the Left Behind Novels and the LaHaye Empire.* New York: Soft Skull Press, 2006.

Stephens, Elizabeth. "Homicide by Police: Coping with Traumatic Death." *Journal of Autoethnography* 1, no. 1 (2020), 111–121, https://doi.org/10.1525/joae.2020.1.2.111,

Stern, Danielle M. "Communication Is…Privilege." In *Communication Is…Perspectives on Theory*, edited by Adam W. Tyma and Autumn P. Edwards, 191–202. San Diego, CA: Cognella, 2020.

Stern, Danielle M. and Linda D. Manning. "Grieving Kathy: An Interactional Autoethnography of Cultivating Sustainable Organizations." In *The Routledge International Handbook of Organizational Autoethnography*, edited by Andrew F. Herrmann, 271–286. New York: Routledge, 2020.

Stewart, Jane A. "The Model Public Bath at Brookline." *American Journal of Sociology* 5, no. 4 (1900), 470–474.

Stuart, Forrest. "Introspection, Positionality, and the Self as Research Instrument: Toward a Model of Abductive Reflexivity." In *Approaches to Ethnography: Analysis and Representation in Participant Observation*, edited by Colin Jerolmack and Shamus Khan, 211–238. Oxford: Oxford University Press, 2018.

Sue, Derald Wing. "Microaggressions: More Than Just Race." *Psychology Today*, November 17, 2010, https://www.psychologytoday.com/us/blog/microaggressions-in-everyday-life/201011/microaggressions-more-just-race.

Sue, Derald Wing and Lisa Spanierman. *Microaggressions in Everyday Life*, 2nd ed. Hoboken, NJ: John Wiley & Sons, Inc., 2020.

Summers, Andy. *One Train Later*. New York: St. Martin's Press, 2006.

Szwabowski, Oskar. "Forget All Criteria." *International Review of Qualitative Research* 12, no. 4 (2019), 476–481, https://doi.org/10.1177/19408447211002780.

Tamas, Sophie. "The Shadow Manifesto." *International Review of Qualitative Research* 10, no. 1 (2017), 110–113, https://doi.org/10.1525/irqr.2017.10.1.110.

Tanner. Amy E. "Glimpses at the Mind of a Waitress." *American Journal of Sociology* 13, no. 1 (1907), 48–55.

Tierney, William G. "Life History's History: Subjects Foretold." *Qualitative Inquiry* 4, no. 1 (1998), 49–70, https://doi.org/10.1177/107780049800400104.

———. "Get Real: Representing Reality." *Qualitative Studies in Education* 15, no. 4 (2002), 385–398, https://doi.org/10.1080/09518390210145444.

Tillmann-Healy, Lisa M. "A Secret Life in a Culture of Thinness: Reflections on Body, Food, and Bulimia." In *Composing Ethnography: Alternative Forms of Qualitative Writing*, edited by Carolyn Ellis and Arthur P. Bochner, 76–108. Walnut Creek, CA: AltaMira Press, 1996.

———. "Friendship as Method." *Qualitative Inquiry* 9, no. 5 (2003), 729–749, https://doi.org/10.1177/1077800403254894.

Tillmann, Lisa M. "Speaking into Silences: Autoethnography, Communication, and Applied Research." *Journal of Applied Communication Research* 37, no. 1 (2009), 94–97, https://doi.org/10.1080/00909880802592649.

———. *In Solidarity: Friendship, Family, and Activism Beyond Gay and Straight*. New York: Routledge, 2014.

———. "Revisiting 'Body and Bulimia Revisited.'" In *Handbook of Autoethnography*, 2nd ed., edited by Tony E. Adams, Stacy Holman Jones, and Carolyn Ellis, 431–442. New York: Routledge, 2022.

Tirrell, Lynne. "Storytelling and Moral Agency." *The Journal of Aesthetics and Art Criticism* 48, no. 2 (1990), 115–126, https://doi.org/10.2307/430901.

Tomaselli, Keyan G., Lauren Dyll-Myklebust, and Sjoerd van Grootheest. "Personal/Political Interventions via Autoethnography: Dualisms, Knowledge, Power and Performativity in Research Relations." In *The Handbook of Autoethnography*, edited by Stacy Holman Jones, Tony E. Adams, and Carolyn Ellis, 576–598. Walnut Creek, CA: Left Coast Press, 2013.

Townsend, Thomas W. "A Groundhog Moment: Examination of a Pivotal Emotional Singularity." *Qualitative Inquiry* 25, no. 2 (2019), 100–110, https://doi.org/10.1177/1077800417750678.

Townsend, Thomas W., Angela Duggins, Brandon Bragg, Tessa McCoy, Juliette Guerrault, Jessica Newell, and Hannah Tiberi. "The IRB's Stone Wall: Rollercoaster of Doom." In *The Routledge International Handbook of Organizational Autoethnography*, edited by Andrew F. Herrmann, 366–382. London: Routledge, 2020.

Townsend, Thomas W. and Kallie Gay, "Expendable and Indispensable: Thoughts on Being Non-Tenurable Faculty in These Uncertain Times." *Journal of Autoethnography* 2, no. 2 (2021), 248–255, https://doi.org/10.1525/joae.2021.2.2.248.

Tracy, Sarah J. *Qualitative Research Methods: Collecting Evidence, Crafting Analysis, and Communicating Impact.* Hoboken, NJ: Wiley Blackwell, 2020.

Tresca, Michael J. *The Evolution of Fantasy Role-Playing Games.* Jefferson, NC: McFarland, 2014.

Trujillo, Nick. "Teaching Ethnography in the Twenty-First Century Using Collaborative Learning." *Journal of Contemporary Ethnography* 28, no. 6 (1999), 705–719.

Trujillo, Nick and Bob Krizek. "Emotionality in the Stands and in the Field: Expressing Self through Baseball." *Journal of Sport and Social Issues* 18, no. 4 (1994), 303–325, https://doi.org/10.1177/019372394018004002.

Tullis, Jillian A. "Self and Others: Ethics in Autoethnographic Research." In *Handbook of Autoethnography*, 2nd ed., edited by Tony E. Adams, Stacy Holman Jones, and Carolyn Ellis, 101–113. New York: Routledge, 2022.

Tullis Owen, Jillian A., Chris McRae, Tony E. Adams, and Alisha Vitale, "Truth Troubles." *Qualitative Inquiry* 15, no. 1 (2009), https://doi.org/10.1177/1077800408318316.

Tunçalp, Deniz and Patrick L. Lê. "(Re) Locating Boundaries: A Systematic Review of Online Ethnography." *Journal of Organizational Ethnography* 3, no. 1 (2014), 59, https://doi.org/10.1108/JOE-11-2012-0048.

Turkle, Sherry. *Alone Together: Why We Expect More from Technology and Less from Each Other.* New York: Basic Books, 2011.

———. *Life on the Screen.* New York: Simon and Schuster, 2011.

Turner, Lydia, Nigel P. Short, Alec Grant, and Tony E. Adams, eds., *International Perspectives on Autoethnographic Research and Practice.* New York: Routledge, 2018.

Valentine, Riley Clare. "Blankets, Rosaries, and Cajun French: The Impacts of Researching Far-Right Online Discourse on the Researcher." *Journal of Autoethnography* 4, no. 3 (2023), 315–329, https://doi.org/10.1525/joae.2023.4.3.315.

van Eijk, Marieke. "Studying Health Care Institutions: Using Paperwork as Ethnographic Research Tools." *Ethnography* 23, no. 4 (2022), 539–558, https://doi.org/10.1177/14661381198715 83.

Van Maanen, John. *Tales of the Field: On Writing Ethnography.* Chicago, IL: The University of Chicago Press, 1988.

———. "The Fact of Fiction in Organizational Ethnography." *Administrative Science Quarterly* 24, no. 4 (1979), 539–550, https://doi.org/10.2307/2392360.

Vande Berg, Leah and Nick Trujillo. *Cancer and Death: A Love Story in Two Voice.* New York: Hampton Press, 2008.

Voltaire,*APhilosophicalDictionary*(1764),https://archive.org/details/aphilosophicald03voltgoog/page/n247/mode/2up.

Vonnegut, Kurt and Suzanne McConnell. *Pity the Reader: On Writing with Style.* New York: Rosetta Books, 2019.

Vuong, Ocean. *On Earth We're Briefly Gorgeous.* New York, Penguin, 2019.

Wallace, David Foster. *A Supposedly Fun Thing I'll Never Do Again.* New York: Little, Brown and Company, 1997.

Walvoord, John. *Armageddon: Oil & the Middle East Crisis.* Grand Rapids, MI: Zondervan, 1991.

Wandix-White, Diana. "The Impact of Teacher-Student (Dis)Connection on Black Student and Teacher Identity Development in U.S. Schools." *Journal of Autoethnography* 1, no. 3 (2020), 234–251, https://doi.org/10.1525/joae.2020.1.3.234.

Watson, Alix R. "Good ol' Boys and Their Analog Networks." In *Organizational Autoethnographies: Power and Identity in Our Working Lives*, edited by Andrew F. Herrmann, 125–143. New York: Routledge, 2017.

Weaver-Hightower, Marcus B. "Waltzing Matilda: An Autoethnography of a Father's Stillbirth." *Journal of Contemporary Ethnography* 41, no. 4 (2012), 462–491, https://doi.org/10.1177/0891241611429302.

———. "Analyzing Self and Other in Autoethnography: Telling Secrets about One's Stillborn Child." In *How Qualitative Data Analysis Happens*, edited by Áine Humble and Elise Radina, 3–17. New York: Routledge, 2019.

Weick, Karl E. "Systemic Observational Methods." In *Handbook of Social Psychology: Theory and Method*, 3rd ed., edited by Gardner Lindzey and Elliot Aronson, 567–634. New York: Random House, 1985.

White, Donna. "Behind Bars: An Investigation of Bartenders in Missouri-St. Louis." *Lambda Alpha Journal* 30 (2000), 56–86, https://soar.wichita.edu/bitstream/handle/10057/1902/LAJv.30_.p56-86.pdf.

Whitworth, Colin. "Sissy That Performance Script! The Queer Pedagogy of *RuPaul's Drag Race*." In *RuPaul's Drag Race and the Shifting Visibility of Drag Culture*, edited by Neil Brennan and David Gudelunas, 137–151. London: Palgrave Macmillan, 2017.

Whyte, William Foote. "On Making the Most of Participant Observation." *The American Sociologist* 14, no. 1 (1979), 56–66, http://www.jstor.org/stable/27702360.

———. *Street Corner Society: The Social Structure of an Italian Slum.* Chicago, IL: University of Chicago Press, 2012.

Wilhite, Allen, Eric A. Fong, and Seth Wilhite. "The Influence of Editorial Decisions and the Academic Network on Self-Citations and Journal Impact Factors." *Research Policy* 48, no. 6 (2019), 1513–1522, https://doi.org/10.1016/j.respol.2019.03.003.

Wilkes, Rima. "Dialogic Autoethnography: A Professor Goes Internet Dating and Learns about Positionality." *Journal of Autoethnography* 3, no. 1 (2022), 65–83, https://doi.org/10.1525/joae.2022.3.1.65.

Wolcott, Harry F. *Ethnography: A Way of Seeing*, 2nd ed. Lanham, MD: AltaMira Press, 2008.

———. *Ethnography Lessons: A Primer.* Walnut Creek, CA: Left Coast Press, 2010.

Woodley, Helen. "The Use of Kierkegaard as a Stimulus for Autoethnographical Journal Writing." *Journal of Autoethnography* 3, no. 4 (2022), 459–474, https://doi.org/10.1525/joae.2022.3.4.459.

Woods, Jacob. "A Gay Man in A Hypermasculine Kitchen: An Autoethnographic Account." *Masculinities: A Journal of Identity and Culture* 11 (2019), 98–120, https://dergipark.org.tr/en/pub/mjic/issue/56064/770510.

Wyatt, Jonathan and Tony E. Adams, eds., *On (Writing) Families: Autoethnographies of Presence and Absence, Love and Loss.* Rotterdam: Brill, 2014.

WYNC Studios. "Musical Language." *Radiolab*, September 24, 2007, https://radiolab.org/podcast/91512-musical-language.

Yalom, Irvin D. and Marilyn Yalom. *A Matter of Death and Life.* Stanford, CA: Redwood Press, 2021.

Yanow, Dvora. "Organizational Ethnography and Methodological Angst: Myths and Challenges in the Field." *Qualitative Research in Organizations and Management* 4, no. 2 (2009), 188, https://doi.org/10.1108/17465640910978427.

Young, Stephanie L. and Art Herbig, "'I Am Also a We': Exploring Queer Worldmaking in *Sense8*." *QED: A Journal in GLBTQ Worldmaking* 7, no. 2 (2020), 69–93, https://www.muse.jhu.edu/article/773400.

Zappa, Frank and Peter Occhiogrosso. *The Real Frank Zappa Book.* New York: Simon and Schuster, 1989.

Zibricky, C. Dawn. "New Knowledge about Motherhood: An Autoethnography on Raising a Disabled Child." *Journal of Family Studies* 20, no. 1 (2014), 40, https://doi.org/10.5172/jfs.2014.20.1.39.

Index